GRINGO LESSONS

GRINGO LESSONS

Twenty Years of Terror in Taos

Bill Whaley

NIGHTHAWK PRESS
TAOS, NEW MEXICO

—

FIRST EDITION 2015

—

Library of Congress Catalog-in-Publication-Data

Gringo Lessons: Twenty Years of Terror in Taos / Bill Whaley — 1st ed.
Whaley, Bill (December 27, 1946 –)
Illustrations by Nora Anthony
Published by Nighthawk Press, Taos, New Mexico
Cover and book design by Kelly Pasholk, Wink Visual Arts

Library of Congress Control Number: 2014958824
Hardcover ISBN 9780986270611
Paperback ISBN 9780986270604

1. BIO026000 Biography & Autobiography: Personal Memoir
2. HIS036130 History: United States - State & Local - Southwest
3. HIS037070 History: United States - Modern 20th Century

—

Dedicated to La Gente de Taos

"Life is not what one lived, but what one remembers and how one remembers it in order to recount it."

—— GABRIEL GARCIA MARQUEZ

Acknowledgments

Below I acknowledge those who inspired and/or affected the publication of this book. Although the book is twenty years behind schedule, I'm in haste to complete it before anymore potential readers, i.e., Arsenio Cordova or Gene Sanchez, die. I miss both Juma Archuleta, the Chicano Barber, and the admirable gallerist and actor, Steve Parks (RIP), both of whom always asked after the Gringo's manuscript. I am grateful to the Sacred Mountain for allowing me to participate in the spiritual cycle of death and rebirth *aqui en Taos*.

For ten years, Nora Anthony translated words into images for *Horse Fly* stories and columns, connecting the spirit of place and people to Taos. With the artist's gracious permission, I am honored to reproduce some of my favorites in *Gringo Lessons*.

Joan Ackermann encouraged me to return to university. Thanks to Kent Barker for the author's photo. Tom Collins shared the pain and pleasure of radio, print, and theatre. Elizabeth Crittenden Palacios referred me to the "man from Rinconada." Suzanne de Silva stabilized, added, and subtracted; she kept *Horse Fly* alive and stinging. Jane Engel proofed the *Fly* and the book. Stella Gallegos kept me informed. Nobody is more hospitable than Marie Louise Lekumberry, the etxekoandrea of the J.T. in Gardnerville, Nevada.

Dr. Hussain Haddawy of UNR taught me to consider antinomies and suggested I write *Gringo Lessons*. Ed and Trudy Healy expressed their faith. Dory Hulburt edited mucho copy. My mother, Elizabeth Johnson, started me on a love affair with literature by taking me to the library as a child. Knox Johnson taught me how to look, listen, and ride a horse. Helen Johnson bailed me out. Rebecca Lenzini published the book. Jean Mayer rescued me from existential angst and taught me to ski. "Dr. Bob"

Merrill of UNR taught the finer points of detective fiction. Luisa Valerio Mylet in Taos made me giggle. Catherine Naylor reminded me to pay attention to my prose.

John Nichols set an example. Dr. Tom Nickles of UNR taught me how philosophy makes you laugh. Thanks to Paul O'Connor for asking me to edit *Taos Portraits*. Jo Owens sent me on my way. Kelly Pasholk designed the best parts. Jules Sanchez provided emergency proofing services for the *Gringo*. Barbara Scott read, remarked, and edited a version of *Gringo Lessons*. Despite my horrid handwriting, Cora Lee Shaw, my teacher in fourth and eighth grade, found something worth reading.

Vicki Sink, UNR colleague, joined in the search for the meaning of life. Andy Stiny, peripatetic and exemplary journalist, filled in the gaps at coffee shops. Taylor Streit, curmudgeon, has a unique take on this "special place." Dr. Peggy Urie said, "go teach" to us UNR graduate fellows.

Robin Watkins read *Fear and Loathing* to me in the fabulous Mustang. Deb Villalobos-Whaley endured lovingly and loyally. Fitz Whaley offered insight on sport, philosophy, and popular culture. Steve White introduced me to greater Taos lo' these many years ago.

To all I am grateful for the experience.

— Bill

CONTENTS

Introduction

"Taos is a great place to visit but you wouldn't want to live here."

— FLAVIO

1

Since I did not want to be interfered with by the authorities, I skipped out of college in Colorado and lit out for the Southwest territory—Taos, New Mexico—in the fall of 1966. I wanted to go skiing before Uncle Sam caught up with me and sent me off to confront my mortal interests in Southeast Asia. During my sojourn as ski bum in Taos, ideas about the immoral war and images of my peers, their spirits trapped in coffins, persuaded me to join the Taos National Guard. Consequently, I found myself mired in a ridiculously long existential journey in search of freedom and cultural adventure among the denizens of northern New Mexico.

At Fort Garland, Colorado, I turned south and followed the highway along the western edge of the Sangre de Cristo Mountains, where small towns sink into semi-arid high desert, where mesas and volcanic formations roll endlessly west like waves in an ocean. The sun glares down on you even as the sky and land tempt the spirit; you begin to shed your old skin during the drive into New Mexico.

Others of my generation, artists and hippies, searchers and second homers, entered the Taos Valley from the south, coming north along the canyon of the Rio Grande from Española and Santa Fé. On the west side of the great river, you see the old railroad bed of the Chile Line, the tracks rising and falling with the undulating terrain. As you enter from the south, you reach a point on Pilar Hill overlooking Taos Valley below the Sangre de Cristos, where you can see how the Rio Grande Gorge snakes north and the valley lies out in front of you on either side of the gorge, looking as if a pagan god had reached down and ripped open the uneven sage-strewn floor. The Rio Grande slides south at a low point in what is known as the Rio Grande Rift—a barely discernible geological feature, some twenty miles wide and 16,000 feet beneath the surface of the Gorge. The river itself has been cutting away into the earth and eroding the canyon for almost three million years.

Enter the valley from the west and you cross the Rio Grande Gorge Bridge, a local terminus for despair, which hangs 650 feet above the river on Highway 64, about ten miles northwest of the Town of Taos. Just as the river continues to erode the Gorge, so the rift—unseen—continues to shift and widen. Geologists say that tectonic forces will one day tear the earth asunder on either side of the rift and the North American continent will split and fall away, shift east and west, leaving a much bigger gap than the one fugitives see in their rearview mirror as they hightail it up the canyon, escaping east through the Sangre de Cristo Mountains.

The Sacred Mountain hovers over adobe houses, stick-built hovels, and myriad metallic havens, even as the multi-story Taos Pueblo rises up out of the earth's crust. Just as the natural world charms the senses and relaxes the viscera, so the tolerant attitude and reversal of mainstream values, born of the historic indigenous culture, infects and frees newcomers to experiment with life. The snow-covered peaks on the eastern border of the Taos Valley turn bloody pink in winter and the western horizon glows in the splendor of burnished sunsets. When you travel the east-west trails of the high desert between the Rio Grande Gorge and the Sangre de Cristo Mountains, the breeze causes your skin to tingle and wakes you up from the catatonic condition born of mainstream America. While you look up at the double rainbow above the Sacred Mountain or stare across the horizon into the fireworks at sunset, you feel liberated. Liberation is a virus that gnaws at the soles of your feet and finds an entry, a hole in your skin; it crawls up your legs, worms its way up your spinal column, and infects the blood streaming from heart to brain, creating a metaphysical stew of ideas that entrap you *aquí en Taos*.

Life in Taos is as unpredictable as a Reno dice game. Half a century later, as I look back at the clash between the naive idealist and natural-born skeptic, I recognize that Taos is the perfect place for a dropout, adrenaline junkie, or existential entrepreneur who would confront chance and fate. Just as nobody told me about the Rio Grande Rift then, nobody tells tourists today that Taoseños live between a Superfund site, Mother Moly (home to Chevron Mining's recently closed molybdenum mine, twenty-five miles to the north), and Los Alamos National Laboratory (LANL), fifty or so miles south, where scientists play with the genie unleashed from Oppenheimer's bottle, up there on the Pajarito Plateau among the spirits of the Anasazi diaspora. If Mother Moly pollutes the Red River and the Rio Grande with toxins, so LANL burns depleted uranium and pollutes the thin, dry air. The besieged denizens of Taos gather in kivas and churches, galleries and cantinas, where they pray to ancient gods, whether called the Great Spirit, Jesus and Mary, or the bacchic nectar captured in a can of Budweiser.

2

Today the timeless adobe abodes slowly come into relief at dawn and display their earthy contours, while briefly sparkling at twilight before fading away under the cottonwood trees at night. Soft flames from piñon fires light up the velvet darkness. The stars above and lights below look like fireflies. At Taos Pueblo the drum beats and the dancers repeat the timeless rituals celebrating the native emergence. The descendants of Spanish farmers irrigate their fields with the water that slips down streambeds from the snowmelt: *agua es vida.* Call it holy water as it dribbles down creeks and spills out of *acequias* into the *vega*, turning kernels into cornstalks and buds into apples. The runoff leaks into the Rio Grande and follows the great winding watercourse down through the mountains and deserts, funneled by concrete aquifers between El Paso and Juarez, and maybe reaches the Gulf of Mexico. Maybe.

Natives tolerate newcomers because of the struggle to survive—the thin topsoil, a short growing season, and capricious weather patterns have created a culture where money is as scarce as water in a parched desert. The indigenous Native cultures traded with other tribes and, later, with the Spanish occupiers, the mountain men, and *los Americanos*. So the hippie invaders of my generation and today's second-home transients help subsidize the subsistent economy. The politicians count coup at government offices, transferring the dough from tourists and taxpayers to *la familia*. As a culture of tolerance unleashes a cycle of idiosyncratic human behavior, alternately compassionate and retaliatory, so the multicultural folk of Taos swear by their own code and the freedom to disobey, whether the law is imposed by God, custom, or a constitution.

3

The problem of beauty bedeviled me in Taos. Why was I so frequently depressed when the landscape presented such spiritual promise? Sooner or later, one learns what D.H. Lawrence, the coal miner's son, said about New Mexico: "It had a splendid terror, and a vast far-and-wide magnificence which made it way beyond mere aesthetic appreciation." After spending eighteen active months, off and on, in the area Lawrence fled, I stayed off and on for twenty years and then came back for another twenty. My experience proved Lawrence was right to flee.

During the '60s and '70s we waited for all things possible, if not probable, to happen. While tradition mesmerized native residents, we transients got high on the local laissez-faire. Whether descendants of the Spanish conquerors or Taos Pueblo Indian, whether Anglo artist or black sheep, we all rooted around in Taos, struggling to live among our perverse tendencies. Regardless of the laws of physics or finance, gossip and the oral tradition prevailed. Imagination as agent and Magic Realism as form gave shape to the pattern of experience, for most Taoseños live in a way that trumps all reason.

By the early '80s, I was engaged in mopping up my financial sins, and by the end of that difficult decade I had returned to university, where I studied my errors through the lens of the Western tradition. In the beginning I had believed what Jean-Paul Sartre said: "Man ... exists only in so far as he realizes himself, he is therefore nothing else but the sum of his actions, nothing else but what his life is." I returned to Taos in 1998 and experienced what Emerson said: "Man is only half himself, the other half is his expression."

While *Gringo Lessons: Twenty Years of Terror in Taos* focuses generally on my adventures as an entrepreneur, the aspiring essayist in me hastens to add that an interest in survival and sanity turned me into a more studious observer of Taos when I returned to publish and edit a monthly journal called *Horse Fly*. By the time I finished writing *Gringo Lessons*, I knew what Montaigne meant when he wrote, "I have not made my book any more than it has made me." I also confirmed through experience what my friend Flavio never tires of saying, "Taos is a great place to visit but you wouldn't want to live here."

Prologue

"I knew you could run, Blackie."

1

During the best time of year, long before I visited Taos, the forests, meadows, and waters of Lake Tahoe formed my involuntary perceptions. In *Roughing It,* Mark Twain calls Lake Tahoe "the fairest picture the earth affords." My experience in Taos encompassed enduring unrest and conflict while my memories of Tahoe represent solace and serenity. Still, the climate of Taos felt similar to the clarity and coolness I felt at Tahoe.

Each Memorial Day, refugees from the hot, windy valleys in Nevada and California flee to the high country of Lake Tahoe.

Cool air greets you. Wind rushes through the green branches on the hundred-foot-tall ponderosas. Summer rain, smelling of fresh pine, drips down on your skin and the High Sierra meadows, watered by mountain creeks, refreshed me and my horse. High among the peaks, springs seep up like fountains between the granite and the grass. Streams flow down the mountainsides through the meadows and converge to form Trout Creek. You can still see the hard-packed dirt trails cutting into the riverbanks of the Trout Creek meadow, where we kids crossed the creek on horseback or lay down on our bellies to drink our fill from the swirling snowmelt. The sweet snowmelt slid by our noses and ended up a mile downstream in Lake Tahoe, a deep natural reservoir of cold emerald-green and turquoise-blue water.

In late spring, there were two cattle drives into the high country. In one day, we made a quick trip from Carson Valley, up and over Kingsbury Grade to the Sierras with the yearlings. Later, we camped overnight with a few hundred head of white-faced Hereford cows and calves before climbing up and over the pass and trailing down the steep granite grade to South Lake Tahoe.

At times, a lively calf might suddenly spin 180 degrees and take off like a bullet shot out of a gun. No matter how many Washo Indian cowhands were present, I'd get the cussing out from my stepdad, Knox Johnson. On the ranches, they always say "family members can't quit."

Bounce, the one-armed Washo Indian and a year-round hand, acted like a foreman for the crew, and sometimes spoke to me in his native tongue. I never learned the lingo, but remember the refrain "ain't it?" pronounced more like "ennit?" When I wore my chaps, the Indians used to tease me. "Billy, why you wearing that dress, ennit?" They'd laugh as my face turned red. Mostly, I remember how Bounce would stop for a smoke, pull out his white sack of Bull Durham tobacco, with its blue, ribbon-bound rolling papers. He used the stump of his left arm as a balance on which to lay the paper for the delicate operation. He poured the tobacco and carefully licked the edge of the paper to roll a cigarette. Even if it was windy, whether on foot or horseback, he could roll one, ennit?

"Hey, Billy, Knox gonna give you hell, ennit?" said one of the Washo hands. Sure enough, Knox came riding up, on his big roan, Blueberry, glowering at me on my black horse, aptly named Black Beauty.

"Goddammit, Billy, why'd you let that calf get away?"

"How'd I know it was gonna take off?"

"You gotta know before he does it."

That was long ago, before the landscape gave way to asphalt, automobiles, wedding chapels, and high-rise, glassed-in casinos at the state line. At Stateline, Nevada, where Nevada and California conjoin, and the casino culture spells out its ode to Lady Luck, the dealers and the tourists poured out of the clubs to watch us pass. They greeted us with smiles and snapped our pictures.

We sat up higher in our saddles, tipped our straw cowboy hats down over our eyes, and pulled back on the reins to make our tired horses prance. "Ho, ha, Bossie!" we'd yell at the lagging cows and calves. The crowds loved Sheriff George Byers, who caught up with the cattle drive at the bottom of the Tahoe side of the grade for the final leg of the journey, the short ride, a mile or so past the Stateline gambling clubs to the pine rail corrals. George, thanks to his prosperous paunch, seemed bigger than his six-foot-plus frame. He wore a big white Stetson and a sidearm. "Go get 'em, George!" they'd yell. He sat on his palomino, doffed his hat, and acknowledged the applause. They always printed his picture on the front page of the local paper.

As the cattle moved south and headed up the unpaved county

road now called Pioneer Trail, the tired cows, tongues hanging out, began to pick up their white faces. They could smell the fresh grass in the meadows and the cool water in the creeks. After the long, slow, twenty-mile trek, the sweaty, burnt-red beasts began to trot. Their bawling voices exulted "moo, mooo, moooo!" anticipating a summer in the cool green high country.

2

My parents, two sisters, and I spent the summers in a one-bedroom log cabin with a sleeping loft on the Trout Creek meadow. Bounded on the north and south by sagebrush hills with intermittent stands of ponderosa pines, the broad green meadow glinted in the morning dew and the sun, while Trout Creek, meandering through willows and deep grass, was deep enough to serve up swimming holes for boys and girls riding horseback. Barefooted, my toes squeezed the fine dirt that stained the skin a dirty gray.

I can still feel the scars from scraping my bare legs against the sagebrush and trees when my horse got away from me. The breeze blows in from the lake and cools the log cabin and the place where I used to sit at the old picnic table under the pines, looking up at the sandy saddle between Freel Peak and Job's Sister, the highest peaks in that part of the Sierras. On the southeast corner of the cabin, there's a handprint in the poured concrete corner with my name and the date—Sept. 29, 1952—which marks the year my stepfather laid the first two logs of the cabin. He and his Washo helpers cut the trees down and pulled the logs out of the forest, crashing through the brush with a working team of draft horses, a black Percheron and a sorrel-colored Belgian.

Knox and the crew stacked up the logs first, then cut out the doors and windows and added a huge brick fireplace. Knox, whom I called Knoxie to his face but Dad behind his back, chose for the fireplace mantle a long, hand-hewn, twelve-inch beam, a beam he found among the ruins of the Sierra House pony express station. The smaller beams in the cathedral ceiling came from the old Baldwin boathouse on Lake Tahoe.

Just up from the cabin on Blue Lake Avenue, which adjoins Highway 50, I hung out at Upham's Trout Farm (the fish pond, we called it). The tourists fished and paid by the inch for their freshly caught trout. I cleaned hundreds of farm-raised rainbow trout between sneaking tiny bites of frozen horseflesh from the bait jars. It has a sweet taste. For my duties, I got paid fifty cents, maybe, topped off by a Sidewalk Sundae ice-cream bar at the end of the day.

Other days, I caught my black horse in the pasture next to the trout farm and rode out across the meadow and Trout Creek, through the forest and up to the back entrance of the Trout Creek riding stables, operated by Art Davenport. Art's cowboy hat carried several years of dust on its broad brim and his stomach suggested he lived on flapjacks. He supervised the donkey ring, where kids went round and round for twenty-five cents, and he entertained their parents with one story after another. Tourists paid a dollar an hour to ride the horses, but could look at the two-headed calf or six-legged sheep for free. Sometimes I guided the dudes out on the trail or got down off my horse and shoveled manure into a beat-up wheelbarrow. At the end of the day, Art bought us kids a soda pop for helping out.

The trout farm is still open just down the street from the log cabin on Blue Lake Avenue, but the riding stable, like the strawberry patch where you paid fifty cents a basket for the fresh-picked fruit, was vanquished long ago by first a supermarket and then a super drugstore. Still, behind the shopping center and throughout the meadow and forest, I can see the trails, the same bent trees, a rock or depression in the earth that remind me of those days spent so happily in the cool shadows of the log cabin. I guess I've been headed back to that cabin every summer from then until now, sometimes physically, sometimes in my daydreams.

3

Back then, we used to race our horses up and down a dirt road where Al Tahoe Boulevard cuts through the forest from Highway 50 to Pioneer Trail. Once, a bunch of us who hung out at the stable all got on our horses and went out to see a proposed race between two college-age kids who had been bragging about their steeds. They were from Sacramento or the Sierra foothills and had a lot of fancy riding gear—boots, saddles, tie-downs, and martingales. I was about ten or eleven and riding Black Beauty bareback, clad in tennis shoes, a tee-shirt, and jeans.

When we got up to the starting line, they asked me if I would count down for the race. Something came over me. "I'm going to race," I said. They looked at me, surprised, and shrugged. Older kids and adults would always say something like, "Hey, nice pony, kid." They didn't really look at my horse, not really, which was way bigger than some pony. They couldn't see the rider, either. Somebody else started us and we took off. Black Beauty loved to run and she kicked their asses in the quarter mile.

"I didn't think that old mare had it in her," said one of the college kids grudgingly.

I leaned over and patted her neck and whispered in her ear, "I knew you could run, Blackie." All I had to do was turn her loose and cluck my tongue. She did the rest.

Early on I learned that riding horses was a contact sport. I fell off, got bucked off, scraped off on trees, and run away with until I jumped off. The horse usually stopped after getting rid of the rider. You just got back up on the horse. Horses have a sense of humor.

By midsummer, a timeless rhythm took over our lives, especially when we visited the pristine sandy beaches. In the afternoons at Lake Tahoe, we would swim out to rafts set on pontoons and get up and dive back into the clear, frigid water. Speedboats roared by carrying famous singers like Peggy Lee. The valley basin at 6,200 feet slopes down to the broad sandy beaches that stretch out below the 10,000-foot peaks, marked by patches of snow left over from winter's dress. The famously cold water in Lake Tahoe warms up in late July and August.

When Knox started irrigating the meadow, the water got deep enough behind the wooden dam to swim our horses in Trout Creek. For kicks we chased trespassers: I worked out a neat trick and could make my horse stop and rear up. The fishermen or suburbanites on foot were scared to death of a small kid on a big horse. At night, riding without saddles or bridles, we played hide and seek on our horses among the thick willow bushes in the pasture next to the Trout Farm.

Whether riding, fishing, or swimming, the days passed lazily through morning sunshine and afternoon thunderstorms. Sometimes at night we went to the drive-in and watched double features or played miniature golf. Or we lay out under the stars and peered into the firmament, asking each other questions.

"Who made the sky?"
"God."
"Who made God?"
"I forget."
"Damn. The only guy who knows forgot."

4

By the end of summer, you could smell the burnt aroma of dead, brown, pine needles. The cattle began to drift down from the high meadows. Roundup time. I'd get my orders from the boss, Knox: "Go get that old cow with the torn ear that always hangs round the flat rock by the big tree next to the manzanita bush by that turn in the creek across from that bunch of rocks up at the Fountain Place." Sure, I said to myself, next to the place where the old chipmunk lives. Maybe my horse knows where that cow is, I thought to myself. And sometimes she did.

Knox knew how to think like a horse or a cow, knew where they liked to hang out, where they were headed, and when. He was six feet, four inches, and had wrists and arms the size of overgrown saplings. Nobody else could ride his horse. I could chase horses all day and not catch them. He'd walk up to them in the middle of a 200-acre pasture and bridle them.

In preparation for the fall cattle drives, Knox hired a farrier named Cecil to file the hooves and nail iron horse shoes on the feet of the horses in the pasture next to the Trout Farm. Cecil did okay with the first six horses. But then he ran up against Knox's two favorites, Blueberry and Queenie. Cecil got the two horses all tangled up in ropes. Hooves were flying. He yelled and cussed. When Blueberry and Queenie tried to bite or kick him, the horseshoer whacked back with his rasp. I wondered what the tourists at the Trout Farm were thinking during the man vs.

beast battle late that afternoon. Finally, Cecil says, "Goddamn sonofabitch, you tell Knox he can do it." He packed up and left the two horses, tied up, glaring, their nostrils quivering, soapy sweat drying on their heaving chests. Knox came by later, said a few words, and the two horses stood there like docile lambs. He scraped their hooves, filed them, and nailed on the iron shoes. It was like magic.

After Labor Day, all I could think about was how my summer friends left for the valleys and how quiet everything got at Lake Tahoe. And I always remember how wonderfully cool and free the summers were for a young boy. He lives there still, inside my heart, alongside Trout Creek in a log cabin.

Nostalgia

At twenty-two, I had made the best deal of my life.

1

In late August of 1964 my folks drove me away from the rural ennui of Carson Valley in a 1959 Chevrolet station wagon with red and white tail fins east across Nevada, Utah, and into Colorado on Highway 50 to Colorado College in Colorado Springs. Despite Knox's admonishment to "look at the scenery," I napped or read in the backseat. After dropping me off at the freshman dorm so I could start two-a-day football practices, the family—Knox, my mother, and two younger sisters—continued driving south through Colorado into northern New Mexico.

Between football practices, a postcard arrived from Taos. I don't remember a personal message but I do remember the image. The background, reproduced in vivid color, depicted a sunny blue sky. In the foreground, two skiers in fur hats (Jean and Dadou Mayer), floated down a steep slope on clouds of dry powder high above the desert valley. A notice on the back of the card memorialized the thousand-year-old Pueblo and referred to the Spanish culture featured on the historic Plaza as well as the significance of Taos as a trade center for mountain men. My mother and my fourth-grade teacher had turned me on to Western history and that postcard touched something deep and inchoate inside me.

Two years later, in the fall of 1966, disappointed by my own behavior and crushed by disillusionment, I dropped out of college at the end of football season, and figured I'd go to Taos, where I had skied the previous spring. Enchanted by the warm sun, light powder, the challenging slopes and the ease of living, I counted on a few months' grace before the draft board caught up with me. My girlfriend from college, Susie, and I went down and spent the weekend at the Don Quixote motel on Kit Carson Road in Taos. The double room cost $4 a night. I drove up to Taos Ski Valley, looking for a job. At the Hotel St. Bernard, I met owner Jean Mayer, who was also the technical director of the ski school; he called TSV founder Ernie Blake and suggested they hire me on as a parking-lot attendant. I got the job and was told to report to work when it snowed. Jean knew a place I might live and gave me directions to the valley of Valdez, halfway between the town of Taos and Taos Ski Valley, where I rented a three-room adobe for $15 a month. I tucked away the rent in an envelope and stuck it in the front door each month but never saw who picked up the greenbacks.

After the football season I had engaged in a few anti-social acts on campus before I officially withdrew. So the dean and the president of the college got together, officially withdrew my withdrawal, and kicked me out. Friends from college helped me move my books and belongings down to Taos. I returned to Colorado Springs for a round of parties to celebrate my escape.

In mid-November, I hitchhiked south along the east side of the Rocky Mountains from Colorado Springs, got out of one car at the Walsenburg exit, and caught another ride up and over La Veta pass to the Fort Garland below Mt. Blanca. A third driver chauffeured me south through the oldest town in Colorado, San Luis, where today the bronze figures sculpted by Huberto Maestas march up the hill, stopping now and then to reenact the Stations of the Cross.

South of San Luis, a pickup stopped. The driver dropped me on the south side of Costilla, just across the Colorado-New Mexico state line in Taos County. Next, a Spanish-speaking *vato* in a lurching, low-slung car, offered me a ride and a slug of sweet wine. We made a conversation composed of grunts and gestures.

Woozy, I got out at the blinking light intersection, three miles north of Taos, where the state highway travels north and east to Arroyo Seco, Valdez, and Taos Ski Valley. A friendly TSV employee gave me a ride to the cattle guard which separated the Hondo canyon from Valdez, a hundred yards or so from my adobe digs. Valdez, a verdant valley filled with patchwork farms separated from each other by crooked barbed-wire fences, was ten miles from the Swiss-Alpine ski resort, complete with imitation Austrian chalets, log-cabin lodges, and a few boxlike neo-Americano condos. While I waited for winter to begin, I sat in the warm fall sunshine on the front stoop and read Jane Austen novels, slightly bemused by the narrator's ironic attitude toward the characters.

One November day, I got a ride ten miles to town and the driver let me out at one of the four stop signs that marked the entrance to Taos Plaza. Clockwise, from the northeast corner, there were four gas stations at the intersection: a Union 76, a Chevron, a Conoco, and a Phillips 66. I entered the historic Plaza and stepped over the two-foot-high concrete wall that kept motor vehicles from parking on the interior loosely laid flagstones. A bronze war memorial cross dominated the southeast quadrant. In the northwest corner a partially submerged concrete building served as headquarters for the town police below and a platform for speeches, dancers, and musicians above. If you looked up through the bare limbs of the cottonwoods, you could see a tattered American flag that flew night and day, thanks to a special dispensation from President Lincoln and the U.S. Congress—in memory of Kit Carson and a band of loyalists who defended Old Glory against Southern sympathizers at the time of the Civil War. The weather was mild, the afternoon sun warm. You could taste the smoky aroma of wood fires riding on the breeze.

In the pueblo-style La Fonda de Taos hotel on the south side of the Plaza, the magnificent two-story walls in the lobby were hung with paintings. In the rear of the lobby, I entered the Los Conquistadores lounge, where I met a slim, black-haired bartender, an artist I came to know as Jim Wagner. He served me a cold bottle of Dos Equis without asking this 19-year-old for an ID. The rich dark taste of that German-Mexican brew slid cooly down my throat, the bubbles bursting in my nose. It was four in the afternoon.

From a black leather stool, I stared at the wooden shields decorated with the names of native Spanish families who had descended from conquistadores. About five p.m. Wagner closed the bar and invited me to join him on the north side of the Plaza at La Cocina, where I met a mixed group of simpatico Taoseños—doctors, bankers, Indians, Spanish politicos, and fast-fingered con artists—all killing time between the summer and winter seasons. Folks might ask you what you did but they rarely listened to the answer. The lively talk, jokes, and glib retorts made for hospitable conversation. I don't know who bought the drinks.

I left around ten, hitchhiking for home. At the blinking light intersection, a Cadillac slowed to a stop. The man behind the wheel wore a gray suit and tie, his hair was neatly combed, his nose slightly hooked. He dropped me at a fork in the road, west of Arroyo Seco. Later, I learned he was J.P. Brandenburg, president of the First State Bank in Taos. From there, an older Spanish farmer in a beat-up pickup gave me a ride past Seco to the rim above Valdez. I walked the rest of the way down the dirt road under the moon.

Moonlight filtered through the cottonwood branches and created shadows, blurring the side entrance to the adobe house next to an apple orchard. The hypnotic Rio Hondo gurgled, its sounds softened by a curtain of thick brush. The scent of sagebrush and sweet rotting apples mixed with the aroma of clean pure water filled the air.

The three-room house had a single electric light bulb, a rusty potbelly stove in the bedroom, and a wood-fired cook stove in the kitchen. Outside, a three-hole outhouse without a roof or walls sloped back lopsidedly into a thicket of brambles. At night the stars appeared like a diadem in the sky.

In the mornings you could glimpse a vast sweep of mountain and desert, arroyos, canyons, and mesas. The landscape ran west from the Sangre de Cristos toward the horizon where the sky touched the earth. The sunsets ignited a mix of orange and red in tribute to the baroque and the beautiful. Upon closer inspection, the desert, mountains, and valleys created a topographical anomie of awe and terror, or the sublime, as mentioned by Lawrence. But then I had neither read his remarks nor did I have the experience to understand.

The dramatic power of the landscape liberated the body and elevated the spirit just as Lake Tahoe did, though the air was thinner and purer in Taos. Tahoe is ringed by the 10,000-foot Sierras, whereas in Taos the 13,000-foot peaks of the Sangre de Cristos dissolve into desert, and the desert stretches out toward the horizon, breaking briefly for the dive deep into the chasm of the Rio Grande Gorge. The glaring sun and deep blue sky, the wind and dust, sagebrush, sand, and walking rain offer an ever-changing spectacle. In the canyons and arroyos, tall, green-leafed, long-limbed cottonwoods cling to life next to the streams and irrigation ditches known as *acequias*. Root systems drink from the aquifers below the seeping *acequias* and arroyos, nourished, like the meadows and fields, by the intermittent rain and snow, which is stored in the watersheds, formed and sheltered by the forests on the sides of the mountains.

Though I hadn't seen the spring or summer when the pastel wildflowers bloom, I saw the end of autumn as the leaves fell and the earth bared itself. The golden-yellow and orange foliage, the deep-blue sky and warm sun mesmerized me. The aspen trees turned into flame amid the dark-green pines on the slopes of the Sangres. My internal organs beat more slowly and rhythmically. I could breathe; gravity seemed less forceful.

The temperature dropped, the snow and ice appeared. While waiting for ski season to begin, I sat in front of the warm fire and my nostrils filled with the sting of piñon smoke. Still the daytime temperature soared and sweat rolled down my forehead at noon-time. The presence of earth in the walls and floors of the adobe house grounded me. Outside, the sensual light entered my soul and body. The blue sky above and the cool thin air brought the sun closer and closer.

There was a kind of ease in the landscape and culture, which I sensed rather than understood. The mysterious villages and neighborhoods were filled with unpredictable folks, some friendly, some not so much. The slope-shouldered adobe houses, narrow unpaved washboard roads, pickup trucks groaning under loads of firewood, stock racks tied together with baling wire—all these things jettisoned conventional ideas about pride of property. The fence posts were crooked and the barbed wire sagged. Local farmers practiced the arts of husbandry with an attitude of benign neglect. Small herds of cattle raised themselves in ragged grassy pastures. What the locals called barns looked like sheds set slightly askew on bumpy ground.

Back in Carson Valley I was used to tidy square barns and fences that marched in straight lines, the cattle and horses well-supervised and fat, barbed wire stretched as tight as a violin string. In Taos the unorthodox approach to farming and ranching, sagging fences and leaning sheds, expressed a tolerance for the human spirit and its foibles. The hospitable natives and the lack of conventional mores among the Anglo artists were antidotes to the up-tight attitudes of mainstream America. Then the World War II generation "out there"—the so-called authorities—seemed intent on killing off its younger progeny by sending them off to fight in an ambiguous foreign war, a war which had lost all credibility.

In Taos, the older folks hauled wood, looked at the sky, and occasionally drank beer. Nestled among the meadows next to the mountains, close to town, Taos Pueblo embodied stillness and endurance. The Pueblo's adobe bricks, marked by time, worn by the rain and sun, seemed as remarkable as its people, whose timeless story inspired faith in the collective human experiment. Even then I had begun to hear about the influence of the Sacred Mountain. The fragile-looking farm sheds or melting adobe architecture exemplified the adaptable cultural forces of the natives and the omphalos of Taos; the Plaza, with its bars full of idlers, was a welcome escape from the fruitless society back in America.

In Carson Valley, my family had moved off the ranch to town when I was in the seventh grade. We no longer spent the summers up there at Lake Tahoe, where developers chewed up the historic trails and forests of my childhood. The secretary of the draft board lived across the street from my house at 210 Circle Drive in the town of Gardnerville.

So I looked at the scenery as I waited for the Christmas season to come and work to begin. I walked south and west up the dirt grade, past Leo Valencia's gas station to the village of Arroyo Seco, where I bought beans and loaves of semi-round Spanish bread. At the Craft House, weavers sat inside among the looms, spinning yarn or creating the warp and woof of multicolored belts, blankets, and pillows. The guys sitting outside the bar on the hoods of their cars, drinking cans of beer, looked through bleary eyes and taunted the newcomer.

"Hey, gringo, *tienes cerveza, cabron?*"

"No, gracias."

Across the Rio Hondo at the flat-roofed adobe-style Hacienda de Valdez, I got a job staining walls for two days with my neighbors Steve and Linda White. I met Steve, thanks to a letter of introduction from a college mate, Steve Ailes, who took me in hand when I tried to join the U.S. Marines. "Whaley," he said in his raspy voice, "you've got a better chance to live if you join the army." His father was Secretary of the Army under President Kennedy. Ailes knew Steve White, aka Whitey, from their summer camp days spent in San Cristobal, a rural neighborhood north of Taos, where Craig and Jenny Vincent, two alleged communists, re-educated wealthy rich kids in the ways of progressive politics. The former summer campers, Steve and Linda, played folk music in local cantinas and seemed like wise adults to me.

The night before Thanksgiving, my co-worker, neighbor Larry Crowley, and I finished up the work. The blue-eyed, dark-haired Crowley entertained me and Steve with his laconic question-and-answer discussions about alternative life scenarios. Larry had rented an adobe not far from me, where he parked his school bus. He and his pregnant wife, Wendy, who had a young daughter from a previous relationship, planned to deploy to a local commune, New Buffalo, when her time came to seek guidance from the friends of natural childbirth.

2

In mid-December I began hitchhiking up the gravel road to Taos Ski Valley, where I started my job as proud parking-lot attendant. Three cooperative spirits guaranteed the nourishment of body and soul during that first Christmas. TSV founder Ernie Blake donated a lift ticket; Jean Mayer gave me a sit-down lunch; and Sergeant Ed Pratt (U.S. Army, retired) of the Hondo Lodge matched the cost of the St. Bernard lunch and supplemented my survival at the rate of two dollars a day. My three bosses instructed me to keep the parking lot organized and the day-skiers out of the hotel driveways. Before the crowds arrived I helped ski-pack the empty slopes and made a few turns in untracked snow. I shoveled snow with the ad hoc ski patrol and even helped haul the occasional broken-legged skier down the mountain in an aluminum toboggan.

That Christmas the TSV ski area had the only snow in the state and we had the crowds to prove it. Three hundred or more cars arrived each day, challenging my ingenuity in the makeshift dirt lot. My co-worker, a young native from Valdez, got paid the princely sum of eighteen bucks per day. We pushed, pulled, and parked cars while cajoling inexperienced drivers from the flatlands. One day I got the bright idea of carrying a rifle to better express my authority. The gesture stimulated less grumbling and more results from resistant drivers.

Though ski bums were considered second-class citizens by TSV executives, i.e., Ernie, to me they personified an honorable trade. While the Spanish-speaking employees took the money and went home, the ski bums lived at the hotels or in employee housing and received free skiing in exchange for assisting with slope maintenance, or sweep, the practice of searching the slopes for tardy or lost skiers at the end of the day. TSV employees, in turn, were given dinner, and they dined with hotel guests. Occasionally a dispute broke out between TSV management and the hoteliers. "You didn't send enough ski bums out for sweep or to help pack," countered by "You sent more employees to dinner than you claimed." Or "So-and-so is obnoxious and drinks too much" and "So-and-so skis closed trails." During the holidays skiing for staff was verboten.

Taos Ski Valley founder Ernie Blake turned out to be a make-shift Jewish aristo, who wore a military-style cap and epaulets on his jacket, masqueraded as an officer in the Prussian army, and barked out orders in a Teutonic accent on the public address system: "Day-skiers, you must have your lift tickets ready." Day-skiers, a necessary evil, subsidized the ski operation for high-class hotel guests. Ernie warned the staff to "watch out for the swindlers" and frequently ordered employees into the parking lot to check for stolen rental skis.

The temperature dived to twenty degrees below zero during the Christmas holidays. After coming home from my duties at the parking lot or tending to my bar tab at the St. Bernard, I lit a wood fire in the potbelly stove and buried myself in blankets with a slight opening for my nose. The fire lasted less than an hour. But with enough liquor, I could sit on the snow-covered privy and howl at the moon. Once I slept in the shower of the Ski Valley's trailer, which had accommodations for six men on one end and six women on the other. Another time, a guest invited me to recline under his bed in the Hondo Lodge. A warm place to sleep was the very stuff of luxury.

On Christmas Eve, as I sat at the bar of the St. Bernard, two Ski Valley employees (Dick Hodges and Hardy Langer) periodically interrupted their holiday feast to bring me delicious morsels surreptitiously wrapped in red dinner napkins. The endless bar tab, thanks to Mayer, kept me in benumbed spirits. Despite my disheveled appearance, my status as a ski-area employee, i.e., ski bum, attracted some surprising company from the sweeter sex.

On December 27, I turned twenty. In early January, I visited Bud Creary, TSV's chief dozer operator, who doubled as ski-shop manager. My skis, a pair of used Head 360s, were scratched and pockmarked. Bud said he'd sell me some relatively new used Head GS skis for a hundred bucks. I counted out $99.90 in Christmas cash, birthday checks, and change. He conferred with Ernie over the phone and I was sent out to find the balance. Jean's secretary, Virginia Welch, at the Hotel St. Bernard, loaned me the dime. For years Bud and I laughed about the parsimonious attitude of TSV but at the time I was bitter. Bud once told me and my running buddy, chief avalanche man John Koch, that if we quit drinking we'd both be rich and successful in less than five years. Later we took the vow, but we still remained perpetually broke.

The number of skiers declined in January, and my parking lot duties were limited to weekends. I had plenty of time to ski but I couldn't pay the rent and eat on twenty bucks a month. Virginia convinced Jean to hire me to shovel snow, sweep the floor, carry luggage and groceries, and hump kegs of beer up to the St. Bernard from the delivery trucks. For these tasks I received a warm bed, three meals a day, and $100 a month plus tips—a veritable fortune.

Officially promoted to ski bum, I was proud indeed. Ernie, however, was not so happy, saying in his Prussian voice, "You can't quit working for me and go to work for the Hotel St. Bernard. I must charge you for your lift ticket." When I crossed the border into France, Jean gave me an advance of $60 to buy a ski pass. Ernie's distaste for me didn't prevent him from handing out free lift tickets to Susie, whenever she visited. He also invited her to ride up the lift with him. When the St. Bernard bartender and brother of Jean's glamorous teenage wife from Mexico quit, I got promoted to bartender.

A St. Bernard guest complained about my rude behavior and told Jean that he could make more money if he hired a professional. "We're interested in a way of life here," Jean said. "If you don't like it, you might be happier at the Hondo Lodge." When the Prussian police, masquerading as ski patrolmen, threatened to take away my pass for skiing too fast, Mayer bristled with Gallic indignation: "Nobody can tell you how fast you can ski." For a boss like that you could go to war, no questions asked.

The draft board called in late January 1967, and the Army declared me fit for duty. Soon they would send me a draft notice. My friend Whitey cooked at weekend drills in Taos for the local National Guard. Whitey, Susie and some other friends urged me to consider joining the weekend warriors.

Although I was opposed to the Vietnam debacle, I had some hazy Hemingway idea, an idea that every young man owed himself the opportunity to join his peers and test himself in battle. After seeing a picture in the *Saturday Evening Post* that featured shiny metal coffins piled up on a dock in Southeast Asia, I got a bad case of claustrophobia and visited with Sergeant Elueto Maestas. My friends from college were chasing around the country looking for openings in the Reserves or the Guard. In Taos I just walked in the door and signed on the dotted line. Though I was a terrible soldier, the local guys put up with the crazy gringo and laughed, especially later, when he made antiwar speeches during monthly drill.

There must have been an angel hovering above the mountain that first Christmas season in Taos. Strangers touched me and became friends so I stayed. It happened by choice and by chance. I've never felt that cold again.

3

In the fall of 1967 at Fort Knox, I qualified on the rifle range and graduated from basic to on-the-job training, where, between bouts of reading paperback novels, I learned to check light bulbs in M-42 and M-60 tanks. After 120 days of active duty, the U.S. Army gave me travel papers and an air ticket back to New Mexico, where I rejoined my national guard unit in Taos. Behind the bar at the Hotel St. Bernard, I celebrated my twenty-first birthday and silently rejoiced at becoming a lawful bartender.

When the Russians elevated Alexander Dubcek to the leadership of the Czechs in January of 1968, the so-called Prague Spring began. But the allusions to spring were as false as the claims of victory in Vietnam by the United States when the Tet Offensive began. By late February, CBS's Walter Cronkite revealed the sordid truth on national television about U.S. military losses. We didn't find out from Seymour Hersh for eighteen months about the March 1968 My Lai massacre. But the vibrations of the atrocity resonated in our subconscious minds since we all knew the government inevitably lied.

When Robert Kennedy announced his candidacy, hope made a brief appearance, but hooked to angst, given our collective Dallas memories. President Lyndon Johnson surrendered to the shame of Vietnam and quit the presidential race. John Koch and I registered to vote at the Old County Courthouse on the Plaza in Taos as Republicans because we despised LBJ. On April 4 they shot Martin Luther King dead at the Lorraine Motel. Though RFK quieted the mobs in Memphis, the ghettos nationwide exploded.

In late April came word that my friend and roommate in college, Jim Turner, had stepped on a land mine or got hit by a mortar and killed in Vietnam. The tall, gangly, bespectacled Turner, whose trajectory at Colorado College was similar to mine—high hopes followed by disillusionment—had joined the U.S. Marines. Jim's college friends, Lex and Anita, Susie and myself, his sister, mom and dad, and others attended the funeral west of Pueblo in the mining town of Westcliffe up in the Rocky Mountains. While the clouds passed overhead, the U.S. Marine honor guard fired a twenty-one-gun salute. We all shared in the shock. In the '90s, a facsimile of the Vietnam Memorial Wall toured and stopped in Carson City, Nevada. I found Jim's name carved in black and wept. By then, in graduate school at University of Nevada, Reno, I had begun to study the history of human nature and realize the role that chance played in one's fate. He died and I lived—there's no justification for it.

That summer of '68 I attempted to redeem myself by applying to rejoin my peers at Colorado College and "get back in so I could get out"—legitimately. Susie graduated with her (our) class in June, but due to a hangover I missed the ceremony. The football coaches conspired with me and wrote letters to the administration; they even got me a job behind the bar at the Broadmoor Golf Club. There, thanks to Hank, the head bartender, I began to learn the trade and contemplated a career behind the plank.

Then, after his June primary victory, they shot Bobby Kennedy in California. The tactics of assassination, the extension of politics by other means, frequently intervened in the political process during my formative years. The violent deaths of JFK, Malcolm X, MLK, RFK, and friends in Vietnam produced in me an attitude bordering on nihilism.

Desperate, scared of the future, and confronted by emptiness behind the face in the mirror, I played my hole card in search of respectability. Susie and I eloped in August. The CC president rescinded his note of expulsion and re-admitted me, the newly married cynic. He dismissed my priors—fights, absenteeism, and the drunken forays—as youthful transgressions. I loved Susie, but knew there must be something wrong if she loved me back. Our parents hoped she'd be a good influence on me. I hoped so, too.

When Jim's mom and dad, a well-read union machinist and a gentle housewife, came up to Colorado Springs from Pueblo, they brought us a box of fresh apples as a wedding gift. Mrs. Turner asked, "Why did Jim go?" I didn't know exactly. But she began to die the day she heard of Jim's death.

At the Democratic convention in Chicago late in August, Mayor Daley slammed the door on Democrats and democracy. The cops rioted and beat up demonstrators, passers-by, and even TV news announcers. The Republicans had put up Richard Nixon earlier at the convention in Miami. But as Norman Mailer said, "Even the drinks tasted bad in Miami in the fever and the chill."

That fall at CC I slipped away from political science and signed up for courses in literature, earning a "C" in English Romanticism and "Bs" in 20th-Century American Literature and an American Theology course subtitled "Death of God." Since God had withdrawn his blessing from America, I withdrew my consent to the mainstream milieu at the end of the semester. This time I officially resigned from Colorado College.

Susie and I headed south, back to another place in another

world. I told her the trip to Taos was temporary, though I was looking for a life peppered with action and adventure and needed a place to stand, behind the bar at the St. Bernard, or sit, while looking up at the mountains from Taos Plaza. I wanted to feel the breezes ruffle my hair and prickle my skin. I didn't know then that the place and people had tainted my soul with notions of the uncanny. And the drinks always tasted good in Taos.

4

Sing, Mother Nature, of a time when the winter snows buried man and ski bum under the long lifts at Taos Ski Valley; sing of skiers who sailed off ridge and rock and flew like raptors between tall pines, riding the downdrafts, down from the cliffs, riding down, down, down through powder as light as angels' breath; sing of those who crashed and burned but rose again to ski another day despite hangnail or hangover; sing of a time when women wore miniskirts and men traded their souls for first tracks on ski runs named Al's, Snakedance, Longhorn, or Lorelei.

The New Year, 1969, began with cold temperatures, and January was as dry as the desert that stretched from the foothills of the Sangre de Cristo Mountains to the sunset mesas in the west. One evening toward the end of the month, I stood behind the bar working my trade at the Hotel St. Bernard. Taos Ski Valley's only real ski patrolman, John Koch, hunched slightly over the bar and gripped a glass of Coors lightly in his gnarled paw. I leaned forward on one elbow. Between sips, we spoke.

"Koch."

"Whaley."

"Will it ever snow again?"

"Ask the Indians at Taos Pueblo."

"They say it used to snow here."

"So they say."

He squinted at the ceiling and wiped off his thick eyeglasses with a bar towel. Koch frequently described ski conditions as "snow-packed and sanded." You could get plenty of edge in the dirt but the rocks gouged out your skis. During dry times, Mayordomo Blake sent out calls for volunteer teams of semi-sober ski bums to man the shovel brigades. A motley crew of bartenders, waiters and waitresses, layabouts, and anarchists hauled loads of snow out of the tree-laden dells on toboggans, distributing their hard-won booty on dirt patches in a cover-up operation.

The old man, as Koch affectionately referred to Ernie, knew how to keep costs down by employing full-time shovel men as part-time lifesavers or ski patrolmen in exchange for a lift ticket, the occasional meal, a warm place to sleep, and the infrequent shower—except for Koch, the full-time man. In long-johns, a moth-eaten multicolored wool shirt, and duct-taped gray parka, with dirty ski cap pulled down, Koch worked the mountain from morning till night. At the bar he discussed the complexities of mountain operations, when to open this slope, what slopes needed work in summer, and which trees needed surgery by chainsaw.

One evening in late January, as we lamented the previous generation of skiers who had settled the valley with its snow-buried cars and lodges, the door of the St. Bernard Rathskeller burst open. Dadou Mayer brandished a handwritten sign: "14 inches, still snowing." We cheered and drank more beer. An hour later, he was back: "21 inches, still snowing."

Between going outside to gaze with wonder at the sight and continuing to quaff down the suds, Koch became increasingly nervous. He had attended U.S. Forest Service avalanche sessions the previous fall. "Whaley, this whole fucking mountain is avalanche prone," he whispered, "including the area below the catwalk above the beginner's hill. Christ." His blue eyes bulged behind his dirty specs. "The whole thing could slide by morning if it keeps snowing." I shuddered. The St. Bernard served as the goalie at the foot of Al's Run and Snakedance, two notorious slopes that pitched skiers headfirst downhill along with boulders and new-fallen snow.

Once the storms broke, it snowed every other day for a month but only at night. The days were sunny and warm, the air and snow as dry as light summer rain on the desert. You could hear the soft swish of fast-moving skis in the serene winter wonderland, followed by the sound of boom, boom, boom as Koch dropped his bombs, a tactic to avert avalanches by starting them first, sans skiers, at the top of each slope. We only lost one guest and one staff member to the reaper that winter but the piquant scent of danger only added to the excitement.

A ski movie made by Warren Miller, *The Outer Limits,* became our organizing principle. Among others, the film featured Dadou dancing down the slopes like a bird and Jean blasting through the snow with the powerful leg and arm strokes of a human dynamo. Though I tried to ski the mountain in the purest and most stylish manner, Dadou frequently reminded me that I merely skied from recovery to recovery. Still it was as close to heaven as a heretic could get that winter of '69.

While dropping down the fall line of a steep slope—say Longhorn, Castor, or Pollux—or making a turn at fifty to sixty miles an hour on Al's or Snakedance, you prayed that your skis would hold and that your burning thighs would defy gravity. Tossed skyward you pumped the air with your poles or tried to grab a tree branch to keep from hurtling into thin air. If you fell, you wouldn't see your ski buddies until nightfall at the bar. If you lost control and headed directly toward a stand of pine trees, slightly out of control, thighs shaking and goggles fogging, you looked for a slice of daylight that meant grace. You always sat back slightly so that your tips would ride up out of the snow over the stumps and logs, landmines left over from trail-clearing projects. Ski up and off a huge bump, and pray for safe passage despite rocks, trees, and other skiers who might be concealed by moguls and boulders. You memorized the mountain so you could lose the skier behind you by taking a safe line over a windblown spot around a blind corner.

While skiing at top speed, two colleagues would jostle and fight for the lead just as the trail narrowed and dived between the trees and ran a dogleg right over the headwall down into Longhorn. The winner made the first strike down through a few hundred yards of fresh powder while the loser crashed, smothered and suffocating—was left for dead in the deep snow. As you plunged forward through three or four feet of light snow and it billowed up around torso and face, goggles fogged. You could sense the trees and boulders but couldn't actually see obstacles. When it was really deep, you just pointed your skis straight down the steepest slopes and continued in slow motion.

Dr. Al Rosen, who skied with an oxygen bottle on Al's Run, set the standard of how to breathe in the billowing snow. The rest of us tried snorkels and bandannas. Finally, you just held your breath, focused on the snow snakes, prayed to the angels, and pounded down, losing control, then jumping up to regain equilibrium. If you skied fast enough, you might beat the avalanche that started above and behind, the one that buried your buddy. Such were our ethics and the sport of godlike skiers. To ski as fast as possible was to live. Then you got drunk at night.

At dry-land clinics behind the bar at the St. Bernard, Jean and Dadou spent hours discussing and demonstrating *Le Technique*, how this foot or that knee should adjust itself to the ski, saying, "*Ici, mais pas ici*" (here, but not here)—how this hand or that leg should move ever so slightly. Ernie called the Mayers' passion for technique "an affectation" and refused to let them teach their ideas lest they infect instructors or guests, though after Jean-Claude Killy won three Olympic gold medals in Grenoble, he relented somewhat. Ernie himself skied solidly with a slight stem, hinting that stability was superior to style.

The first year at the St. Bernard Jean once asked me, "Do you have fun the way you ski?" Humbled by the insult, I hastened to attend ski school—a privilege accorded ski bums. Dadou said that if it weren't for my strong legs, I wouldn't be much of a skier. I thought if I had skinny legs like Dadou, I wouldn't be caught outside the boudoir in shorts.

Classes with Jean included the top skiers among the guests and the occasional drop-in instructor. When we arrived at a slope with uncut powder, Jean would say in an exaggerated Gallic accent, "I want you to get an idea, an image of how I ski, so that you can feel what I do, how I seduce the mountain." Then he would turn to me. "Bill, on me. *Allez, à l'attaque.*" Off we'd go down Al's Run, the paying customers floundering behind. On the way up the mountain, Jean taught the scattered members of his class from the lift. "George, a little more weight on the inside foot. *La merde*, Frank, look, look where you're going. Ben, please, not like that; like this. Susan, don't lean on your poles. Bend your ankles. *Oui, c'est bien.*"

On that morning in February of '69, in my third year at the St. Bernard, I finished my breakfast chores about 9:30 a.m. My hands were red and chapped from washing glasses for all three meals. Just as it takes ten ski patrolmen to do Koch's work today, so it takes ten St. Bernard employees today to do my job. The sun shone, the sky was blue, the temperature crisp, and the lift crew had just spent two hours digging out the two chairlifts from under several feet of fresh snow.

The road between the Valdez cattle guard and the Ski Valley, some ten miles, was mostly impassable, except for the legendary lift operator, one-eyed Lee Varos, who could spot a ticket thief a hundred yards away or drive through miles of drifts, maneuvering his old truck like it was a Snowcat. Long before the craze for four-wheel-drive SUVs, two-wheel-drive trucks filled with sand or rocks for ballast were driven by men and women as if GM and Ford made chariots for the gods.

That morning the best skiers in the Valley—Jean, Dadou, and Tony Bryan, a former college ski champion—were also digging their learn-to-ski-better students out of the snow banks. Airborne Fred Fair, a powder nut and free-form aeronautical test pilot from town, was delayed by the closed roads. The Thunderbird Lodge diva, Frau Elizabeth Brownell, waited for Fred. Koch was high above on the slopes, pop-out snappers and blasting caps in hand, dropping bombs and trying to get the upper hand on the mountain. Yes, Koch's job today takes ten men and several howitzers.

So, I alone got first tracks while charging down a dozen slopes. Today, the ski patrol rates these slopes by posting fearsome double black diamonds to warn off neophytes. Then we just called them by name: Al's, Snakedance, Inferno, Edelweiss, et al. When Koch opened the upper slopes, I cut through fresh powder on Longhorn, Lorelei, Castor, Pollux, Reforma, Blitz, and two unnamed chutes in West Basin. By noontime I had exhausted my quest for orgasmic conquest and collapsed into a state of enchantment behind the bar.

There were other great days that winter when we ski bums showed up for upper sweep at 3:20 p.m. or lower sweep at 4 p.m. When he saw the sunburnt and windswept snow on Longhorn, Young Cho, a Korean Olympian and the nominal head of the ski patrol, inevitably complained, "My skis too stiff." But the bums of the St. Bernard, drunk or sober, were scared of neither rotted snow nor rocks and ice but skied—recovery to recovery—any slope, opened or closed, despite conditions of slush or potential holes hidden beneath the surface. Oh, yes, we only cried out to Thor for more godlike opportunities.

It might snow again, but the winter of 1969 gave me enough powder to last a lifetime. When it snows today, the powder junkies fill up the lift lines before the bell rings at 8 a.m. Extreme skiers today run up and over the cliffs, climb higher and ski faster, half bird, half human. But in those days, a single man made his way more leisurely up the mountain so he could set downhill speed records of singular achievement, an achievement shared only with the angels. The ghostly voices still mutter from the rafters at the St. Bernard about the snow, the best there ever was, when men were men and some of the skiiers were women— Lizzie from the T-Bird and Mary Anne, the goddesses of yore.

Oh yes, that's the way it was in the winter of '69.

5

At the end of the ski season in 1969, Susie and I made the pilgrimage to Mexico for rest and rehabilitation. In late April, we found ourselves living out of our VW camper, sleeping, sunning, and reading on the beaches of Guymas, Mazatlan, San Blas, Puerto Vallarta. Eventually we turned back and drove north up to the heart of the revolution in Berkeley and San Francisco. I loved to read the fiery rhetoric in the Black Panther Party newspaper or the *The Berkeley Barb*, which tone could be captured in a vivid front page illustration—the one-fingered-salute aimed directly at "the man." I entertained myself with pamphlets distributed by the Third World Liberation Front at San Francisco State. My hippie acquaintances from Taos could be found in the Haight-Ashbury district where they participated in the annual celebration of summer love at concerts in Golden Gate Park, topped off by ingesting quantities of acid, which test they claimed confirmed the validity of findings from the Book of Revelations. We also visited People's Park, where suburban-urban kids were learning about the business end of the shovel.

"Hippies ought to get a job," said my darling wife. "They look at us like we're tourists."

"We are." In my National Guard haircut, I knew myself. "Besides, we don't have jobs either."

"What are you going to do?" she sneered. "Hang out and follow the revolution?"

"What else can a college drop-out do?"

As we drove east toward Lake Tahoe and Carson Valley on Thursday, May 15, 1969, we heard on the radio how Gov. Ronald Reagan had ordered in the troops to destroy the People's Park.

"Where are we going?" she asked.

"Back to Taos."

In Gardnerville, my mother, in a moment of insight, said to me, "You'll never amount to a thing." I was reminded of the hostile greeting the dropout received after returning from Taos the first year, a member of the National Guard. I had, she said, disgraced the family by refusing to serve on active duty. She didn't much care for Taos then, the dirt and the brown people, the others who "were different." But she had sent me the postcard. Knox was himself different and had visited Taos way back in the late thirties with his mother. He told me if we ran into something we wanted to do, an idea about a small business, to let him know.

Though the revolution continued spinning crazily "out there," time stood still back in Taos even as the seasons had changed. The red and blue wildflowers had bloomed amid the yellow-brown mesas. Purple lilacs blossomed and the smoky scent of sagebrush drifted in from the desert. The *vega* had turned the valleys into a lush green blanket. Rumpled dust and dirt, no longer whipped up by the fierce April winds, settled down under cool bracing breezes. Dented pickup trucks bumped along dirt roads next to sagging barbed wire fences in front of the slumping adobe houses.

Sure, Susie was dubious, but I got a job, tending bar at the venerable La Doña Luz Restaurant, a block east of the Plaza, and was thrilled. We moved into the Cañon neighborhood, east of Taos proper, renting a makeshift abode from Fred Fair, who Koch claimed specialized in creating alternative forms of cash flow. "He just goes out and generates it, Whaley."

Under Fred's direction a year earlier, Larry Crowley had assembled the house in Cañon out of ammunition boxes filled with perlite. Gallerist and glamour girl Tally Richards—from Atlanta via New York and Las Vegas—did a test drive of the house and referred to it as Walden. Piñons and cottonwoods grew round the house, set down among the sagebrush hills, only minutes east of Taos Plaza. Years later, I learned that the pungent aroma emanating from the woodshed in back of the house was caused by ripe bails of Mexican marijuana.

A couple of weeks after I began tending bar, Whitey dropped in for lunch. "Willie," he said, "how'd you like to go into business for yourself?" He had a line on a bar, Ramon's Room, on the north side of the Plaza behind Tano's bar, next door to the Fernandez de Taos Bookstore, two doors east of the La Cocina. Steve played guitar and banjo while singing like a combination of Gordon Lightfoot and Ian Tyson. "What do you think? I'll play music, you tend bar, the girls can alternate as cocktail waitresses."

After work, driving home, I was so drunk with the idea of my own place that I could hardly see the road. I resigned immediately from La Doña Luz and apologized to my boss for the change in plans. Our landlord, Arturo Martinez y Salazar, a soft-spoken gentleman, exemplified the notion of dignity. He rented us the back room made famous by Ramon Hernandez, whose flamenco guitar style faded as age and drink caught up. For ten percent of the gross as rent, due at the end of each week, we got a fully equipped bar, use of a $40,000 liquor license, and a line of credit. We opened the doors for about $300, the cost of a juicer and fresh fruit for margaritas, baskets for popcorn, a few candles, and minor repairs to the joint's tables and chairs. Our agreement was verbal and both sides honored the terms. Under the portal on the north side of Taos Plaza, the Ramon's Room sign was replaced by a new one: The Living Room.

Before the tourists arrived in June, Vern and Leota Matheny, the owners of La Cocina, let their gang go early, and they frequently adjourned to our place: musician Antonio Mendoza; the world's greatest cocktail waitress, Ruthie Moya; and the black bartender, Jay Johnson. Asked about his reception in El Norte, Jay used to say, "New Mexico's the only place in America where I'm considered an Anglo." The usual artists, occasional writer, dilettantes, and world travelers filled up the rest of the calfskin chairs. Whitey fiddled on his guitar while I filled orders for drinks.

Each morning I experienced the freedom and the thrill of being self-employed. As I added up the columns of debits and credits on scraps of paper from the night before, Whitey and I always came up winners. We had a 60-40 split. He made about $150 a week and I took home $100. I still had $1500 in the bank from the winter season at the St. Bernard. It was the last time I would be truly solvent in Taos for half a century.

During the day, we—Whitey, Linda, Susie, John Koch, and

other friends—drifted from a late breakfast at Spivey's (Michael's Kitchen today) to a late lunch at La Cocina (now Taos Cowboy). We had all the time in the world to talk and listen to the dreamers and the farmers, the artists and hippies, who filled our ears with tales about the Taos way. After the bars closed at 2 a.m., we met at the R&R Truck Stop a couple miles south of the Plaza to soak up the suds with a dose of burgers and fries.

In late May, my buddy Koch alerted me to the gallery scene. "Whaley," he said, "on Saturday you can drink all day for nothing and get enough to eat to last a week. And maybe get laid, too." Though New Mexico blue laws prohibited liquor sales on Sunday, you could still buy anything you needed at George Sahd's Ranchos Trading Post. If there wasn't a private party on their day off, the downtown bar crowd went to the movies at the Plaza Theatre. The clubs and cantinas seemed as exotic to me as the café life depicted by Hemingway in *The Sun Also Rises*.

Our friend Jim Wagner ran off to Phoenix to start a new life along with his amigos, tin man Andy Ivory (aluminum siding sales) and the black Anglo, Jay Johnson. Wagner and crew were gone for ten days. On the eleventh night, when Wagner walked into our bar, Whitey began playing, "By the time I get to Phoenix...." to much applause. Wagner's abrupt departures from and sudden returns to Taos throughout the century became a part of his own inimitable legend.

In the middle of June, I was driving around Taos Plaza when a cricket chirped in my ear: the movie theatre on the south side of the Plaza was for sale. In the spring of '69, during a conversation with Koch and me at the St. Bernard Rathskeller, Larry Frank, an L.A. ex-pat and aspiring filmmaker, and pilot Fred Fair had planted the seed that nourished the idea of buying the Plaza Theatre. Fred had made a public name for himself by defying regulations against flying under the Rio Grande Gorge

Bridge—even as the agents from the FAA above watched and caught him in flagrante delicto. The air-taxi iconoclast flew the politically incorrect Larry—alleged buyer and collector of santos, retablos, and bultos—around northern New Mexico. The collection sold decades later for $3 million, thanks to Governor Bill Richardson's post-mortem intervention on behalf of Larry's widow, Lycée.

That morning I stopped on a dime and parked. In the Plaza Café that adjoined the Plaza Theatre, I met Bill Beutler, who owned the business and rented the theatre building from J.P. Brandenburg, owner of the First State Bank across the street. Beutler and his wife said they wanted $25,000 for the theatre and adjoining Plaza Café. If I came up with $7,500, they would finance the balance on a five-year note with payments of $202 a month. Over at the bank, J.P. said he'd rent the 400-seat movie theatre and café, with its four booths plus five seats at the counter, for $600 a month. The monthly rent included natural gas for heat and cooking. J.P. mentioned how he and Floyd Beutler, Bill's dad, once made a profit of $3,000 in a single year from popcorn sales. "The town needs a theatre," said J.P.

My running buddy, John Koch, who was as comfortable with plastique as Coors in a can, assured me he could come up with half the down payment by tapping a trust fund. The trust had been set up for higher education, but, as John said, "They just tell you lies in school." The Navy had rejected John's attempt to become a Seabee engineer due to his father and grandfather having been German—though each received classified security clearances during WWII. After John rejected their rejection of his application, the Navy mustered out the volunteer.

I still had the $1,500 saved from working at the Hotel St. Bernard and my folks said they'd loan me $2,500. While Koch, the mechanical genius, would operate the projectors, Susie and

I agreed to run the box office and manage the café. I wrote out a check that same day for $1,000 in earnest money and gave it to the Beutlers. The $6,500 balance was due in two weeks—while I was away at National Guard summer camp.

"What do you guys know about running a movie theatre?" somebody asked us that evening at The Living Room.

"Show good movies."

Everyone laughed.

Whitey hired a couple of folk singers to replace him, and we found a bartender to replace me during the pilgrimage to Guard summer camp in Fort Bliss and the follies in Juarez. The alarm clock interrupted visions of movie stars dancing in my head at 5 a.m. "Report for duty, Private Whaley!" Back then civilians slept secure in the knowledge that the National Guard was awake.

6

We reported for duty one block north of the Plaza at the Armory, an old gym with offices that was connected to the motor pool and garage by a hallway, which included the mess (kitchen). My head ached and nausea welled up in my stomach. I belched in short bursts, like a World War II M42 air-defense rocket launcher. The sergeants shouted: "Stand at attention! Port arms! Right shoulder arms!" We threw our O.D. (olive drab) gear and duffel bags into the back of an O.D. deuce-and-a-half.

As the convoy rumbled south into the swirling desert dust, the thermometer climbed toward 100 degrees. Flat on my back, I dreamt of my glorious life serving drinks and showing movies. But the exalted entrepreneur jumped when gung-ho school-teachers and insurance salesmen barked. The real adventure de Taos had begun.

As the sand at Fort Bliss blew across the outdoor kitchen behind the cook's tent, I scrubbed pots and pans from sunup to sundown the first weekend. On Monday morning I followed the M42s out to the range in an ammo truck and humped metal canisters filled with rockets for the soldiers who, locked and loaded, spent the day blasting drones. That evening the company clerk told me I had a message to call Susie.

"John's bank won't release his money."

"What about our half?"

"I got the check today."

"We close at 5 o'clock Friday."

"What are you going to do?"

"Maybe Mr. Brandenburg will loan us the money."

Tuesday, I humped more ammo, sweating through the 115-degree heat. My stomach churned all day. At 7 p.m. John called.

"Did you talk to Brandenburg?"

"The Beutlers won't let anybody see the books. They're telling everybody we'll never make the deal."

"Talk to Ramming about a delay." John Ramming was our attorney.

On Wednesday evening, Susie called. "Their attorney doesn't like our attorney."

"How's the bar doing?"

"Packed. Maybe we should stick to the bar business."

"And lose our money? No way."

"What are you going to do?"

"Ask for leave."

The desert was quiet. I could see the C.O. (commanding officer) sitting in the headquarters tent at his field desk.

"Sir, may I speak to you for a moment?"

"What is it, Private?"

"I made this offer on a business, the local movie theatre in Taos. I stand to lose a thousand dollars. I need twenty-four hours' emergency leave." The captain, an insurance salesman, stared out over the top of his reading glasses. He folded his flabby arms over the bulging belly that poked out of his white t-shirt. He shoved his green field cap with the two gold bars back up over his head. He leaned back in the camp chair.

"There's time for civilian life and time for soldiering."

"Yes, sir. But I didn't realize …."

"You're no prize in this man's army, Private Whaley."

"No, sir. I'm not much of a soldier."

"No."

"Pretty good at KP and humping ammo though, sir."

"Request denied."

My legs wobbled. My skin burned. I don't remember walking back to the barracks. Whitey looked up. "What's up, Willie?"

"Let's go to Juarez and get drunk."

The next day, I scraped away at the scorched bacon and cigarette ash smashed in the brown yolk on the skillet. The wind blew sand across my face into a clean pan. The sun beat down.

"What the hell, Willie, we've still got The Living Room."

Shortly after 7 p.m. I walked slowly toward the phone booth to call off the adventure. First Sergeant Elueto Maestas and Lieutenant Reggie Archuleta emerged from the major's tent. Both turned and walked straight toward me. I put down the receiver.

Sergeant Maestas said, "Better go see the old man."

"Don't make any speeches," the lieutenant said, eyes twinkling.

"Private Whaley reporting, sir." The captain had his back to me. He spun around in his chair and glared. The night before, I had made a drunken speech about the "capitalist warmongers" and how they exploited the brown man in the white man's army.

"I hope I don't regret this, Private Whaley, but they tell me you're a respectable citizen. It's hard to believe. It's not right. But I'm going to give you leave from 0500 hours Friday until 0500 Saturday morning. Get your business done."

I saluted. "Thank you, sir."

My stomach did a somersault as I turned on my heel. I walked quietly out of the C.O.'s tent before sprinting for the phone booth. "Susie, can you pick me up at the airport tomorrow at 1:30 p.m.?"

"I'm supposed to meet with Ramming. I've got errands to run for The Living Room."

"How about John?"

"I don't know where he is."

"There's a flight at 11:30 a.m. I'll rent a car. I should be in Taos by 3 o'clock.

"What are you going to do?"

"I'll think of something."

I hung up the phone and joined Whitey, who was smoking a cigarette on the front steps of the barracks.

"So?"

"The old man is going to let me out tomorrow. I've got to make a deal by 5 p.m."

"What the hell!"

At El Paso International Airport I wrote a check for my ticket to Continental Airlines, using my driver's license and a Frontier Airlines credit card for identification. Frontier issued the credit card to me when I was a college student traveling standby, and a change in fare caused me to be short of funds. Subsequently the airline neglected to bill me for several air tickets. I adjourned to the bar where the air conditioning and a couple scotch and waters settled my nerves. The public address system blared, "Passenger Whaley, please report to the Frontier Airlines ticket counter."

I ignored the page and got ready to board the Continental bird with the golden tail. Two Frontier Airlines employees with white-shirts and pale-faces eyed me. "Mr. Whaley?"

"Yes?"

"May we have your Frontier credit card?"

"Sure. You know, I've never received a bill but ..." I drew out my wallet and peeled out the errant plastic.

"Thank you, Mr. Whaley. Enjoy your flight."

I drank another scotch on board. The airplane arrived in Albuquerque at about 12:30.

"No, we can't rent you a car without a credit card."

"But I've got business in Taos. I'm a businessman. My checks are good."

"Sorry."

I hotfooted it down the pavement two miles under the boiling sun from the airport to the freeway on-ramp. Sweat, sweat, sweat. My thumb got me to Santa Fé. It was 2 p.m. Seventy miles to go. From Santa Fé, a farmer gave me a ride to Pojoaque, about fifty miles from Taos. At three o'clock, a couple of Española *vatos* stopped.

"Where are you going, gringo?"

"Taos."

"Get in, gringo. You got some money? Ha, ha. Here, wanna a shot?" The passenger handed me a bottle of sweet port.

"Thanks." I unscrewed the cap and took a swig.

Somewhere north of Española and south of Velarde, just before the highway enters the canyon, they turned west off the highway onto a dirt road and stopped at a rundown adobe. "We got to see if Miguel wants to come with us." They talked. Miguel had other things to do. Thirty miles to go. It was 3:30. I got out. "Hasta la vista, guys."

"Hey, you stupid gringo," they shouted, "where you going?"

I ran for the highway. My shirt was soaked. I flagged down a fast-moving pickup.

"Where you going, guy?"

"Taos, man. I gotta deal closing at the bank in the next hour."

Gravel spit out from his tires as he pulled away from the shoulder of the two-lane blacktop. "What's up?" He brushed back an errant brown forelock that hung down over a prominent brow.

"Buying the old movie theatre on the Plaza."

He punched the accelerator and passed the first car on the inside curve and the second car on the outside, a rear tire hanging over the Rio Grande. Swirling rapids appeared and disappeared outside the window on the driver's side. On the sidewalk in front of the Plaza Theatre, across from the First State Bank, I stepped down from the pickup.

"Good luck," said the driver.

"Thanks."

Susie nodded at me. John took off his glasses and wiped them on his greasy shirt. "What now?"

We walked into the bank's cool lobby and sat down with J.P. Brandenburg and the Beutlers. The bank clock said 4:15 when J.P. turned us down for a loan. We had no collateral, no books to look at, nothing to secure the $3,750 loan. "What about a co-signer?" I asked. To this day I don't know where that idea came from or if I even knew what a co-signer was.

J.P. nodded thoughtfully. "Who?"

"Jean Mayer?"

J.P. said that it was a fine idea. I dialed the phone.

"'Allo. 'Otel St. Bernard."

"Boss. It's Bill."

"Hey, Bill."

"What are you doing right now?"

"Cooking coq au vin."

"Can you do me a favor?"

"What?"

"Co-sign a note at the First State Bank? I've got until five o'clock here or I lose my earnest money. Koch and I are trying to buy the movie theatre."

"*Quelle heure est-il?*"

"It's 4:25."

"*Bon.* I'll be right there."

Jean arrived at five minutes to five on his 750 Harley Sportster. Perched on the bike, he looked like a tiny grizzly with his thick, muscled torso. He wore neither a shirt nor did he ask how much the loan was. After signing, he said, "I've got dinner on the stove." He was gone. J.P. deposited the dough in the vultures' account. The sellers handed over the keys. We shook hands with, J.P., our new landlord, and walked across the street to the Plaza Theatre. The Plaza seemed strangely silent. I handed one set of keys to Susie and one set to John.

"What do we do now, Bill?" asked Susie.

"They wouldn't let me in the projection room today," said John. "And they took everything out of the concession stand."

"We'll have to open tomorrow night."

"We open The Living Room at 7:30 p.m.," Susie reminded me. "I can't be two places at once."

"The bartender can open. The music doesn't start until after eight. You'll be done selling tickets by then."

"Why don't we wait until you get back?"

"We need to earn money for the rent. Open tomorrow night."

John unlocked the carved, double-wooden doors with narrow glass panels framed by routed wood dividers. An old-fashioned, glassed-in box office, containing a mechanical ticket dispenser, jutted out onto the sidewalk. Inside the lobby, the Spanish tile gleamed dimly between the streaks left by a dirty mop. We walked up and down the two aisles of empty seats into the auditorium. John ducked into the left exit to check out the janitor's closet near the southeast rear door. He came back and said, "They left us an old bucket and a dirty mop." The bathrooms didn't have toilet paper. The dirty, dented silver screen had a couple of small holes but it rose up grandly on the 40-foot-wide dusty stage below the proscenium arch. Fifty-foot vigas spanned the auditorium above the 400 moth-eaten, green-cloth seats between twenty-foot-high adobe walls.

Outside on the sidewalk, next to the box-office, John led the way up narrow dusty stairs to the deserted second-floor hallway, where several rippled opaque glass office doors were closed. Koch opened a steel door and stepped into a room with two large, black Simplex carbon-arc projectors on pedestals. As he inspected the gates, rollers, sprockets, optic bulbs and the burnt carbon rods, he muttered to himself. While scratching his head and wiping his glasses on a sleeve, he said, "Maybe I can figure this out."

Downstairs, Susie poked around behind the counter of the café that adjoined the theatre lobby. Four white molded-plastic booths with red naugahyde seated a total of sixteen people, plus there were five knee-high stools at the counter. The equipment included a French fryer, grill, hot-dog roaster, refrigerator, freezer, and sink. The café was clean as a whistle. "The cook, Sally Gonzales, and her sister Frances, the waitress, want to work for us."

"Hire them," I said. "Open it up later in the week."

At 5:30, John and I got in his '58 flatbed truck. "Let's go, man. I can't miss that plane." As we backed up from the diagonal parking place in front of the Plaza Theatre, Susie pounded on the hood.

"You're both crazy, you bastards!"

"Show business," I yelled out the window. Once again I was roaring through the canyon, this time in an aging flatbed truck, but still driven by another American maniac. I braced my feet against the floorboards and hung onto a metal brace between the torn cloth hanging from the cab's roof with one hand, clutching a can of Coors with the other. At seventy miles an hour, glasses slipping down his nose, Koch reached under the driver's seat and pulled out a McDonald's hamburger, wrapped in its signature paper. "Albuquerque, last week, Whaley. They improve with age."

"Think of your health, man. That burger will kill you."

In Santa Fé, we stopped at a distributor's warehouse and bought concession supplies. I wrote a check for almost 300 bucks. Koch borrowed $10 for gas. "How do we pay the rent?"

"J.P. told me we could sign the lease when I got back. We should have enough money by then to cover it. Susie and I can live off the bar."

About thirty people attended the first showing of *Camelot* on Saturday night. Koch broke the film, he said, maybe 100 times, and told me how the sticky, un-oiled sprockets mashed the movie at will during each change-over from one projector to the other every twenty minutes. As Koch's expletives dropped down on the heads of the audience from the open portholes in the projection room, the moviegoers broke up with laughter. The bar crowd said he only fried the celluloid a mere ten or fifteen times on Sunday night. Koch said he pitied the next projectionist who got the fragmented print of *Camelot*.

When I got back to Fort Bliss, Whitey asked, "So, Willie, you pull it off?"

"Mayer, man. A friggin' miracle."

"Now what?"

"Susie thinks we're in over our heads," I said. But at twenty-two, I had made the best deal of my life.

7

At the end of National Guard summer camp we loaded up the O.D. trucks with our duffel bags and rolled north from Fort Bliss. As the miles passed, the temperature dropped and my sluggish body revived. On Sunday afternoon, we received the company commander's benediction: "Companyyyyy ... dismissed!"

Back home in Cañon, under the cottonwood trees, Susie wouldn't get out of bed and come downstairs. "We're stuck in this goddamn place," she said. "I knew it."

"We can try it for a while, then leave."

"You'll never leave now."

"To go where?"

"Back to school."

"To learn what?"

"You can work tonight. You sell tickets. John can't get the money. How are you going to pay the bank?"

"I'll think of something." I drove into town alone and parked in one of three parking spaces in front of the posts holding up the sagging portale at the theatre. The one-sheets and stills in the glass display cases announced current and coming attractions. Inside, the cement floors shined, courtesy of Koch. During the first few minutes of the movie, I heard two teenagers talking in the back row. I whispered a couple of warnings and asked them to stop talking, then: "Shut up or I'm going to throw you out."

"Try it, gringo."

I grabbed the two boys and dragged them out of their seats and up the aisle. Their girlfriends screamed.

"Hey man, we paid our money."

"Here's your money," I said to them in the lobby. "If you behave you're welcome to come back." During my tenure at the movies I threw out drunks who rolled beer bottles down the concrete floor or hippies who smelled bad and mothers who wouldn't keep their kids quiet. From time to time, I evicted locals—Anglo and Hispanic—who felt compelled to comment during intensely dramatic scenes. The Taos Pueblo Indians rarely said a word.

The cheers from the hundred or so members of the audience for *The Shoes of the Fisherman* were not meant for Anthony Quinn's portrayal of the pope but for Koch's performance: he didn't break the film once that Sunday night. During July, Susie and I worked at both the movie theatre and The Living Room. The Plaza Café ran itself under the supervision of Sally and Frances. My teenage sister, Mary, came out and worked as a waitress in August. Early that month Whitey and I parted ways at The Living Room. Business partnerships rarely lasted in Taos. Nobody knew what the rules were or how to account for the wiles of human nature. Of my more than twenty enterprises in Taos, however, my brief experience at The Living Room is memorable for its consistent profits.

The theatre did well enough in July so that we paid two months worth of rent the first of August. Then, each night after locking up, Susie and I relaxed at one of the local clubs, listened to music, and paid for drinks and tips from the dark brown First State Bank bag. One afternoon, Susie woke me up from a nap. "John just phoned from Albuquerque. He won't be in to do the projecting. He says he's done."

I had given up on Koch getting the money for his share of the down payment, but I thought we'd save enough in salaries to pay off the bank loan. In my office desk upstairs I found Beutler's list of part-time projectionists and started calling around, leaving messages with wives and mothers. At five to eight—showtime— I was still selling tickets.

"I'm going home, Bill. You shouldn't sell tickets under false pretenses."

Just then, a friendly man standing adjacent to the box-office window said in a quiet voice, "Hello, my name's Fermin Vigil. My wife said you needed a projectionist tonight." He still wore his gas company uniform. Susie reappeared, shook her head, and smiled. During my almost twenty-year career in the movie business I never learned how to run the projectors and I never missed a show.

At the box-office, I met the local film and literary crowd. Peter Duval and Jack Parsons were in town trying to raise money for a movie based on Frank Waters' book *The Man Who Killed the Deer*. John Nichols, whose novel *The Sterile Cuckoo* had been turned into a movie, introduced himself. "Great job you're doing here, man. Are you going to bring some Buñuel movies, too?"

"Sure, "I said. "Whatever you want. And Bergman and Fellini."

Each month, I dropped off my monthly movie calendars and free passes at supermarkets and smaller shops, including John Ranier's grocery store at Taos Pueblo, as well as gas stations throughout the valley and in Questa, Peñasco, and Ojo Caliente. At Safeway, the checkers slipped calendars in the grocery bags and congratulated us on the orderly way we ran the theatre: clean bathrooms, prompt show times, no roughhouse.

In Carson Valley, northern Nevada, where I grew up and became acquainted with rural life, the sun hangs above you like a huge bright orb in the blue sky and shines down on the snow-capped Sierra Nevada Mountains, baking the haymakers and hay haulers in summer. Sit on a tractor, chug around a field, chop hay all day. The tractor burps and coughs or the truck drones ... on ... and on ... and on. Sweat drips down under your hatband and dribbles off the end of your nose. Buck a thousand bales, drag them, muscle them, stack them on a wagon or a truck. Pull into the barn. Stack the bales, suck in the dust and bird droppings high up among the rafters next to the birds and bats. As soon as one dark-green alfalfa or grass-hay field is finished, there's another hundred acres on the other side of the barbed-wire fence, and one-hundred fifty acres beyond that one.

During days between the belching smoke from the tractor or the beer fumes in my stomach, I entertained visions of beach-bound bodies lying in the sand and sun fifteen miles away at Lake Tahoe, but at night I could attend the movies as the antidote to what Karl Marx called the repetitious "idiocy of rural life." In Carson Valley—named for Kit Carson, the intrepid tracker and Indian fighter from Taos—I watched movies at the single-screen Nevada Theatre in the town of Gardnerville. The Washo Indians sat upstairs in the balcony and the white people, downstairs. I don't remember where the Chinese families sat. You always tried to sit back under the upper deck lest your red brothers hawk spittle down at you. In the company of two Washo Indian ranch hands who worked for Knox, I once evaded the aging usher and sneaked upstairs to watch a movie. The seats were in a shambles; a whole row leaned forward or backward if two people got up at the same time. No wonder our Washo brothers felt compelled to protest with spit balls from the balcony.

But the magic of the movie house transformed my sensibilities and restored my equilibrium. The experience was cathartic—similar to reading a novel, riding a horse at breakneck speed, or skiing a high-speed nonstop run down a steep ski slope. Upon leaving the movie theatre, I felt restored.

The first movie that made an indelible impression on me was *Shane*. At the climax, Shane (Alan Ladd) shoots Jack Wilson (Jack Palance) and the bullet sends the bad guy sprawling back against the wall of the saloon. Shane spins the barrel of his pistol in a triumphant gesture. Joey (Brandon de Wilde) pleads with his hero, "Come back, Shane. Dad needs you. Mother wants you." But Shane tells his young friend Joey "there's no going back from a killing." The hero rides up the pass into the mountains and vanishes.

But when I woke up in the morning, I was stuck, like Joey, with the homesteaders—back on the tractor or the truck in

Carson Valley. Shane had ridden up and over Kingsbury Grade, probably to look at the babes on the beach. I'd start riding round and round the fields again. The sweet smell of alfalfa can sicken you. The rhythmic sound of the crickets at night only reminds you of the pastoral prison.

At Colorado College I saw foreign films, like Ingmar Bergman's *The Seventh Seal* and Francois Truffaut's *Jules and Jim*. Though these films evaded my understanding, they liberated my sensibilities. In Taos I began reading criticism and reviews about the art form while studying the empirical effects on audience members. One summer at Colorado College I had attended a lecture about movies by Pauline Kael, *The New Yorker* critic and one-time Berkeley film exhibitor, who wrote sizzling prose that recreated the experience of seeing movies and focused on the way film reflected cultural attitudes. In *I Lost It at the Movies,* her 1965 collection of reviews, she noted that the "art of the critic is to transmit his knowledge of and enthusiasm for art to others" and secondly that "any honest man can perform the critical function to the limits of his taste and power." Kael, a philosophy major at UC Berkeley, encouraged one to consider how the movies provided the public with possibilities—new ways of living and thinking.

The counterculture considered film a sacred art form and in the '60s the saints had names like Buñuel, Fellini, Truffaut, Bergman, and Bertolucci. In the '70s, Americans like Robert Altman, Martin Scorsese, and Francis Ford Coppola joined the pantheon. Literature and film appealed to my restless imagination and sure enough, as the years passed, I began having trouble distinguishing between fiction and reality.

Though I booked movies based on my analysis of what the movie critics wrote or in response to advice from knowledgeable friends, the opinions of film salesmen, carefully considered, were more reliable in terms of results. Still, what played well in

Manhattan or Peoria didn't necessarily match the tastes of moviegoers in Taos. I always paid close attention to requests at the box office and attempted to translate local tastes into practical success.

I met at La Cocina a white-haired 20th Century Fox film salesman with a glistening eye and the homonymous name of Dick Fox, who set me straight over cocktails about the business of running a movie theatre. Courtesy of his expense account, Ruthie kept his glass and mine full in the air-conditioned comfort of the lounge. Dick laughed when I told him I had ditched the ticket stubs without recording the numbers. He said the film distributors hired spies to spot-check audience attendance at movie theatres and explained the system of flat-fee guarantees versus minimum percentages, what box-office reports meant, and how your house expenses affected the percentage you paid. We discussed 20th Century Fox's *Lady in Cement,* starring Frank Sinatra and Raquel Welch, which grossed $500 in three days—twice what *Shoes of the Fisherman* had garnered in a week. After Dick left, I recreated the ticket sales figures and filled in the box-office reports. I attributed the generosity of his spirit both to his character as well as La Cocina's fabled hospitality.

Over the years, La Cocina's staff, the management, waitresses, and Ruthie Moya could make nervous parents, dining with their long-haired or raggedy-ass child, feel as if their progeny was a respectable member of this eccentric community. There was an unacknowledged conspiracy of us against them. A smile or recommendation from a waitress carried more weight than a letter from a banker.

When the July bills arrived in mid-August, the distributors charged us the maximum percentages, saying they'd never seen such high grosses in Taos—even at the Kit Carson Drive-In. Per Dick Fox, I submitted my overhead of $2,500 a month, which included rent, salaries, and utilities. Subsequently, the distributors lowered the charges from sixty to thirty-five percent.

The Beutlers booked July, but I chose the movies for August. The kudos and the money poured down like rain during a summer thunderstorm. The urbane film aficionados appreciated the foreign or specialized art films that we mixed in with the usual commercial titles. Evelyn Waugh's satire of the funeral industry, *The Loved One,* did good business, as did *100 Rifles,* the western thriller featuring NFL great Jim Brown and sexpot Raquel Welch. Sidney Poitier in Columbia's *To Sir with Love* and Dustin Hoffman in *The Graduate* did big business. *Guess Who's Coming to Dinner* with Tracy and Hepburn was another success.

The Plaza Theatre generally featured films for short playtimes —Sunday-Monday, Tuesday-Wednesday, and Thursday-Saturday. Multiple weekly changes meant less risk—if it was a winner, I could always bring it back. We charged $1 for adults and fifty cents for children twelve and under. For the kiddie matinees we charged twenty-five cents—cheap for two hours of babysitting. While the moms shopped the Plaza merchants and the dads attended to their duties at the Plaza cantinas, we sold out two kiddie matinees almost every Saturday afternoon. Our ticket gross doubled from $2,500 in July to $5,000 in August.

Each day I traveled back and forth across the Plaza from the theatre on the south side to La Cocina on the north side, becoming increasingly familiar with the three scarecrow-thin *viejos* who sat on the wooden bench with their scrawny necks and shirts buttoned up to their necks under their straw cowboy hats; they grinned and mumbled back when you said *"Buenos días."* Surly teenagers in cotton shirts, pegged jeans, and black Beatle boots slouched along the two-foot-high walls that surrounded the central park fixed with flagstones and cottonwoods. A hippie who panhandled responded to advice about "getting a job" with the standard comment, "Far out, man." You'd spot a Pueblo Indian dressed up in clean-washed braids and his Penney's blanket wrapped round the waist, posing for tourists who wore brightly colored jump suits tucked tightly over bulging stomachs by wide silver and turquoise Concho belts. The daytime drinkers who spilled out on the sidewalk at Fernandez de Taos made guttural remarks like, "What are you looking at, *gringo?*"

Mostly I enjoyed my blind luck that first summer in Taos—a seemingly magical place far from my youthful frustrations in Nevada and my failures as a college student in Colorado. Unlike in Carson Valley, I woke up to a beautiful wife, charming digs in Cañon, and a historic 400-seat theatre on the Plaza, along with new friends and the constant elixir of music and conversation. Between the buzz and the beer, I had all day to recover from hangovers. Most of my friends were older by five or ten or twenty years. Though the fires raged in the ghettos of urban America and napalm ignited the green velvet jungles in Vietnam, there was a sense of otherworldliness in Taos. I felt free of the bigotry of my redneck roots and liberated from the conformity of the America I imagined ensconced behind white-picket fences. The high desert and mountains appealed to the senses and café society on Taos Plaza stirred the imagination. While living in never-never land, I washed down spicy enchiladas with Dos Equis. Though tomorrow was never as sweet as yesterday, we in Taos never tire of invoking the memories.

8

The day after Labor Day, the tourists disappeared and the kids got called back to school. The receipts at the Plaza Café dropped during the day and the box-office revenue for movies plummeted at night. We abruptly leased the café to George Fowler, a local handyman and extra in *Easy Rider,* who played a deputy sheriff in the scene where Jack Nicholson's character gets out of jail at the old courthouse across the Plaza. In trade for renting the café, George swept and mopped the theatre.

In late August, the season had begun changing and swayback pickup trucks trundled back to the villages filled with firewood from the mountains. The wood stacks outside adobe houses grew in depth and breadth toward the end of September. The foliage changed from green to yellow, gold, and red. Smoke curled up each morning from the chimneys and stovepipes. Cal Loving, the co-owner of La Cantina, a bar across the alley from the Plaza Theatre, purchased La Cocina from Vern and Leota Matheny. Cal's lovely wife, Mary, a nurse from Maine, and her two daughters, Meredith and Vicky, joined him for the ride. On Monday nights, we idlers gathered at La Cocina to watch football with

Howard Cosell, Dandy Don Meredith, and Frank Gifford.

The Beutlers, who still operated the Kit Carson Drive-in, offered to sell me five acres, the screen, concession stand, the projection equipment, and business for $60,000. It was a helluva deal. The drive-in sold more in concessions—popcorn and cokes—than we grossed in ticket sales. A glance at the number of cars and you could see the undercount the distributors had mentioned to me. I approached a couple of people half-heartedly, including my stepfather, but I couldn't raise the money. Les Dollison, a fellow from El Paso who owned several small-town hard-top and soft-top theatres throughout the state, purchased the drive-in, or so-called "soft-top." At La Cocina, Les tutored me on the ins and outs of theatre management. In the mid-'80s, Wal-Mart bought the drive-in property for a reported half-million dollars. I was right about the deal, but youth undermined my credibility.

That fall syndicated film critic Chaucer Henderson joined the theatre staff and wrote enigmatic one-liners about the movies: "See it ... to believe it" and "I dare you to watch" such and such. He might even compare a movie star to a well-known local. Film fans read Chaucer's comments on the backs of the calendar quizzically or smiled knowingly and winked at my pseudonym.

In October, Susie and I accompanied friends Steve and Linda White and Mark Daily and his partner Jan Akolt to Sandra Wilson's Gallery on Canyon Road in Santa Fé for Mark's first show. Mark rented the Blumenschein studio on Ledoux St. in Taos and lived on lima beans. Since he managed to sell a few paintings that evening, we celebrated by dining at The Compound restaurant, where the former Hotel St. Bernard chef Claude Roth cooked. Claude joined us for dessert.

Then we adjourned to Santa Fé's Hotel La Fonda, where guitarist-singer Antonio Mendoza, who had transferred from Taos to the City Different, called on Whitey to sing a few songs. When the bar closed, we decided to rent a hotel room to avoid driving home that night. As we were checking in, a slight scruffy figure in Levis, a jean jacket, and cowboy hat came up and re-introduced himself to Whitey, reminding the entertainer that he, Dennis Hopper, had spent a previous summer filming *Easy Rider* in Taos. He invited us to join him and his companion, Michelle Phillips of the Mamas and Papas, in his room.

Michelle got out her guitar and began to strum. Dennis attempted to build a fire in the kiva fireplace. Susie giggled and he glared at her. Michelle sang *Me and Bobby Magee.* As we left, Whitey whispered that Michelle was "off-key. Terrible guitar player." The lyrics, "Freedom's just another word for nothing left to lose," always appealed to my existential attitude. We had heard that Bonnie Evans Bell, Mabel Dodge Luhan's granddaughter, sold the Mabel Dodge house to Dennis for $200,000 above the asking price.

Mabel Dodge had arrived in Taos toward the end of the second decade of the 20th century and established a salon at her house for social engineers and luminaries from the world of art and literature, including D.H. Lawrence. It became a place filled with *Utopian Visions,* according to scholar Lois Rudnick in her book of that name. In 2009, during the seminar called Dennis Hopper and Friends at the Harwood Museum, the actor mentioned that he only paid $140,000 for the rambling Southwest salon. Both Luhan and Hopper believed the transcendent vibrations from this house and holy place—Taos—could renew the spirit of mainstream America ... and the world. We are still waiting.

The November sky turned ashen white. Tony Bryan, a Colorado College mate, entrepreneur, and ski instructor, suggested that we go partners in the grocery delivery/garbage pickup business.

Since the road to Taos Ski Valley was unpaved and intermittently maintained, truck drivers preferred to drop the freight at Montoya's Texaco Gas Station near the blinking light. Montoya and son, both of whom wore the famous Texaco Star, rented us a storeroom for freight delivery. Tony provided a four-wheel-drive Dodge power wagon with horse trailer, and I provided a strong back. In the mornings, I picked up groceries and kegs of beer on my way up to ski. At day's end, I'd empty garbage from the various hotels into the trailer and head for the dump in the middle of town behind the Kit Carson Drive-In.

The Ski Valley scheduled its opening for Thanksgiving day in 1969. Walt Disney's *Never a Dull Moment* was scheduled to play that weekend, along with *The Incredible Sex Revolution* for the "midnight show" at 10:30 p.m. The Tuesday-Wednesday change was a Spanish-language double feature called *La Chamuscada* (The Scorched) and *Amor a Ritmo a Go Go* (Love to Dance Go Go). The film distributors promised me that the Thanksgiving holidays would bring a bump in ticket sales and said the Christmas releases would ignite attendance.

But the fireworks came early when the phone rang at 1 a.m. on Thanksgiving morning. "Hey, man. This is Steve Williams at La Cantina. Your joint's on fire." Susie stayed in bed. I got up and remember dressing as if in slow motion. When I drove up to the theatre I could see the volunteers from the fire department hacking away at the hand-carved double wooden doors with short, red-handled fire axes. They asked me to unlock what was left of the front door. When they pulled the doors open fresh oxygen poured in and the flames exploded. They dragged their thick rubber hoses into the lobby and sprayed water up and over the auditorium into the inferno. Black smoke billowed out the front door and ballooned up into the deep blue-black sky. The flames leapt high above the seats and gobbled up the fifty-foot vigas.

At 7 a.m. the volunteers retreated to the Walgreens Drug Store, catty-corner to the theatre, for coffee and brandy. J.P. Brandenburg showed up in khakis—the only time I saw him without a suit. Attorney John Ramming (who had never sent us a bill for drawing up the contract and lease for the theatre), Clark Funk of Funk's 5 & 10 and the Don Fernando Curio Store, and Bob Krongaard of the Lilac Shoppe, all helped fight the fire. By daybreak, only the facade and three lonely walls stood up against the sky. Smoke and black soot covered the café, the offices, and the projection room.

Later, the volunteers told me that the Plaza Theatre became a case study in what not to do. They could have saved the place if they had kept the front doors shut and gone in the back where the fire started. Earlier that Thanksgiving evening, at 6 p.m., the Taos Art Association's playhouse, an old barn a couple blocks away, also burned. The state fire marshal said both theatres were torched by arsonists.

• • •

As I sit here writing these words I am staring—literally—at old movie calendars from 1969, smudged with soot from the fire. The fire left me feeling marooned with unfinished business. I spent years trying to recreate the best deal I ever made and the feelings of excitement associated with that extraordinary year. Though I always wanted to leave Taos, and succeeded for short periods, I kept coming back. And I still haven't figured out why.

The Exile

"Whaley, you gringo, what the hell are you doing in this bar?"

1

Some thirty-six hours after the arsonists torched the Plaza Theatre on Thanksgiving eve, 1969, this gringo whined his way up the slopes of Taos Ski Valley on the chairlift with the light-footed skier and hotelier Dadou Mayer, who suggested that I check out the vacant theatre in Ranchos de Taos, where the L.A. expat, Larry Frank, had curated a foreign film exhibition during previous summers.

After skiing and completing my rounds as TSV grocery delivery man and garbage pick-up service, I unloaded the day's refuse in the town dump. Next I stopped by Montoya's TV and Radio Repair shop on South Santa Fé Road and asked Raymundo, the owner of the shop and landlord of the El Cortez Theatre, if the vacant picture palace was available. He said it was for sale, but offered to lease me the narrow auditorium with its 330 wooden-back seats, six on each side of the aisle, for $200 a month. In the event that a buyer came forward with an offer, the lease included a "right of first refusal." I agreed to the deal and went home to tell Susie, whose long blond tresses fell down, down over the hollows in her long pale face. Her blue-green eyes filled with despair. "I thought we were finished here," she said.

"I haven't got any place to go," I replied. "Everyone here treats me good." In Taos, where the tyranny of tolerance prevails, they keep giving you second chances. When the cops stopped your weaving automobile in those days, they might ask, "Think you can drive home okay?" When Los Taoseños allowed me to join the National Guard, I always believed they saved my life, or at least my sanity. What I didn't know was that the Sacred Mountain keeps you alive to serve the metaphysical spirits of El Norte.

With all due respect for science and empirical evidence, the Sacred Mountain, as all Taoseños know, gives you permission to jump in and test the waters. As Taoseños say, it is "better to beg for forgiveness than ask for permission." My opportunities, the episodic adventures of the entrepreneur, and the culture of tolerance taught me much about the foibles of human nature and more about fate and chance.

First paradise tempts you, as it had me. I got a job at the ski valley and became, however briefly, a member of café society and the business class on Taos Plaza. Then Father Salazar denounced me with his fire and brimstone sermons from his pulpit at the Cañon Brethren Church in the fall of '69, reportedly telling his congregations that the new overseer of the Plaza Theatre was a "yuppie or hippie in disguise." Finally Zeus lit me up with his lightning bolts and reduced me to reality. Veterans of bar-stool wisdom warned me of the two-year rule: if you survive the first two years then you'll know whether you, a *pendejo*, can find a home in this paradox of paradise. The suffering begins, not because your karma is so bad but because pain is good for the soul, hence my exile to Ranchos de Taos.

On weekends the Ranchos rowdies gathered at the two dance-halls, El Cortez Tavern/Old Martinez Hall next to the theatre, and Andy's La Fiesta Lounge on the east side of the historic church. Sunday mornings parishioners picked their way between broken, bloodied beer bottles. As the tale of my entrepreneur-ial adventures unfolded across the decades, my twenty-one months in Ranchos turned out to be a gift for a student of neo-phyte Chicano cultural studies, which studies included advanced courses in street fighting and the application of the equalizer—a convenient chair, bottle, club, or attorney.

The double doors below a broken neon sign opened for busi-ness on February 1, 1970 at the El Cortez Theatre in Ranchos de Taos, next to the north-south highway, by the post office, across the street from the famously photographed and paint-ed San Francisco de Asis Catholic Church. The aroma of dead cockroaches, patchouli oil, and the sweet scent of urine greeted moviegoers even as they marveled at WPA social realist murals on the morphic adobe walls under a leaky roof. The space heater roared on and off, competing for the ears of the audience as the voices of movie stars blared forth from the single audio speaker behind the nipped and torn screen.

Upstairs a small projection room housed the large black me-tallic cylinders for the carbon-arc Simplex projectors, carbon copies of the old Plaza Theatre machines. The ratchets rattled and rolled in time to the idiosyncratic beat of the 35mm film as it passed by the apertures, thanks to operators Fermin Vigil and Steve Rivera. Fermin, who responded to an emergency call when my buddy and projectionist John Koch resigned, taught the trade to Steve, a National Guard *cuate*.

In Ranchos, folks referred to the Town of Taos as Sodom and Gomorrah or had never visited Taos Ski Valley. Other Ranchos residents were sophisticated politicos with influential connections to state government in Santa Fé, which politicos ignored in public their more unorthodox relatives—say, gang-bangers—which relations I learned more about later during the *Horse Fly* years. Despite a lack of competing cinemas, the relocation of my business from Taos to Ranchos reduced attendance by fifty to seventy-five percent. At the El Cortez Tavern next door, the number of asses on barstools frequently outnumbered paid moviegoers in my seats. As the staff exited the theatre, moviegoers were often seen huddled over disabled vehicles. Vandals slashed tires and batteries disappeared even as fractured windshields appeared. Without knowing it, I had stepped into El Norte's version of the barrio.

2

In February, 1970, Sun International Films four-walled (rented) the El Cortez theatre outright for a family fracas film called *Cougar Country* and saturated Albuquerque television with regional advertising, unbeknownst to me, who had no television set. Cars and pickups began parking up and down the highway and all around the St. Francis church that Friday night. We were prepared for maybe one hundred ticket buyers, but the sudden onslaught of hundreds of men, women, and children outside, clawing against the glass doors shocked us. I called the state police, who hastened over to help with crowd control. By the second show at 9 p.m. I managed to get everyone lined up two by two, while also taking reservations over the phone. Inside the tiny lobby, across from the men's and women's bathrooms—toilets only—the staff pitched in behind the L-shaped concession stand and sold out a month's supply of candy, cokes, and popcorn during the two-day run.

In March, *Easy Rider* made its Taos debut and most of the seats were sold for an unprecedented ten-day run of the locally filmed movie. The opening scene features Antonio Mendoza, the La Cocina musician, who plays a Mexican drug dealer and sells white powder to Billy (Dennis Hopper) and Captain America (Peter Fonda) at a disconsolate location better known to locals as La Contenta, a bar in El Prado, north of Taos. The La Contenta regulars posed as extras and watched the fictional transaction from the front porch at the local cantina. Each evening these same gap-toothed hombres showed up at movie time, grinning and giggling, to sign autographs and receive plaudits from their fans. Though the distributor got seventy percent of the gross, *Easy Rider,* thanks also to concession sales, was the financial highlight of the El Cortez exile.

Due to malodorous habits, I convinced the Hog Farm communards from the Peñasco Valley, about thirty miles distant, to call before coming to the movies so we could segregate them from the local population. The happy hippies agreed to restrict their movie diet to Tuesday nights when art or exploitation films played to only ten or fifteen fans from the greater Taos area. The sixties were over, but the hippies, including the ones who rode the bus out of Woodstock to Taos, haunted the greater area for decades with dreams of an alternative America.

After the El Cortez Theatre opened, and since I wanted more time for skiing and running gates, I recruited Larry Crowley to take over my partnership with Tony Bryan in the TSV grocery and garbage business. By promoting himself as an authentic hippy garbage man, Larry parlayed the business into a cottage industry complete with trade in recycled material from the back of a large flatbed truck. The ingenious Blue-eyed Crow rigged up a wire-fence contraption on the empty flat bed. After making his rounds and piling up the garbage, he would attach a chain to post and wire fence then drive out from under the load, leaving the garbage neatly piled up for burial by bulldozer at the town dump.

While waiting my turn to race slalom on Porcupine at TSV, a ski patroller came up and told me that Susie, who worked as a ticket agent for Fred Fair's air-taxi service, had broken her leg skiing on Reforma, under the second lift. The year before, a friend had crashed on the same slope and died of a broken neck at Holy Cross Hospital. When I arrived at the hospital three doctors were standing at the foot of her bed. She was writhing in agony and screamed like a banshee when one of the docs tried to pull off her ski boot without undoing the buckles. I yelled, "You sonofabitch," jerked his hand away and shoved him back against the wall.

Doctors Rosen and Pond, veteran skiers and leg fixers, took over while I called some docs in Colorado Springs who fixed knees and legs for my football teammates. They recommended a chemical engineer-turned-surgeon, Dr. Kosicki, who operated out of the St. Vincent's Hospital in Santa Fé. He inserted a steel rod in her femur to hold the bone and wired her leg to the end of the bed, where she said she enjoyed virtual visits from Prince Valiant, prompted by the pain killers.

After three weeks in hospital, Susie hobbled home on crutches to the house in Cañon, where she slept downstairs on a couch with her Siamese cats for weeks before she could climb the stairs to the loft bedroom. The emergency service, hospital stay, and surgery cost about $4,000. Insurance man Dave Polson had persuaded us to purchase a thousand-dollar deductible policy. We piled the balance owed onto the Plaza Theatre debt left over from the fire and scraped by on popcorn revenue.

When the Kit Carson Drive-In, located between Taos and Ranchos, opened in early spring, attendance at the El Cortez Theatre turned from a trickle into a seep. Then things got worse.

In early May, a friend phoned from La Cocina to say, "Your landlord is down here celebrating the sale of the El Cortez Theatre to Dennis Hopper." I had a right of first refusal written into my lease, but nobody called or gave me a chance to match the $25,000 offer. That weekend I had a National Guard meeting in Springer on the east side of the Sangre de Cristos. I put on my O.D. fatigues and left to consider the end of life in Taos.

Despite her crutches and distaste for Taos, Susie raised hell and got hold of David "The Good" Hopper who served as the enfant terrible's business manager. David, his wife Charlotte, and their two daughters frequented the movie theatre and, in contrast to the Hopper hangers-on, appeared to be quite sane. He told Susie he'd look into the matter.

That weekend fifteen inebriated National Guard soldiers from Taos kicked the shit out of two Anglo cowboys at a bar near the Springer armory. A fellow guardsman, New Mexico native, and Chicano from Santa Fé, said he was sickened by the sight. I filed away the massacre in my memory bank as a reminder to keep the previously mentioned "equalizer" ready at hand. You might not win all the battles but you could increase the odds of survival.

At the Brandenburg and Ramming Law Office, the up-and-coming young Republican, John Ramming, dressed sharp in Western trim—bolo tie, white shirt, Levis, and boots—while the enfant terrible sat there in his stuntman costume from *The Last Movie*—Levis, boots, long hair, and a disheveled cowboy hat. From his shoulder hung a leather bag, where he concealed, it was said, a .45 pistol. I wore my Army haircut above the ears, Levis, a blue shirt, and low-cut, black Converse tennis shoes.

Ramming had not billed me for the legal work he'd done on the lease and purchase of the Plaza Theatre business back in the summer of 1969, but I thought he was still my attorney. He and his new client knew I didn't have the wherewithal to match Dennis's $25,000 offer. Dennis said I could cause a lot of trouble for his current project—viewing the edits of *The Last Movie*—and he also mentioned that I could sue him if I didn't like the done deal. Ramming leaned toward Dennis and nodded.

Although showbiz buzz estimated the actor's share of profits on *Easy Rider* at millions of dollars, the famous director offered me free rent for the summer, a deal worth six hundred dollars. Since the rent rebate gave me some breathing room until I could think of something, I said okay. David Hopper told me that he and his secretary would take over management of the theatre in September. Later, much later, the secretary herself worked for me at the new Plaza Theatre box office, where she also provided me with supplements.

That spring and summer I spent a lot of time touring the Taos environs on my 175-horsepower Bridgestone motorcycle or driving around with Jack Parsons in the latter's worn-out Porsche. The photographer temporarily turned filmmaker told me about his experiences at film school in London and his relative, Elsie Clews Parsons, who figured as the basis for the anthropologist in Frank Waters' *The Man Who Killed the Deer*. I backed Jack to the tune of a few hundred dollars in a venture he named The Green Tree Gallery of photography. We rented space from the Taos Art Association for $150 a month in a building just north of the Taos Inn. Jack fixed the place up and managed to sell one photograph before we closed the venture at the end of August.

When September arrived, David and his secretary assumed

management of the El Cortez Theatre. I wished them luck and left for San Francisco to find work. While I was holed up on Nob Hill with a friend from college, the millionaire Harvey Mudd dropped by *The Taos News,* where Susie waited for me to find a job in the city. She worked as a receptionist, bookkeeper and supervisor of the newspaper boys. Earlier that winter I'd stopped by Taos East, the condo complex managed by Tony Bryan, and met Harvey, who I solicited for help to rebuild the Plaza Theatre. But the heir to the Cypress copper fortune demurred. Now he told Susie he wanted to invest. Shortly after Harvey left, David called her saying they would pay me $400 a month to return and manage the El Cortez Theatre. Our landlord, Fred Fair, told Susie he'd sell us the house we rented, and six acres, for $15,000, and he offered to finance the down payment.

Suddenly we had prospects. Years later when I saw *Godfather III,* and Michael Corleone (Al Pacino) says, "Just when I thought I was out, they pull me back in," I realized how the pattern of temptation and seduction kept me in Taos. Whether enchanted or entrapped, and though I tested the rapids in other places, I always washed up on the ancient seashores, now deserts and valleys, of Taos.

At La Cocina, Ruthie welcomed me back, "Hi, hon." Weren't we all in love with this vision of loveliness, the dark hair and eyes, a hospitable smile, both sexy and maternal? Owner Cal Loving reopened my tab and the usual suspects—architect Gene Sanchez, artist Jim Wagner, picture framer Dave Nesbitt, teacher Gil Archuleta, and artist-draftsman Woolcott Ely moved over and found an extra barstool for me.

One early Sunday morning, December 13, 1970, the House of Hopper called to arrange a midday screening of the latest edit of *The Last Movie*—Dennis's *auto-da-fé* about life imitating art. Depending on the director's mood enhancers, the narrative structure of this work in progress changed frequently. Call it mimesis unhinged.

That particular Sunday, Dennis surprised us first with a screening of Alejandro Jodorowsky's surrealistic *El Topo,* a panoply of provocative imagery which, following its Ranchos debut in the USA, opened on December 18 at the Elgin Theatre in New York, becoming the progenitor of the midnight movie cult. Though Dennis's movie seemed tame compared to Jodorowsky's paean to heaven and hell, the experience of watching *El Topo, The Last Movie,* and the regularly scheduled film that evening *Fellini Satyricon,* reminded me that the enfant terrible was in good company. Ultimately, Universal took the final cut of *The Last Movie* away from the wayward auteur and edited it into episodic units absent Dennis's unrequited vision. After watching the three films, eyeballs spinning, I could barely find my way home that evening.

Due to a friendly relationship with a La Cocina part-timer and TSV ski school supervisor (much to founder Ernie Blake's chagrin), I was invited to become a ski instructor in the winter of 1970 and again in 1971. When my ski-instructor friend, Tony, broke a leg, he turned over his high-paying guests to me and

I scored at the top of TSV income ranks for private lessons at Christmas.

(TSV Inc. retained sixty percent of the gross income from privates, while a group lesson for six or seven people, which was worth twenty-five or thirty-five dollars to the ski corporation, paid the instructor nine or ten dollars for two hours work.)

The more praise I received from guests, the more fault Ernie found. At the Hotel St. Bernard my frustration, aided and abetted by beer and brandy, stimulated further anti-authoritarian outbursts whenever I bumped into one of Ernie's toadies. My relations with my colleagues in the ski school suffered from my wise-ass tongue. For instance, in imitation of Mayer, I might turn to a colleague and ask, "Do you have fun the way you ski? No, seriously?"

In January the skies were deep, pure blue, and nary a cloud appeared for ten straight days. Each day the temperature soared to ten below zero by three in the afternoon. We used hair dryers to warm up our ski boots at lunchtime. Koch's memorable words— "snow-packed and sanded"—described the winters of 1971 and 1972, ski seasons that ended more or less in mid-March.

The mid-winter drought also dried up our well in Cañon, so we hauled water from Jim Farrell's Conoco gas station on the Plaza. Fred Fair's now ex-wife, Hueri, rented out the big house up the hill in Cañon to artist Ken Price and his wife, Happy. Happy showed up at our door to complain about the dry well we shared. We told her to haul water like the rest of us. She and Ken had moved to Taos with small children and shortly moved out in search of a studio and house with running water. Happy has reminded me more than once of my rude manners.

That winter of 1971, Dennis addressed some UNM film students in Albuquerque, who embarrassed Mr. Hipness by mentioning that his own El Cortez Theatre had shown *Paint Your*

Wagon, a retro musical western featuring Clint Eastwood and Lee Marvin. One couldn't fault the student critics, but among exhibitors and distributors there was a quid pro quo. Show this dog so I can tell my bosses, and we'll let you show the winners. Though I explained the ins and outs, Dennis didn't seem interested in the arts of distribution and exhibition. The *Easy Rider* sociologist also told me, "You shouldn't show Buñuel's *Viridiana* on a Sunday." Few (if any) native Taoseños attended Buñuel's anti-Catholic art film, since *la gente* preferred Mexican movies with comic stars like Cantinflas or singing cowboys like Antonio Aguilar. Dennis reminded me that we lived in a good church-going community, ignoring the history of violence that we all endured, including Dennis himself who, due to anti-social behavior, got beaten up and thrown in jail.

He ranted on and said he didn't like my showing *Soldier Blue*, a movie that depicted in graphic detail the Sand Creek (Indian) Massacre, which always attracted a large crowd from Taos Pueblo. During discussions about *Soldier Blue* or *Flap* (aka the politically incorrect movie first named *Nobody Loves a Drunken Indian,* with Anthony Quinn), my friends from Taos Pueblo said that regardless of the violence, they liked seeing images of Native Americans on the screen. The politically correct outsiders, like college-educated insiders, turned out to represent censorship and paternalism and lacked the native-born and bred Taoseños' self-deprecating humor. Several of my politically incorrect Hispanic and Pueblo friends have said they cheered for the Cleveland Indians and Washington Redskins because they appreciated the name recognition. After listening to one of Hopper's rants in late winter 1971, I told Dennis to go to hell, hung up the phone, and quit.

3

By the spring of 1971, Harvey had begun construction on the Plaza Theatre but the dream was turning into a nightmare. Back in January of 1970, a friend of Whitey's who owned a chain of movie theatres in Missouri had described to me a new business model: the twin—two screens, one projectionist, and one concession stand. Subsequently, I scrounged up $450 from the popcorn revenue at El Cortez Theatre and paid a theatre architect from Denver to consult with me in Taos. The architect visited the burned-out hulk on the Plaza and drew up a simple design for two auditoriums with 200 seats each, a common projection room, concession stand, and bathrooms. He estimated that the entire project could be built for $85,000. J.P. Brandenburg said he would sell me the Plaza Theatre for $75,000 and offered to finance the package, because, he said, "the town needs a movie theatre."

After Harvey offered to take on the project in the fall of 1970, we discussed my ideas less and his utopian concepts more. He intended to divest himself of the Cypress mines stock inherited from the family, and reinvest the cash in Taos: movie theatre, low-income housing, and the remodel of the Dunn House property—today's boutique shopping complex adjacent to Bent

Street. In turn he wanted to set up two companies, Ponderevo Inc. and Pelican Inc., one for the construction of new buildings and one for operating the businesses they housed. The profits from Harvey's Taos enterprises were meant to fund an environmental organization called the Central Clearing House in Santa Fé, the predecessor to today's enviro advocates at the Western Environmental Law Center. Harvey and his compatriots fought the good fight against the coal-fired power plants, which poisoned the air and created haze in the deep-blue skies above the four corners region of Arizona, Colorado, New Mexico and Utah. He also told me that I was the leading candidate to manage his Taos enterprises. Susie was dubious of the millionaire, but I still dreamed of recapturing the magic of 1969.

During negotiations with J.P. Brandenburg, I suggested that Harvey offer to buy the adjoining building on the west side, which had a common wall with the theatre and shared access to the basement and second-story offices. Dave Polson's insurance agency occupied the ground floor, but he wanted to move. J.P. agreed to sell the corner building of more than 5,000 square feet for $75,000.

A liquor-store business in the corner of McCarthy Plaza, owned by Joe Sanchez, was also for sale, and we discussed opening a delicatessen and wine shop in the street-level café space. Upstairs, we planned to install a bar with a few stools and tables overlooking the Plaza, while remodeling two offices as private viewing rooms, one for each theatre, where food and drink could be served to film fans. Harvey bought Joe's liquor license and inventory.

There were only three parking spots in front of the theatre so we met with Saki Karavas, owner of Hotel La Fonda and the vacant lot behind the theatre building. Saki wore a dark suit and tie, and his head shone under the dim light in his hotel bedroom.

He was renowned as a tough negotiator, but he was also broke. In the tiny room, stuffed with books, paintings, and memorabilia, including original Lawrence manuscripts, Harvey and Saki sat in chairs with their knees almost touching.

"You've got to have parking. I'll sell you the lot behind the theatre for $85,000."

"Too much. I'll give you 65,000."

"80,000."

"70,000."

"I'll meet you halfway. 75,000."

"70,000."

Sitting behind Harvey on the Greek's bed, I looked at Saki and shrugged my shoulders. Saki shook his head, "Tsk, tsk."

Outside on the sidewalk, Harvey said, "I blew it, didn't I?"

Never before or since would Saki negotiate in such a reasonable manner. The asking price for his ten D.H. Lawrence paintings increased from $30,000 to $300,000 to $3 million during the 35 years I knew him. Artist Ken Price and musician Ry Cooder saw the price of a bullfight poster rise from $500 to $1,000 to $1,500 on successive days (still that poster became the cover of Ry's album, *Borderline*). As Saki always said, "Some have the cookies, some have the jar." At the time, he had the jar but no cookies.

At La Cocina I mentioned to Woolcott Ely the need for a crane to install steel girders for the Plaza Theatre roof come spring. The tall, slender, slightly balding artist-draftsman had a heightened sense of justice and was known to stand up and yell epithets at dastardly villains on the screen. He said he flew too many combat missions in the South Pacific during WWII. After he was decommissioned, they hooked him up to electro-shock treatment and consequently he could drink more scotch to less effect than any five La Cocina regulars combined. We were all jealous. Woolie worked for an architectural firm founded by partners Gene Sanchez and Ben Benson. Bill Mingenbach eventually joined the firm as a partner. The firm designed Taos's new county courthouse on South Santa Fé Road. Woolie said that Alec Grosstete of La Mesa Builders, the contractor for the courthouse, would have a crane in Taos come spring. "I'll mention it to him," said Woolie. Years later, Woolie, ever the gentleman, apologized to me for what happened next, the accidental meeting of Ming and Mudd.

At about 4:15 p.m. that fateful day, I left La Cocina and walked across the flagstones of Taos Plaza toward Hotel La Fonda. Woolie, Alec Grossetete, and Bill Mingenbach ambled slowly west along the sidewalk under La Fonda's portal to meet Harvey Mudd in front of La Cantina. I had arranged the meeting to save money, specifically to coordinate the use of a crane, scheduled to be used at the new county courthouse, designed by Ming, and hoped we could time the placement of beams and roof structure in the spring. But when Harvey's heavy wallet met Bill's fantastical imagination a forest fire of cash-and-carry ideas turned my simple remodel project into a bizarre complexity. Alec, who got the job, told me later, "It was a first-class project, nobody skimped or cut corners." He didn't tell me how much the contractor profited from change orders due to Ming & Mudd's imaginative whimsy.

By mid-1971 the Plaza Theatre building had morphed into a Rube Goldberg variation with multilevel spaces designed to accommodate a two-story restaurant for Herff Applewhite's Sunshine Company. Harvey was taken with the tasty omelets and grits prepared under Herff's watchful eyes at Hotel La Fonda. Herff and Harvey bonded over the grits and their common dislike for the Greek. And so the two street-level theatres of 200 seats became one, but that one was located below ground level in a basement. A second art theatre of 80 seats on the second story, separated by labyrinthian stairwells and several doors, remains unroofed and eternally unfinished. The upstairs became a proposed bar and restaurant while a courtyard for outdoor seating further complicated the labyrinthian levels.

Herff abandoned the project shortly after construction began and his legacy in Taos can be considered benign compared to the headlines he made in 1997 at San Diego. There, he and his partner, Bonnie Nettles, co-piloted a last ride for a crew of thirty-eight up and away in an attempt to catch the Comet Hale-Bopp. The event ended in a mass suicide known as the Heaven's Gate affair.

Today the Ming & Mudd memorial accommodates mice and pigeons, standing water and moribund dreams. A poet and dramatist from Boston bought the albatross in the early part of the 21st century, but later abandoned it and Taos. As this book goes to press the Plaza Theatre Building remains unroofed and vacant.

4

In Ranchos de Taos, the church and plaza sandwiched between two dance halls reminded one of a western movie set—except there was no sheriff or marshal in town. In the spring of 1971, a tall, shaggy-haired, substitute English teacher, Ken Jenkins, began talking to me about leasing T.P. Martinez's El Cortez Tavern, a cantina, and Old Martinez Hall, a dancehall, both in the same building, adjacent to the El Cortez Theatre.

Ken had retreated to Taos from L.A. to write a book about the Manson family massacre, but spent most of his time doing research at La Cocina. He and his wife, Nancy, she the schoolteacher and breadwinner, lived across the street from the El Cortez Theatre in an adobe retreat under the watchful eye of St. Francis de Asis, where they kept company with a porcine pet.

Prior to Ken's arrival, Fargo Gerard, a leather worker and recurring character in my life, lived in the same place. After a movie, I sometimes ambled over to discuss Yeats's poetry or George Stevens' *Shane,* while sharing a bottle of scotch with Ken.

Ken said we could get two bars from the Martinez family for the price of one—the daytime tavern and nighttime bar and dancehall—for a total of $600 a month. He figured the income from El Cortez Tavern, with a couple of pool tables, should pay the monthly rent, and that we would make a ton of money by scheduling Spanish wedding dances and rock bands in the Old Martinez Hall. The huge two-story wedding dancehall came complete with WPA murals, like the images inside the theatre, and could accommodate five or six hundred concert goers. A neighborhood clientele—pool players, pensioners, miners, errant husbands, artists, and layabouts—made the tavern their home.

In the newly remodeled lounge, connected to the tavern by interior double doors, the bar for the dancehall featured muted brown look-a-like adobe bricks framed in polished brown wood. The dancehall itself retained a hardwood floor below giant vigas and a sizeable stage between thick, high adobe walls, in a hall where kids once played basketball.

The summer before, Luis Valdez's Teatro Campesino performed a commedia dell'arte version of *Viva la Huelga* in Old Martinez Hall to raise money in support of farmworkers' great sugar-beet strike against Coors in Colorado. Consequently, the locals switched: "Coors? No mas. Schleetz, *ahora.*"

Harvey put up the $5,000 seed money for the project. Edmundo Martinez, the managing brother and veteran employee of the New Mexico Department of Motor Vehicles, made a phone call to Santa Fé and the liquor license approval sailed through the bureaucracy in a day or two. Years later in the first decade of the double aughts, a Teutonic lass, La Martina, spent a small fortune buying, remodeling and fighting with the locals to gain liquor license approval. When I stepped behind the plank the first of May at the El Cortez Tavern, the aroma from the partitioned-off pissoir wafted up and out, over the pockmarked linoleum floor and stained hardwood bar. I remember muttering to myself: "Whaley, you gringo, what the hell are you doing in this bar?"

Generally, Ken worked the tavern days while I tended the newly remodeled bar at night and managed the wedding dances on Saturdays. The wedding dance season was notable for its hand-to-hand combat inside between waltzes by members of the wedding party and parking lot fisticuffs outside between *los vecinos*. One of our bouncers, Manuel "Pablito Red" Trujillo, fancied himself a politico, and didn't like to make enemies or lose potential votes by throwing out troublemakers. The concept of "native Taoseño" and "bouncer" was a contradiction in terms, like prohibiting the customary "conflict of interest" among *primo politicos*.

Several dancehalls in Taos competed for the wedding dance business then. Los Compadres, on the town's northern boundary between Taos and El Prado, was numero uno. The owner, Martin Vargas, fancied slicked-back hair, sported a cigarette holder, dressed in a fancy suit, and drove around town in a black Cadillac. I wore scruffy Levis, a shirt with a collar, and drove a VW bug. Martin looked down his nose at me, though in person the shorter man looked up.

The wedding parties scheduled receptions on Saturday afternoons from about two o'clock and dances for the evening from eight o'clock. But the hours were as flexible as the guests were adaptable. The general public paid a dollar at the door. According to custom, wedding parties paid a fee for the use of the room and were charged for the band. Since revenue from door charges covered the cost of the band and the operating expenses, I waived the customary fees to become more competitive and booked the popular Visarragas dance band from Peñasco. Soon happy couples snatched up the available Saturdays at Old Martinez Hall and the summer season sold out.

In the Tavern, *los viejos* (the old guys), aka *los tios* (the uncles), dressed in coats, ties, and fedoras, arrived at nine or ten in the morning, and after one or two drinks engaged in friendly games of pool or fisticuffs aimed at resolving long-forgotten feuds. Weightless as shadows, they caused little damage to each other or the furniture. Around noon, a daughter or grandson would show up to walk *los ancianos* home.

Draft beer cost a quarter or fifty cents and mixed drinks seventy-five cents to a buck. We ordered new pool tables and Ken organized tournaments with trophies, pool cues, and cash as prizes. The pool guys who furnished the tables retained fifty percent of the grosses. When I asked one of the locals, retired sheepherder and schoolteacher Pat Martinez, why business was so good, he said, "Because you have no history of screwing people."

Pat was fond of saying, "I'm bilingual, I speak neither Spanish nor English." Members of the older generation referred to themselves as Spanish, but the younger guys, especially the ex-cons and the college boys, called themselves Chicanos. Applying the word "Spanish" or "Chicano" to the wrong individual—even if related—could mean a fight: "I'm no Chicano, *cabron*!" I never heard the term Hispanic or Latino, and "Mexican" was considered a dirty word. An exchange of insults between born and bred *vecinos* (neighbors) captures the socio-ethno conflict in a nutshell: "Who you calling a Mexican, you Indio?"

In the mid-sixties at the Central Catholic School gym in Taos "they" said Fats Domino had scored a full house. Ken and I convinced each other that we might get rich by booking oldies.

Friends put us in touch with friends in the L.A. music business and soon enough Susie and I found ourselves at the Hyatt on Sunset, where Lewie and Hank Wickham, La Cocina favorites from Albuquerque, headlined the lounge act.

When the word got out in L.A. about the country concert producers, hungry rock promoters got in touch with us. Based on guesswork we signed a contract with Ricky Nelson and the Stone Canyon Band for three nights at a cost of $7,000 plus rooms at the Taos Inn, and we agreed to spend $1,000 promoting the gig. Ricky's hit tune, *Garden Party,* was soaring on the charts.

Back at the Taos Inn, the Morris Brothers, Ken and Gary, whose folks had operated the Walgreen's Drugstore on Taos Plaza, told us about a furniture maker in Juarez who would make cocktail tables for us, cheap. Fred Fair was busy so another local pilot, Oren Olinger, flew Susie and me to Juarez, where we dined on fresh shrimp, drank Dos Equis, and visited the artisan in a nondescript back alley. So we deposited about $225, for custom-made plywood cocktail tables, costing $6 each. He said he'd call the Morrises when the seventy-five tables were ready for delivery.

The most honest man in Juarez did call and my buddy John Koch and I headed off to Mexico. We stopped off at the same hotel for fresh shrimp, drank more Dos Equis, and bought a couple bottles of Metaxa brandy for the return. We found the alley, paid off the balance of $225, and piled up the tables in an asymmetrical pyramid on the back of the flatbed. A long line of vehicles preceded us at customs and I urged Koch to bypass them. He gunned the engine, swerved in and out of traffic, and made it to the front of the line, where he pulled up and stopped. Drunk as an Irishman, I got out and proffered a bottle of brandy to the embarrassed customs agents, who immediately stamped the bill of lading.

While Koch drove, I slept. John's monologues gradually merged with the early morning dawn and woke me up. He seemed woozy so I took away the beer and started him on the brandy to sober him up. We arrived at Old Martinez Hall in Ranchos and unloaded. Years after abandoning the Ranchos adventure, those plywood tables from Juarez continued to turn up and haunt me at bars around town.

We spent $1,000 promoting Ricky on radio all across El Norte and the show drew about seventy-five people per night at $5 a head. Few locals bought tickets. The hippies stayed in their communes. I had paid Ricky $3,500 in advance, but after the Friday night opening we had barely $1,000 in cash and the balance of $3,500 was due on Saturday night. So I called the pool-table guys. They drove up Saturday morning and gave me a bag with twenty-five hundred bucks. It took all summer to repay the advance.

Dennis came to the concert and reassured me, "Don't worry about it, smile." Ricky asked me if I could arrange for him to meet Mr. Easy Rider, so I called the house and Dennis showed up for a tete-a-tete at the Taos Inn. After introductions, the actor and the singer gave each other the Hollywood hug and retired to a corner table.

Later that summer I visited Bo Diddley in Las Lunas, just south of Albuquerque. Previously, about fifteen of us, including Dennis, caught Bo and his singer, Cookie Vee, one night at the San G. during François de Menil's film shoot for an unreleased movie starring French actor Pierre Clémenti (*Belle de Jour*). That night Bo did a virtuoso show of the *Shake, Rattle and Roll* and burned up the oxygen in the room.

"What do you think, Mr. Diddley?" I asked Bo, standing beside his suburban-like detached garage-studio. He wore a costume cowboy hat and thick spectacles.

"I ain't doing much. I'll take the door."

I agreed to spend a grand (again) on publicity for the three nights. When Bo's drummer didn't show, Dennis Long, a former hippie and schoolteacher from Arroyo Hondo, played backup. Due to a second emergency, Mr. Long accompanied Earl "Fatha" Hines in the late '70s at the TCA. Bo did a terrific show and we only lost $1,000 on the weekend.

At the end of the three-night Bo Diddley concert, the hippies, tired of taunts and bullying by the locals, got in their pickups or picked up axe handles and some really big rocks. Engines roared, tires squealed, and they charged the locals, who, in turn, armed themselves with shovels, tire irons, and hunting rifles. The evening fracas was reminiscent of the famed gun battle at the Old Mountain View saloon when the hippies shot it out with their Arroyo Seco neighbors.

Customarily, it was worth a hippie's life or a haircut if he wandered by Taos Plaza or Ranchos de Taos on the wrong night. School buses filled with women and children got shot up when they arrived in the Taos area circa the Woodstock diaspora. A female hitchhiker might get several kinds of rides on the way to work or while going home to one of the estimated twenty communes. Ex-communards themselves whispered that troublesome members of their tribe "disappeared" in the desert or the mountains.

My first response to a fight or riot was to try and stop the carnage, but the regulars held me back. "Not tonight, Bill. Better stay in here." The Ranchos riot continued for a couple of hours. The state cops arrived—after the rioters had gone home. As a kid I got used to getting bucked off or scraped off against a tree by a disagreeable horse or a horse with a sense of humor. You hit the ground hard, then got back up. The point of football was to get knocked down or to knock somebody down—even if your opponent was a blocking dummy. Skiing included sudden encounters with trees, rocks, and hard-packed slopes. A bar fight seemed like more of the same. The culture of bartending and its ancillary violence just seemed like part of life.

My most intense memory concerns the fight I never had at El Cortez Tavern about midnight. There were no regulars, just four Chicanos, my age or a little older.

"Gringo, *cabron, tiene una cerveza.*"

"Sure," I said.

"You sonofabitch."

"Uh, huh."

"You're a stupid gringo."

I knew that.

"Yeah, we're going to burn down this place just like we burned the Plaza Theatre, *cabron.*"

Long before Clint Eastwood finished off Little Bill's bully boys in *The Unforgiven*, I reacted to those hateful words about the Plaza Theatre. I broke an empty beer bottle on the bar and filled the piss-soaked air with epithets: "Goddamn, sonofabitch, mother-fucker! This place doesn't belong to me." And then I said, reaching full volume, "It belongs to the Martinez family and I don't give a shit, motherfuckers! But if you burn it, I will hunt you down. Even if your wife and kids are at home I will burn your cars and your houses."

"Bill, hey guy, take it easy, we were just kidding."

They were kidding the wrong guy. The Plaza Theatre was my curse and cure—my *bête noir*, the symbol of an inchoate idea, an obsession really, the thing for which I lived.

5

Late that summer I met Harvey for lunch one day at La Doña Luz, a fancy French restaurant that had seen better days. Feeling both guilty and self-righteous, I referred to the Ming & Mudd edifice, the Plaza Theatre, as some architectural Godzilla, saying "It's preposterous and pretentious." Then I uttered the unforgiveable calumny by suggesting Harvey had bad taste.

While working the wedding-dance scene and defending the furniture, I had tried to pay off the losses incurred by the Ricky Nelson-Bo Diddley debacles. I'd brought Old Martinez Hall back from the brink but I couldn't repay Harvey, whose five grand I'd bet and lost in Ranchos. Susie tried to smooth things over, but I was bent by my own indignation. At the downtown Taos Mudd combine, the backbiters bad-mouthed me and the rumor mill said I was out of luck with my handshake deal.

In September, Mudd and I agreed to lay off Old Martinez Hall on a willing cantina fantasist for next to nothing and I retired to my house in Cañon to consider my memories of the toughest summer I ever experienced—tougher than boot camp, tougher than that first winter in Taos, tougher than going broke later. Ironically, the lessons learned about the Taos way—about drunks and bullies, about the differences between the good guys and the bad guys in El Norte—continued to pay cultural dividends far into the future.

Long before the end of summer, Ken had retired from the Ranchos business partnership and rejoined the civilized company of the elbow-benders at La Cocina. Fortunately, Pilo Tafoya, steady as a rock, had taken Ken's day shift behind the bar. Pilo played an indirect role in saving me to serve the ship at KVNM FM radio in the '80s.

Few residents of Ranchos remember Obid Brito, but he

embodied the objective correlative of the compassionate Taoseño. Obid got drunk too early in the morning at the El Cortez then went home or slept it off under a tree, not far from a bottle or a six-pack he hid under a bush. His matted hair fell out under an old cap, his pants were crusted with dirt, sometimes he didn't wear socks or smell too good. Occasionally, one of the pool players would wrinkle a nose, put down his stick, take Obid by the arm and drive him home to his falling-down house. Occasionally Obid appeared freshly shaved and washed. Though passive by nature, he was ready to fight when teased. If he was still around at closing time and it was a warm night, I'd prop him up against an outside wall.

The hipster Manny Ocanas bought tickets for the Ricky Nelson and Bo Diddley shows and attended concerts at the TCA featuring jazz artists like Dizzy Gillespie, Fatha Hines, and Woody Herman. A septic tank hauler and political fixer, he, too, later helped keep FM radio alive in Taos because he knew "the man."

One Sunday, just before noon, which was the legal hour for selling liquor, there was a knock on the back door. Chemo Valerio, hired to plaster the building and remodel the upstairs (a project completed four decades later by the new owner), had a few greenbacks in his hand and said, "Bill, I want to buy a case of beer." Chemo also worked for New Mexico's alcoholic-beverage control agency. If I sold him the beer, I might get busted. If I didn't, I might get busted later. "Here take the beer, Chemo, on the house—you've been working hard."

"You sure?" he asked.

"Sure," I said. In the mid-'70s, when I operated the upstairs Plaza Theatre Bar, the beverage-control guys busted every bar on the Plaza during fiesta but mine.

In the early summer of 1971, woodcarver and furniture-maker Gilbert Vargas took me over to his shop to look at a high-backed wooden banco with a bench-seat that opened up for storing liquor. It was beautifully carved, eight feet long, and solid as a piece of granite. He offered to sell it to me for $1,000—not even half what it was worth. "We can't afford it, Gilbert," I said. "But we can trade."

Gilbert got a thousand dollars worth of credit at the bar. One round begat another. When I saw Gilbert forty years later at Juma's Chicano barbershop in El Prado, he laughed, "That summer almost killed us."

The *banco*, Harvey Mudd's sole return on his Ranchos venture, rattled around the Plaza Theatre building during the late 1970s. My folks got a six-foot-high, 12-by-12-inch liquor cabinet, carved by Gilbert, called the "Taos Tower"—about the only return they received on multiple investments in the adventures of their prodigal son.

At our house in Cañon that fall I slept twelve hours a night. During the day I read, finding solace in books, a lifelong habit to which I still return when my equilibrium needs recalibration. "Reality is the goal," Henry Miller writes, and "art is only a means to life, to life more abundant." Miller's comments confirmed an intuition I had about the relationship between the call of experience and the response to the formal study of literature. But I didn't have the patience to sit still and make the trip.

While discussing my sociological adventures with poet Richard Trujillo of Cañon, the author of the *Tio Zuco* tales, the ex-con told me between beers that "most of these local guys didn't know they were Chicanos until they went to college." In the double aughts of the 21st century, Richard sold copy books of his prose and poetry bar stool, to bar stool, like Walt Whitman, but he quit publishing them in my monthly journal *Horse Fly* "because people can read them for free." Even if he carries poems and stories for sale in a bag today, most people still believe he might have a knife or a gun on his person. The fierce *pachuco/vato loco* survives because he's just a little more disciplined and sensible than all his *cuates*, who turned to hard drugs and needles.

After the eighteen months spent in Ranchos, the environs of Cañon and Taos Plaza seemed as civilized as San Francisco. At La Cocina, Ruthie reassured me, as she did the others each day, with a question and a smile, "What'll you have, hon?" If the Sacred Muse dressed in human clothes she would look a lot like Ruthie.

6

Admission to the Guard in 1967 may have saved my life, but by 1971 I thought (again) that "they" were trying to kill me. As a political science major in the mid '60s at Colorado College, I had read accounts of the French experience by historian Bernard Fall and analyses by the likes of political scientist William Pfaff and Senator William Fulbright, who wrote about the follies of foreign adventurism. The war, historically doomed and politically immoral, threatened the national soul as well as my own mortal interests. "In modern war," Hemingway said, "you will die like a dog for no good reason."

From the early spring of 1967 until the late fall of 1971, except for my four-month active-duty assignment at Fort Knox (August-December 1967), I spent one weekend a month hanging around Armory Street (now Civic Plaza Drive) at Bataan Hall in Taos. Since the chief cook was my friend Steve White, who prepared boeuf bourguignon or stroganoff for the troops, I frequently volunteered for KP. Washing pots and pans kept boredom at bay and me out of harm's way while my colleagues enthusiastically tinkered with the vehicles in the motor pool or the M42 Tracks, vintage WWII antiaircraft weapons which they cleaned and polished in preparation for target practice—shooting down drones.

When the Taos Guard got called up for active duty in June of 1967, I hadn't been to basic training so I wasn't alerted to the emergency confrontation with land-grant revolutionary Reies Tijerina. Still, the guys gave me a rundown on Tijerina, the Aztlán activist who claimed that the American occupiers of the 1840s had ultimately broken the Treaty of Guadalupe Hidalgo, the treaty that brokered the end of the Mexican-American war. So Tijerina annulled U.S. laws and led a gang of activists into the Rio Arriba County courthouse in Tierra Amarilla, about fifty miles west of Taos, where they shot a cop and a jailer, kidnapped a deputy sheriff and a reporter before they vanished.

The State of New Mexico called out the Guard to restore order and protect American occupiers, who worked at the U.S. Forest Service. The shooters of drones and drinkers of beer loaded up their deuce-and-a-halfs and drove west across the Rio Grande Gorge bridge, following Highway 64 across the mesas and up through the mountains and forests over the high pass and down to Tierra Amarilla.

Executive Officer Lieutenant Reggie Archuleta said, "We didn't really know what was going on. We threw up a perimeter, stopped a few cars, and opened their trunks." Reggie shrugged off the experience with a grin.

Another soldier told me, "It was dangerous. They gave us live ammo. You know how we always throw our weapons around in the back of the trucks? It's lucky no one got shot. We were supposed to stop people and question them. There were all these rumors. Some of the guys were scared. These *viejos,* sheepherders, were wandering around in the woods. Most didn't speak English. The state cops said we should hold them. But the *viejos* ignored us and left during the night."

Whitey said the joke was on the Guard initially, because "the banditos were armed but for our own safety we weren't."

The motto of the Taos National Guard was "Safety first." To me, the whole country seemed paranoid except for these non-coms and a few officers from northern New Mexico. Tragedy, it seemed, was avoided due to the common sense of my fellow guardsmen, who by temperament were more intent on having a good time than on apprehending revolutionaries or killing foreigners. Hiding out from sergeants during drill, drinking a few beers, playing grab-ass, and napping were more the rule than the exception.

The unit reported for two weeks of active duty each summer out in the desert at the Fort Bliss firing ranges near El Paso. At night the soldiers made (mostly) authorized incursions into Juarez. One of the local legends concerned a friend of mine, confined to barracks by the C.O. Subsequently, the recalcitrant soldier slipped out of the barracks and crossed the international border to visit *Las Mujeres*. Sure enough the C.O. heard about the AWOL guardsman. The commander, dressed in uniform and driving an army jeep, crossed the border, found the offender behind a locked door in a room over a cantina. He kicked down the barrier and brought the soldier back to the barracks.

During my first summer camp in 1968, a few of us were allowed to drive our civilian vehicles. The NCOs were impressed by my new VW camper; its icebox and fold-up table made for an ideal cantina on wheels. The civilian vehicles arrived at summer camp a few hours before the main convoy, so we immediately changed into civvies and headed south across the bridge to visit the fabled cantinas.

When I woke up the next morning in an El Paso parking lot, I was leaning against a wall in the sitting position. The sun beat down. A hammer pounded my temples. My shirt was soaked. My tongue tasted like the convoy had camped out in my mouth. For the next three hours, hot and sweating, I stumbled through alleys and picked my way among the hundreds of automobiles parked alongside the Rio Grande, a dirty stream that trickled down the concrete riverbed under the overpasses that separated El Paso and Juarez. The watery gray residue looked very different from the cool whitewater that flowed between the cliffs of the Gorge up north.

It was almost two o'clock before I found my VW camper and began following a labyrinth of highways in search of my unit, bivouacked in the desert outback. Helpful gate guards at Fort Bliss called headquarters, located my battalion, and gave me directions. When Captain Lawrence Santistevan—our commanding officer, an exemplary post office employee, and later, mayor of Taos—saw me, he just smiled.

First Sergeant Maestas, however, frowned, for I had been nothing but trouble since the day I reported. On the way to pick up the bus to basic training in August of 1967, after an all-night farewell party with my fire-breathing friend John Koch at the St. Bernard, where we did our best to consume a friendly 15-gallon keg of Coors beer, I had smashed Susie's parents' car into a tree. By the time I got my nose straightened out and cuts stitched up, I looked like a street brawler. Sarge put me on the bus—a day late—and sent me off, but I had to pass through the adjutant general's HQ in Santa Fé. One of the officers called Maestas and dressed him down for recruiting my sorry ass.

Initially, I was one of four Anglos in the Taos Guard. Steve White cooked. Mark Daily, lima bean artist, was a member of an M42 crew. "Whaley-Daily" for no particular reason was a common refrain. Ernie Blake's son, Mickey, posed as an officer. Later, locals Richie Grainger and Frank Delmargo, Taos natives who spoke the local *lenguaje*, joined. Richie used to tell stories about getting off the school bus in Cañon and running all the way home while being chased by the very big brothers of the Medina clan. Even Peter Blake, a gentle soul and the youngest member of the TSV dynasty, threw in with us. More than once, in some cantina, when I was challenged by a mean looking vato, an army buddy came to the rescue: "That's Whaley. I know him. He's okay." Later, some of my army buddies became cops or judges in Taos and deep background sources in the double aughts when I published *Horse Fly*.

As the war in Vietnam dragged on into the '70s, and the antiwar movement gained strength, the local officer corps began exhibiting signs of paranoia. After the May 4, 1970 Kent State student protest, when the Ohio National Guard gunned down four unarmed students who were sixty to two-hundred forty yards away from the troops, the Pentagon decided that weekend warriors, the first line of defense against radical young people, needed more training. While Taoseños slept in on Sunday mornings, we warriors practiced the arts of riot-control drill at the Armory (now Bataan Hall) on Armory Street (Civic Plaza Drive), marching across the hardwood floor, thrusting out our bayonets at imaginary college coeds and longhairs, yelling in unison: "Get back, get back!" The mostly Anglo officer corps warned the mostly Hispanic-Chicano noncoms and troops about the dangerous revolutionaries, La Raza-Brown Berets up at New Mexico Highlands University, a center of Chicano activism in Las Vegas, New Mexico. One alarmist from the Tucumcari headquarters battalion repeatedly warned, "When the balloon goes up ... when the balloon goes up ... when the balloon goes up at Highlands University we must be ready."

Though the class and cultural bigotry was as obvious as the nose on your face, nobody was speaking except me. In a loud voice, I asked my brothers, "Are you afraid of a bunch of girls, who are a hundred yards away?" Or "Remember sticks and stones may break my bones, but names and faces cannot hurt me?"

While my clever remarks coincided with the hour after our liquid lunch, the soldiers warned me, "Eeee, Whaley. The captain [or the colonel] is going to get you." Wiser, older sergeants, like Palemon Cardenas, Juan Martinez, or Jimmy Santistevan shook their heads and counseled restraint.

At Saturday-night wedding dances in Old Martinez Hall, I saw far more violence than anything I experienced as a member of the Guard. My experience as a bouncer raised questions: why do cops beat up drunks and why do some members of the Guard feel compelled to shoot unarmed civilians? I never questioned the courage of combat vets. But a bartender didn't react aggressively unless attacked or forced into defending himself and the furniture against drunken marauders. The cantina code made more sense than the Uniform Code of Military Justice (UCMJ). You don't beat up your customers.

The Taos Guard finally got called up to confront the antiwar activists, rioters, or the members of the "party until you drop" faction at UNM in Albuquerque. I rode around the Duke City in the backseat of a state police cruiser, nervous about the live ammo we had in our clips. After a few hours of surveillance, the cops let us off at the state fairgrounds where we were bivouacked.

Bored by duty and enchanted by the big city, a few of us jumped over the walls and took off for a go-go club. We were drinking beer and studying the dancers' technique as they twirled the silver or red ribbons dangling from their nipples—when the doors of the club burst open. A second lieutenant, who was also a second-grade schoolteacher, and who despised me, led the charge. A couple of troops marched us out. As I slid into the front seat of the jeep, the schoolteacher said to a recent basic-training graduate, "Juan, if Whaley tries to get away, shoot him."

"Juan, are you going to shoot me?" I asked sarcastically. We were trained not to point our weapons at each other. Juan abided by the standby slogan: "Safety first."

The next morning at reveille, I insulted the lieutenant's ancestors in front of the whole battalion, challenged his manhood, and finally accused him of being "uptight." He shuffled his feet and spluttered during my diatribe. Later he charged me with being AWOL and insubordinate under Article 31 of the UCMJ.

When not on duty, I was restricted to the barracks at Fort Bliss that summer. After their revelry in Juarez, the guys stumbled in an hour or two before reveille, telling stories. While waiting for customs agents to approve their passage, they used to tease each other: "Hey Luis, you're too dark. They're not going to let you back in, Indio." Spanish was the language of choice in the barracks, but at the border, Taos natives spoke very good English.

First Lieutenant Reggie Archuleta convened a hearing for my war crimes—going over the wall and cussing out the lieutenant. "Whaley, what's wrong with you? What were you doing? The lieutenant wants to send you to active duty. "

"Reggie, sir, " I said, "you guys are paying me five dollars a day. I'm losing my ass in Taos while I'm down here." The lieutenant, aka executive officer, fined me $30 and confined me to barracks. I stayed sober and spent my time, as usual, humping ammo or scrubbing pots and pans. Later, back in Taos, the second lieutenant/schoolteacher busted me again for a bad haircut or un-shined shoes and whatever else—all of it deserved, though the bust meant I'd lose credit for attending drill.

Each weekend drill counted as four active-duty days, two on Saturday and two on Sunday. Miss four drills in a year and you got sent to active duty in Da Nang or into the desert near Juarez. I appealed the lieutenant's decision to the New Mexico adjutant general, General John Jolly, in Santa Fé. I explained how some rebellious Chicano friends, despite their similar sins, remained unpunished. General Jolly said, "The Anglos complain in the north and the Chicanos complain in the south." He overturned the lieutenant's decision and sent me back to my unit. My behavior at drill, "they said," was a subject of conversation at the headquarters battalion in Tucumcari.

In early fall, our O.D. convoy was returning from Springer when the driver, Richie Grainger, who was wheeling down through the twists and turns of Taos Canyon, gently laid the truck on its side. I was sitting in the back on a pile of duffel bags and whispered to Peter Blake, "Here's your chance." He went to the hospital claiming, reportedly, a back injury, and we never saw him again. His father, Ernie, the TSV founder, later reproached me for being a bad influence.

After four-and-a-half years, the growing tension between conscience and consciousness convinced me to apply for status as a "conscientious objector." Dr. Al Rosen and author John Nichols wrote letters on my behalf to the brass. Rosen had once written an excuse for me to miss a Guard meeting and cautioned me to stay home. But that night I went down to help keep order at Old Martinez Hall and two guys threw a cloth over my head and whacked me with a table. The regulars pulled me out, but due to stitches and bruises I was forced to confess the next morning at Guard duty. After that the officer corps refused to accept Rosen's signature on a medical excuse. Still, Rosen and Nichols wrote that Whaley's moral integrity prevented him from condoning wars of aggression.

The colonel interviewed me. "If a man assaulted your wife or hit you, would you strike back?" he asked.

"Absolutely not, sir. I am a pacifist, morally and by temperament."

As soon as I applied for C.O. status, the military excused me from drill. After four and half years, I was released from military service, with the rank of E-2. You enter basic training as an E-1. The military sent me an honorable discharge in the fall of 1972, saying Pvt. Whaley was "psychologically unable to adapt to military life." Thirty years later, at the ballyhooed opening of El Monte Sagrado's faux Living Machine in Taos, I ran into my onetime commanding officer, Mickey Blake, who told me I had flunked the psychological evaluation when I joined the Guard back in February of 1967. Apparently, the authorities let me out to cover up the cover-up.

<h1 style="text-align:center">7</h1>

While I focused on survival in Ranchos de Taos during my exile from 1970 to 1971, whether at the El Cortez Theatre or at El Cortez Tavern/Old Martinez Hall, on the Plaza I got no closer to the Plaza Theatre than a bar stool at La Cocina. The hustlers and backbiters beckoned by Harvey's fat purse tripped all over themselves in tune to the several-hundred thousand-dollar project. After the ski season ended in 1972, I made an attempt to repair the personal and professional damage with Harvey's pal, Jim Levy, who had returned from a sabbatical in Africa to begin work as Harvey's troubleshooter. Levy himself questioned the

Mudd & Ming absurdities and cut back on bloated construction projects. He closed the Sunshine Company, which had turned from a restaurant into a bar—comedian George Carlin made an appearance—in the extant basement adjacent to the proposed theatre. Bouncers there had the peculiar task of heaving drunks out and up the stairs to the street-level sidewalk on the Plaza. Levy and I met one morning at Foster's Café, east of the Union 76 gas station on the northeast corner of the entrance to the Plaza on Kit Carson Road.

The April sky was gray and dust hovered over Taos Valley. Jim listened politely as I recounted the Whaley-Mudd narrative. We drank coffee and looked out the windows as an occasional car passed by heading east. Politicos Bobby Duran and C.B. Trujillo, along with their buddies Charley Foster, Tiger Trujillo, and Latouf Sahd, played poker in the basement. Levy expressed deep doubt about my so-called moral claims on the theatre and he confirmed that I was out.

Susie and I had purchased our house and six acres in Cañon the year before, financing the mortgage, thanks to Steve Trujillo, at First Northern Savings and Loan. The seller, Fred Fair, who financed the down payment, still owned his house and twenty-nine acres of adjacent property. Strangers dressed in dark suits and white socks variously visited and identified themselves with gold badges as members of the IRS, FAA, INS, the Treasury Department, or U.S. Bureau of Alcohol, Tobacco and Firearms. They asked about the Canadian's whereabouts but we repeated the traditional Taos response: "I dunno."

Susie, who had taken a job as a receptionist and bookkeeper at *The Taos News,* had worked her way up to reporter and now netted about $200 a month. We charged our groceries at Harry Packard's Plaza Supermarket when we were short. I paid off my fall tab at La Cocina with my winter income from ski instructing.

Though our credit was good, our prospects were dim.

We decided to leave Taos (again) and I legged it out to San Francisco (again), where I couldn't find a job (again), so I high-tailed it up to Tahoe, where the family log cabin sat empty and the casinos would be hiring for the summer. At the Sahara Tahoe, I got a job as a cook's helper and began looking at the possibilities of a new profession. Our Taos friend, Tony Bryan, drove Susie and the three Siamese cats out to join me later in June. I took classes in literature and creative writing during the fall at the University of Nevada in Reno. Each morning I read Herb Caen and Charles McCabe, *San Francisco Chronicle* columnists, looking for advice, if not exemplary companions, who could drink martinis, smoke cigars, think and talk and write.

That fall I watched Muhammad Ali live as he worked out at the Sahara for the upcoming Bob Foster fight in November. Ali did standup comedy from the training ring with Bill Cosby, who was booked across the street at Harrah's. At Harrah's stage bar, I listened each evening to Fats Domino, who appeared there to sing his ten favorite songs. For the price of a beer, say three dollars, I, along with a few drinkers, enjoyed an almost private concert.

One day a black suit with white socks from the IRS showed up and emptied our savings account, due to unpaid FICA fees (employer-matched taxes for Social Security) from our El Cortez/ Old Martinez Hall adventure. After working 120 straight days as a cook for the buffet that summer, preparing private banquets ad nauseam in the fall, I lobbied the executive chef for a transfer to the fry line or the gourmet restaurant. When he said no, I packed up my tools and quit.

Winter arrived, the snow fell, and we spent the last of our savings at the vet for three Siamese kittens who had caught distemper and soon died. The snow piled up higher and higher as the sky grew darker over the mountains. The temperature dropped below freezing in December. The great fireplace burned hot and the logs disappeared in smoke up the chimney at an alarming rate. We retreated to the bedroom heated by an Ashley woodstove.

I was reading poetry by Robert Frost—*The Road Not Taken*—when the phone rang and a voice said, "Bill, this is Sally Howell." Sally, Harvey Mudd's new practical person, said she was overseeing his enterprises while Jim Levy managed the newly reopened Plaza Theatre. Accountant Tom Hickey had double-checked the books from the Old Martinez Hall adventure and confirmed my frugal operation, pointing out that I had drawn little in the way of dough—except for a few monthly car payments of $150 each for my Volkswagen bug.

The Mudd combine, Sally said, was losing money on the movie-theatre operation and asked if I had any suggestions. We discussed what and how movies should be programmed and promoted, and how to manage the house. She called back and asked if I would be interested in leasing the Plaza Theatre. Absolutely. By the third phone call, she had convinced Levy, Hickey, and Mudd to offer me a deal.

As the pressure built for a return to Taos, Dr. Gilbert Johns, the director of the summer session at Colorado College, offered Susie a job. If she took that job, I could finish my own education at CC—tuition free. But motherhood was also calling. A few nights before Christmas, we crossed Trout Creek Meadow under a full moon and cut down a celebratory tree. I don't remember praying, but I'm certain we discussed our options with Santa.

Sally called again and we agreed that I would return to take over the movie theatre. I'm not sure if it was the Taos way or my way or Sally's, but we didn't discuss terms or where I would get the money for operating expenses. In mid-January, our trustworthy friend and realtor, Tony Bryan, phoned to say he had a buyer for our Cañon property, the sale of which would result in a profit of $8,500.

"Sell," we said. Once again, we had prospects.

We rented a U-Haul trailer and attached it to our turquoise-colored VW bug for the drive east through blizzard conditions at night on the four-lane highway in Wyoming. Our three adult Siamese cats yowled and crawled over the suitcases and up the backs of the seats. The windshield fogged up. I had a choice of two lanes and settled into the lane on the right. My headlights suddenly picked up the wind-packed snowdrifts that made the left lane impassable. I mumbled aloud, "We could have been dead, dead, dead." But we weren't.

With karma as comforter, or maybe it was a guardian angel, we continued on. I dropped Susie at her parents' house in Denver and made the run to Taos. Between Questa and Taos, the trailer began pushing the VW bug down steep hills, burying the speedometer—U-Haul trailer fishtailing behind. Still, no crash.

Once in Taos, Tony put me up at his mother's condominium at Las Milpas, next to Kit Carson Park. He had closed the deal on our Cañon property. I walked into La Cocina about 9 p.m. and sat down next to Dave Nesbitt. "Hey, can I buy you a beer?" I asked.

"I heard you were coming back," he said. The regulars merely nodded. Lounge singer Lewie Wickham warbled, "How Come My Dog Don't Bark When You Come Around?" Fresh from Missouri, full-bodied Jo Owens rolled her own Bugler cigarettes and watched the crooner with her eager brown eyes.

Pristine Tahoe, set in a basin below the snow-covered peaks in the valley, glistened in various shades of blue-green and gray, while the dirty snow in Taos turned the roads into a quagmire of deep mud puddles and cavernous ruts. Out on the sidewalk in front of Kit Carson Park, Ron Kalom, The House of Taos pizza chef, and I stopped to greet each other when a car drove by and splashed us from head to toe with mud.

"Welcome to Taos," he said.

After changing my clothes, on my way to the offices at the Plaza Theatre, I saw J.P. Brandenburg crossing the street.

"Hello, Bill. What are you doing?"

"I came back to lease the theatre, Jack."

He nodded. "Everybody comes back to Taos."

Taos Plaza

Maybe it was self-indulgence and confusion. Quien sabe?

1

During my first week back in the box office at the Plaza Theatre in February 1973, I got a call from Fay Fuller, who wanted to sell me a 3,000-square-foot house and adjacent rental home on Valverde St. for $60,000. "I don't have that kind of money," I said. Fay said he'd take the $5,000 I had left from the sale of my Cañon property as a down payment and finance the balance. Suddenly I was in possession of a business, a big house with a restaurant kitchen, and as a tenant, Virginia Dooley, R.C. Gorman's mayordomo. So we retired from our rural retreat in the *vega* and cottonwoods of Cañon and joined the staccato sounds of traffic brushing by Valverde Street, a short distance from the historic Plaza. Unlike many of my generation, who had abandoned cities and suburbs for the isolated outback, I had discovered the antidote to the rural ennui of Carson Valley, Nevada in the thriving multicultural community of Taos.

Each morning, I slipped between the gap in the fence by Howard Brandenburg's two-story house (a retirement center today), next to the tennis court (now Taos Public Library), where I strolled across the dirt baseball field (later Town Hall) to Camino de la Placita, walking the few blocks from my house to Taos Plaza. By 1973, a single traffic light had replaced the four stop signs that marked the entrada to La Plaza in 1966. Modest metal trash containers decorated by local artists were placed at irregular distances on the sidewalk under the portals that extended from building to street around the four-sided, enclosed park.

On the northwest side of the Plaza, the early-morning crowd stopped to quench their thirst at Fernando de Taos Tavern— Tano's long bar—open at 7:30 a.m. A couple of picture framers, the dark-haired artist Jim Wagner and his red-haired buddy, prospector Dave Nesbitt, or the long-haired *vato loco* poet Richard Trujillo might emerge to check out the chicks, the market for marijuana, or the weather and the general human condition. As the sun rose higher, more guys tumbled from Tano's to the sidewalk, calling out, "Heepy! Hey, Heepy!" to the longhairs emerging from Volkswagen buses.

Next to Tano's, at the Fernandez de Taos arcade, Señor Martinez y Salazar sold liquor, cigarettes, newspapers, progressive periodicals, and avant-garde art magazines. While I skimmed the subheads of *The Nation*, I could smell the Spanish peanuts in the white metal cabinet, which circulated on a round rack beneath a heat lamp. When I felt flush I bought cashews.

Heading west along the north side of the Plaza, past La Cocina, I stopped to visit John Holland at the Rexall Drug and check out the headlines and sports stories in the *Albuquerque Journal, Denver Post, Rocky Mountain News,* or *The Santa Fé New Mexican.* John could regale you with the latest gossip from the previous night's doings or he might suggest an over-the-counter cold remedy or refer you to a doctor if the problem sounded like scabies and you needed a prescription. You could drink coffee, order a burger, get a watch fixed, buy greeting cards, pick up a birthday gift, or sign a terpin-hydrate form to help a local bass player painlessly pass the day—all at the Rexall.

Next door at El Mercado, Tom McCarthy sold Scotch tape and hardware or gave out free advice about stovepipe length and how to install your woodstove. On the northwest corner in front of his two stores, Funk's Five and Dime and the Don Fernando curio shop, Clark Funk hunched over a broom and swept the sidewalk with steady strokes. As you headed toward the First State Bank, at the extreme southwest corner of the Plaza, you might stop and do some price comparisons, while the oiled, hardwood floors cushioned the sound of footfalls at Gabe Jeantete's hardware store.

At the First State Bank, I claimed my bank deposit bag with the previous night's take from the Plaza Theatre and consigned the dough to the checking account, capitalizing (nervously) on the "float"—or the time that lapsed between the date checks were sent, received, and debited against your account. During the '70s, I got caught up with my bills twice a year—in August and March—then paid off my charge accounts at the Rexall, El Mercado, Gabe's Hardware, and La Cocina.

Some mornings, I might have parked my car for an oil change or repairs at John Nabors' Conoco station. John, a retired El Paso cop, offered cantankerous opinions during a morning fill-up. If

I left my car for a tune-up, he'd drop the car keys off at the box office that evening.

If you had a traffic fine to pay or needed a haircut, you visited with Judge J.C. Montoya at La Fonda Barber Shop on the south side of the Plaza. The Judge, while engaged in the arts of the tonsorial trade, discussed jurisprudence (clip, clip) and threatened you with jail (buzz, buzz) or a fine (clip, clip … buzz, buzz). Finally, J.C.'s frown would turn into a smile, his mustache curling up at the corners of his mouth, and he'd giggle, "five dollars" or maybe "fifteen." The occupant in the barber chair would join in the laughter, as the offender, relieved by the humor, paid the fee for the privilege of entertaining the onlookers.

The First State Bank dignitaries in ties and suits—Eloy Jeantete, Ben Tenorio, J.P. Brandenburg, and insurance agent Dave Polson—walked slowly up the sidewalk under the portal of the theatre and Hotel La Fonda to the Plaza Café (now Robert's Antiques) to meet Clark Funk at mid-morning. They drank coffee and flipped a coin to determine who would pay the tab.

Between 11:30 a.m. and 12:30 p.m., Hotel La Fonda's Saki Karavas emerged, either in his pink bathrobe or dressed in jacket and slacks. He laughed at Clark Funk's early-morning obsession with clean sidewalks. "Some labor with their minds and govern others, others labor with their hands and are governed by others," he'd say.

"Those guys are cheap, buddy," Saki would say about the coin flippers at the Plaza Café. When you dined or drank coffee with Saki, the Greek paid the tab whether he liked you or not. The Leon Gaspard painting of Saki's mother, Noula, hung in the lobby of the First State Bank as collateral to justify the loans J.P. Brandenburg made to Saki to maintain the Greek's lifestyle. Saki never tired of saying, "If you want to live in Taos, buddy, you've got to make a deal."

Saki spent a couple of hours each day opening his mail, bills, love letters from abroad, and unwrapping boxes of shirts from his London tailor, or untying the string on plain brown packages of Cuban cigars from Davidoff's in Switzerland. He read and recited tidbits from the epistles sent posthaste by sweethearts from all over Europe and America, after which he continued with *The London Times* and newspapers from Athens.

After making the bank deposit and checking the movie theatre, I crossed the central park to join friends at La Cocina, nodding to *los viejos*—the old guys—who soaked up the sunshine while sitting on a split-log bench with wooden peg legs. They wore straw cowboy hats, well-worn blue shirts, and faded Levis during the week, but white shirts, coats and ties, and fedoras on Sundays. As they discussed *la vida*, their Adams' apples worked up and down their skinny throats.

You might see two lesbians necking on another park bench, while the pedestrians stepped gingerly over the occasional drunk, sleeping on the flagstones, or around a poncho-clad hippie, accompanied by a flute, who danced to his own choreography. Texans in turquoise leisure suits decorated with squash-blossom necklaces headed to the Don Fernando emporium of Southwestern jewelry. Beat up pickups parked next to Cadillacs. The neighborhood kids eyed braless hippie chicks, the down and out panhandled, and the drunks cadged cash to buy booze at one of several Plaza area liquor stores. Taos Pueblo Indians, adorned with sacred J.C. Penney's blankets, posed for photos and collected tips from tourists. Leo Salazar hawked his famous *santos* on the Plaza or traded the carved figures for liquor in the bars. The cops drove slowly round the park, stopped to talk to friends, and ignored the teenagers who chased the hippies or mugged tourists in plain sight. Grown newsboys Paulie and Felipe entertained the onlookers with shouts and threats about customers and circulation territory. Back on the sidewalk I'd nod to Rosemary Baca, who made her daily rounds from the Taos Inn to the Plaza and around town, an omnipresent cigarette dangling from her lips.

In La Cocina's dining room, there was a big round table with a sign that said "locals only." Our host, Cal Loving, installed a telephone with a coiled line on the wall that formed one side of the arch, where you crossed over from the dining room into the lounge and bar. When the phone rang, the waitress would answer and hand over the receiver to the requested party. Thanks to the in-house phone, the enterprising Bill Moles published his magazine, *High Country News*, from a barstool.

During slow afternoons (or any afternoon) high school buddies from California, Wagner and Nesbitt, discussed their picture-frame business while waiting for architect Gene Sanchez and teacher Gil Archuleta to arrive. Ageless Willie Taylor of Louisiana, dressed in overalls, sat at the bar with his buxom black "niece." He drove a ragpicker truck around town while this customer paid him to pick up the odd item, which he re-sold to that customer just down the street. While serving Willie upstairs at the Plaza Bar, I once asked him if anyone made trouble for him. "No, Bill, not as long as I got this." His eyes twinkled as he pulled a .45 out of his coveralls and laid it on the bar.

The La Cocina bartenders and waitresses carried messages between regulars and irregulars, who checked in to pick up the threads of a conversation regarding a social or business proposal. For years, whenever I heard a phone ring in public I experienced a kneejerk reaction—is that my wife calling? I'm not here. At La Cocina you might see the governor of the Taos Pueblo as well as the governor of New Mexico; Dennis Hopper and friend, Dean Stockwell; artists Ken Price and Larry Bell or R.C. Gorman; James Arness and the cast of *Gunsmoke;* or Dennis Weaver, Marshal McCloud of TV fame. And serving us all was Ruthie Moya, the world's greatest cocktail waitress. The cross-cultural mix of locals and visitors at La Cocina on Taos Plaza represented the venerable members of humanity during this ... the best of times.

2

In the spring of 1973, the new Plaza Theatre opened each evening at 6:30 p.m., and the movie screened twice, at 7 and 9 p.m. (more or less). Adults were charged $1.50 and kids twelve and under paid seventy-five cents. Children under six were admitted free of charge. At the special matinees on Saturdays, all seats were fifty cents. Still, Taos moviegoers waited from six months to two years before getting to see a popular movie at a rate the Plaza Theatre could afford. Hits like *Jaws* or *Star Wars* required a $5,000 minimum and two-week play date versus a seventy percent guarantee of the box-office receipts. The distributor always got the higher figure. An older Fellini film, *8 1/2*, might cost $150 versus thirty-five percent of the gross, in addition to airfreight of another $150 for a two-night screening. Classic cult films on the backlist of major Hollywood distributors, like *King of Hearts* or *McCabe and Mrs. Miller* cost $50 versus thirty-five percent guarantee of the gross for two days. Until the distributors caught on and the guarantees jumped, you could bring a classic back every six months at a tidy profit.

Screening a movie for one or two weeks increased the risk for yours truly in the event of poor attendance. On Thursday-Friday-Saturdays, I booked popular movies like *Billy Jack* or *Blazing Saddles*. A Saturday matinee might include a double feature: *And Now Miguel* with *Jack the Giant Killer*. Sunday and Monday featured crossover exploitation fare—*Kansas City Bomber* with Raquel Welch or Stanley Kubrick's *A Clockwork Orange*; the Tuesday-Wednesday change alternated between artistic sensualities like Pasolini's *Decameron*, a W.C. Fields double feature, Truffaut's *Wild Child*, or the X-rated cartoon *Fritz the Cat*.

In the '70s the Church of the Holy Cinema was a popular destination for mini film festivals, featuring the work of Woody Allen, Lina Wertmüller, Robert Altman, or Russ Meyer and Clint Eastwood. At an early version of the Chamber of Commerce Fall Arts Festival in 1975, the cinema component included classic foreign films by Truffaut and Fellini, the *Apu Trilogy* and the *Children of Paradise*.

For a few years the single screen, 202-seat Taos Plaza Theatre became a virtual twin-screen complex. We featured popular animal movies or conventional Hollywood films, such as the latest in Kung Fu adventures and G-, PG-, or popular R-rated fare at 7 p.m. At 9 p.m. moviegoers enjoyed foreign films, art films, an exploitation R-rated movie, or an X-rated sensationalism like *Deep Throat* or the orgasmic *In the Realm of the Senses*, wherein a woman shears off the male parts at the moment of climax. (Director John Waters celebrated fine dining in *Pink Flamingos* when Divine demonstrated the use of the original pooper scooper.) Like the rest of the country, we showed midnight movies— *Rocky Horror Picture Show*—but at 10 or 10:30 p.m. on Friday and Saturday nights.

The customs of moviegoers varied according to your tri-cultural ethnic group aquí en Taos. The Anglos avoided graphic displays of cinematic violence, while the Spanish filmgoers avoided explicitly sexual imagery. Taos Pueblo residents came to see the movies. If I tried to explain the subtleties of subtitles or ratings to a family of four from the village, they just looked at me like I was another long-winded *ponsigh* (white man).

You might ask how I didn't get busted for showing X-rated movies while remaining a reputable citizen in a conservative church-going community. Taos Mayor Phil Cantu and Town Manager Nestor Gallegos used to tease me in passing while they lunched at La Cocina: "Hey, Whaley, when are you going to bring *Deep Throat?*" While Nestor giggled, Phil smiled benignly.

I called the Mitchell Brothers in San Francisco, who distributed *Deep Throat* and *Behind the Green Door*. The brother who answered wanted to know if I represented the FBI. "How do I know you're for real?" he asked. I mentioned that I lived in Taos and he said, "Oh, OK." Nobody faked living in Taos. The magic of the name acted like a talisman in a not-so-secret society of the artful cognoscenti.

In January of 1977, Linda Lovelace demonstrated her

sword-swallowing act for Taoseños. The crowd, ninety-five percent native Hispanic, stood patiently in line on the stairs, staring nervously at their feet, while waiting for the 9 p.m. show. During the movie, a local waitress from a well-known diner came out to the lobby red-faced, covering her eyes, and said, "I can't believe it. I can't stand it." After regaining her composure, she returned to finish watching Linda's circus act. After the initial thrill of seeing triple X-rated films, Taoseños lost their interest in sex flicks and I discontinued the exhibition of X-rated sensationals.

Successful box-office movies subsidized the losses incurred by art films. While my patrons paid only $1 in 1969 and $3.50 for admission to a film in the '80s, the privilege frequently cost me a couple hundred dollars. The hangover from artistic lust came the next morning when I deposited the meager receipts at the First State Bank. Movies then were both sacred and profanely influential. As Ron Kalom noted, local grocery stores ran out of butter the week we premiered *Last Tango in Paris* in New Mexico.

In the second story of the Plaza Theatre Building, the Mudd Combine operated the Plaza Theatre Bar, commonly referred to as the "Upstairs Bar" or "Airport Lounge." Since they were losing money on the operation, they offered me the bar in May of 1974.

It seated sixty or seventy happy revelers and could accommodate one-hundred fifty for dancing. The stairwells and alcoves provided discreet spaces for dope smokers.

The Combine charged $800 a month plus a percentage of the gross. When the grosses were high during the summer, I paid as much as $3,000 a month in rent for the theatre and bar. Across the Plaza, Cal Loving rented the La Cocina building for $450 a month but did $500,000 to $700,000 worth of business each year. My gross for a year between bar and movie theatre was little more than $150,000.

As I passed the dough from the street to the landlords for rent, I felt more like a moneychanger than an entrepreneur. Still, Susie and I lived a middle-class, if tense life and netted, according to our income tax forms, about $20,000 annually for a few years. More importantly, the Plaza Theatre provided me with the credibility and cash flow for numerous side ventures, including a bar and radio station, TCA theatrical productions, real estate deals, or more nefarious survival schemes, like poker games and selling art on the black market.

The great literary modernist D.H. Lawrence, like our local Hollywood commuters, played an ironic role in my life and times on Taos Plaza. If I wasn't staring at Saki Karavas's collection of Lawrence paintings at Hotel La Fonda, I was showing movies adapted from his novels. Just as Dennis Hopper movies boosted business at the box office, so Lawrence novels adapted for the screen drew crowds.

One night, the long-suffering Susie—"Hey, Blondie" (to the locals)—had taken my place at the box office. We were showing director Ken Russell's adaptation of Lawrence's *Women in Love*. The first show sold out and at about 8:45 p.m. Susie called in a tizzy. "Alex and the gang are terrorizing customers waiting outside for the second show." I got the infant Fitz up out of his crib and jumped in the car. By the time I got to the Plaza, Alex, a 17-year-old kid who wore his hair in an imitation Afro, and his gang of punks were gone. For the next week I kept an eye out for the wannabe gangsters and expressed my displeasure when I saw them. On a Sunday morning at about 10 a.m., I stumbled into Alex by the wooden sidewalk that led from the Plaza to the John Dunn House. He stepped back and tripped over the board-walk. While he lay flat on the ground, I menaced the punk with my cigar and chastised him with my tongue. After my tutorials, the gang moved their mugging operations, more or less, away from the Plaza.

While watching Jack Cardiff's adaptation of Lawrence's *Sons and Lovers*, I remember how impressed I was by Dean Stock-well's portrayal of the young Lawrence. Between the first and second shows, I went upstairs to check on a ruckus in the bar. In contrast to subdued moviegoers seated at cocktail tables who were discussing the high points of literature and film, two guys in straw hats—drugstore cowboys—stood at the bar pounding back drinks and shouting epithets. Lurking nearby, but looking slightly sheepish, stood a familiar figure in jeans and cowboy hat.

"Dennis," I said, "who is that guy?"

"Dean Stockwell," he whispered.

The screamer at the bar looked nothing like the sensitive young man with beautiful eyes portrayed downstairs on the big screen. Dean had tripped on his career and was hiding out with the hard-core denizens of the Taos demimonde and, worse, he had begun, we heard, selling real estate. Years later, when Dean and Dennis starred in David Lynch's *Blue Velvet*, several locals claimed they had watched the two amigos rehearse the scenes in Taos.

At the box office I met screenwriter Leo Garen, who co-wrote *Grassland* (later known as *Hex*). Garen regaled me with tales of trying to make films and television shows in Hollywood. He claimed to have introduced Dennis to Taos, but Dean Stockwell implied that he himself told Dennis about Taos after Stockwell filmed *Sons and Lovers* in 1964 and visited the fabled art village. At the Plaza Theatre, Dennis always looked for me because Susie made him pay for tickets. He'd slide around the box-office door and whisper, "Bill, I want you to meet Nicholas Ray" *(Rebel Without a Cause),* or, "That's Warren Oates." So I'd wave him and his friends in the door. When we screened *High Noon* and despite hand held in front of face, I recognized Julie Christie at the box office.

The Taos Valley looked like a pastoral Eden back in the '70s, but the lovely, snow-covered Sangre de Cristos and the fiery gold-orange glow of the sunsets, even the serenity of the stars hanging in the heavens over the Sacred Mountain, contrasted sharply with the outlaws and troublemakers who came out when darkness descended on the Plaza. As I dragged one smelly patron out and up the stairs from the theatre or held up an inebriated drunk as I carried him or her down the stairs from the bar, I was put in the delicate position of not breaking the neck of the person who was pulling my hair, spitting in my face, or trying to stick me.

You approached the Plaza Theatre Bar, designed by Ming & Mudd, by walking up a broad set of stairs with three landings, ideal hangouts for nighttime muggers. The stairways were decorated with art and valuable Indian pots—perfect for thieves. The lounge had soft comfortable couches where members of the methadone culture nodded off during the afternoon. One afternoon I heard Jim Wagner yelling, "Whaley, he's got a gun! He's trying to shoot me!" Jim grabbed the gun from the junkie and we bounced his head on the table before the miscreant stumbled off down the stairs.

Our patrons sat at custom-built "antiqued" wooden tables, designed by former freelance photographer Shel Hershorn, who had dropped the straight life, though he liked to tell stories about the way he got *Life Magazine* photo credits for Texas Tower shooter Charles Whitman or got the con artist Billie Sol Estes to pose in front of non-existent silos subsidized by the federal government. An eerie painting of a red fox hung above the bartender's head behind the thick plank at the five-stool bar. A fancy sound system filled the room with tunes, courtesy of Bob Dylan or Phoebe Snow. An expensive Navajo blanket covered up the color TV, set in the recess above the stage, when we weren't watching the Watergate drama.

From the picture windows in the bar, you could look down on the Plaza through a curtain of snowflakes in winter or watch the seething masses of tourists and locals in summer. Toward five o'clock, a former New York stockbroker, Dick Gordon (R.I.P.), would leave La Cocina and weave across the interior of the park, negotiate the multilevel bricks, and manage to overcome the tricky stairs. Each day Dick ordered a few Margaritas while watching the five o'clock news before passing out.

When Nixon resigned in August of 1974, a full house jeered as the Trickster flashed the victory sign and climbed up the gangway to his getaway chopper. "Drinks are on the house," I announced. Though we celebrated Nixon's departure, the next day and for the rest of the summer, nary a soul showed up for happy hour and the five o' clock news—except Gordon. Though the Trickster got me in the end, Taos Pueblo got Blue Lake because of Nixon's sentimental feelings for Native Americans.

One night I walked into the bar and saw this skinny coupon-clipper from Oklahoma sitting at a table with his longhaired friend. The two claimed membership in an art and jewelry collective, which had bounced a check for a big bar tab; hence they had been banished. (These newcomers should not be confused with the authentic young artisans, whose credit was A-1, and who were mostly Taoseños from the Mabel Dodge Luhan house; the latter made everyone proud of their collective efforts at turning turquoise, silver, and leather into objects of desire.) I grabbed the interlopers by their collars and hustled them down the stairs. When the skinny one jumped on my back I fell to my knees. I held off the jumper with my right arm while gripping his partner's long hair with my left hand until the latter pulled his head back and my hand came away with a fistful of hair. I dropped the yucky booty and booted them both out the front door.

For the next week, Mr. Long-Hair Bald-Spot walked around town with the remnants of his natural wig in a leather purse, complaining to everyone about my brutality. Magistrate Judge Norbert Martinez, KKIT's afternoon DJ for the Spanish music show, called me to say that the guy had filed a complaint.

"Norbert," I said, "he's nothing but a damn hippie. He and his buddy bounced a check."

"That's what I thought," said the judge. "I'll drop this complaint."

Similarly, one night I was escorting a belligerent Taos Pueblo drunk down the stairs. When I spun him around to keep him off-balance, his bigger, wider sister grabbed my ill-kempt hair from behind and pulled me down on the floor. A good Samaritan intervened and saved me from losing my scalp.

The chief threat uttered by the Chicano locals at the time was: "I'm going to get my brothers and come back. We're going to fuck you up, honky, and kill you." Those friendly farewells were punctuated by the sound of more choice epithets as I shoved them out the front entrance onto the sidewalk and slammed the door.

An acquaintance who hailed from Dallas called me from the bar one night, saying, "Whaley, you better get down here."

"What's the matter?"

"There's a bunch of women dancing with each other."

"It's dyke night," I said. The seeds of Yogy Odus, an all-female rock-and-roll band, were sown on Tuesday nights. Though verbally caustic, the so-called dyke community didn't express themselves as violently as other subcultures—at least in public, though they were a force in the performing arts.

A loyal Hopper fan, upon entering the Plaza Bar men's room, once saved the movie star from an organic shampoo when he stopped a big black guy from stuffing the actor's head down into the urinal. According to Peter Biskind's book, *Easy Riders, Raging Bulls*, Dennis intimidated his Hollywood colleagues. The author quotes Hopper's wife, Brooke Heyward, who describes Dennis as "violent, and dangerous. Extremely dangerous." But Dennis earned his stripes in the Taos community, where he got arrested and occasionally beaten up. Today, he is buried in a back-road cemetery near gangbangers and prominent locals in the nebulous border area between Talpa and Ranchos de Taos, three miles south of the Plaza and not far from the El Cortez Theatre, which he transformed into an art studio.

Then, the town police responded to calls for help—more or less. Since they worked for minimum wage, about $4.25 an hour, I gave them free passes to the movies. But they weren't always willing to risk their street cred' by throwing a local in the lockup on behalf of a gringo bar owner. Like most Taoseños, the cops operated in the shadows of a passive-aggressive culture and believed that Anglos would one day leave their valley, just as Taos Pueblo residents believed the descendants of Spanish conquerors would one day abandon the conquest. Transient émigrés of my generation generally believed they would someday leave Taos to rejoin mainstream America. Since everything seemed temporary and nobody had much to lose, the residents of the demimonde surrendered to their appetites and their passions became unhinged; violent acts followed. To this day it is difficult to find a violent local criminal who has acted up sans stimulants.

The only part of the Plaza Bar experience I remember with affection concerned two special Taoseños. Jo Carey, a tall, thin, energetic cocktail waitress, possessed of humor and intelligence, was second only to Ruthie Moya of La Cocina in the Taos trade of great servers and peacemakers. Leo Santistevan, who cleaned up the bar and lounge, then took a similar job in the theatre, and moved quickly up the ladder to concessionaire and assistant manager. When I began losing my mind, Leo repeatedly answered my calls of distress and helped me keep the ship afloat. Later, as a realtor, Jo Carey rescued me from lo' these many mortgages in the late '80s, through one of the most byzantine transactions ever negotiated in Taos. The transaction was all the more miraculous for the small amount of money at stake in contrast to the exceedingly complex tangle of tax and mortgage complexities. When I asked her how she trained for a job involving such sensitive negotiations among a variety of mortgagees and mortgagors, lien holders, both private and federal, and personalities of both a rambunctious and civil nature, she said, "I was a preschool teacher."

3

In March of 1975 I stopped to talk to Jean Mayer, at the Hotel St. Bernard. Mayer told me how much he grossed in his bar on President's Day, which was more than the Plaza Bar grossed in a month. As I drove down the mountain and turned south toward Arroyo Seco, the sunset glowed golden in the west, and the snow-covered peaks in the east turned blood red. My own frustration boiled over and I resolved to close the bar.

Though the rent got paid promptly each month, I hadn't made a dime from selling booze or sandwiches. The employees were passionate about work, except on Tuesdays, or from 5 to 10 p.m. on Fridays, or if Mom came to town during the solstice. "I can't come in before 7 p.m. No Sundays. I have no experience but I refuse to clean ashtrays or windows. I'm slow but people like me—except for Spanish guys. And I can't stand hippies." Bouncers refused to reprimand drunks and bartenders said the fella passed out in the chair "only ordered one drink." One night, my newly hired doorman stole the bank, some $50 in change, and split before the music started or a single customer had paid to enter. Later, that same doorman was elected county commissioner and engaged in a bout of fisticuffs with a fellow commissioner on the dais at a public meeting.

To catch the thirsty laggards who drifted in from El Patio, La Cocina, the Taos Inn, and other bars that closed before midnight, we kept the Plaza Bar open till 2 a.m. Though the crowds might applaud at the end of a live set, the civilized tone rarely lasted. No matter what kind of music you presented—folk, rock, a classical trio—everyone began to dance and fight. And the fights usually began after the midnight witching hour.

Circa 1966, when I arrived in Taos, a bar fight between two drunks was treated as a simple disagreement. By the mid 1970s, ethnic politics had become an excuse for social diatribes. "You're throwing me out because you don't like 'Indians' or 'Chicanos'—you honky *cabron*." A hippie might say, as he or she stole tips from a waitress or bartender, "Don't you know about aquí en Taos, you capitalist pig?" The Chicanos and Indians talked bad about WASPs, calling Anglos racists, who, in turn, made bigoted remarks about "beaners." The so-called mountain hippies grew increasingly antisocial and disregarded all laws and customs. A new threat to the social order emerged in the persons of returning Vietnam vets—native Taoseños who glared contemptuously at the love-peace crowd. Their eyes said it all and I decided I didn't want to attend the next seminar in social mores.

Between midnight and two, the princes turned into frogs and the princesses grew more beautiful. You couldn't control anybody's behavior—even your own. When my wife began pounding on the door of a waitress's house, where I lay naked in the sheets, I could only mutter like Kurtz in *Apocalypse Now*: "The horror, the horror."

These adventures honed my survival skills—call it moral realism—and constitute memories that helped forge an identity conditioned by walking through the hot coals of experience. The youthful illusions of patriotism and righteousness instilled at my mother's knee, however, created so much inner tension that I sought the solace of drink. Plus, it seemed, I was condemned to financial failure, surely a sign of sin in the conventional society of Calvinist America—feelings that caused me to double down on cognac or scotch as I hastened to escape my nemesis, my guilt, even as the enemy stared back at me each morning from the mirror.

That final evening, a bottle of scotch and the bartender, a handsome and diplomatic lad, kept me company—as he had my wife (she told me later). Downstairs at the Plaza Theatre, Bruce Lee starred in his kung-fu masterpiece *Enter the Dragon*. After the show, the local kids burst through the exit doors, ran up the stairs, and emerged on the sidewalk emitting high-pitched sounds—"*Eeeee!*"—kicking at imaginary enemies and flailing the air chop-socky style. Upstairs, the bartender and I locked the doors at the end of the night and sat at a table looking through the windows at the moon shining over Taos Plaza.

We stared out into the Plaza, and I thought that if the rent had been lower, the staff more dependable, the clientele a bit more civilized, I might have made a go of it. After saying goodnight, I got in my turquoise VW, drove around the Plaza, and parked on the sidewalk between local cantina El Patio and an adjacent building. I was drinking at the bar when a rookie cop I didn't know walked in and asked, "Whose car is parked outside on the sidewalk?"

"My own," I said. He asked me to move it. The cop was small of stature and fresh of face, very young. I was a beaten-up 29-year-old. "Now, if I get in the car, you'll arrest me for drunk driving," I said. Still, I backed up the car and moved it to the parking lot on the east side of the bistro.

"I have to take you in," he said.

"Okay," I said and started to get in the cop car. Then, "No,

I'm not going." I got out and shut the door. He came round the front of the car, opened the door, and tried to manhandle me. I grabbed his collar with one hand and his belt with the other, lifted him up and threw him into the patrol car. Then I returned to the bar, sat down on my stool, and resumed drinking. Suddenly, here came Sergeant Joe Hammer, leading the local SWAT team, brandishing shotguns. I went quietly.

Two blocks from El Patio and the Plaza, at the police station, they fingerprinted me and began to take my picture. With a swing I broke the camera and with a lunge I began to break up their furniture. According to the master scribe of Taos, John Nichols, whose spies were everywhere, I assumed a three-point stance, legs and forearm cocked, and repeatedly extended and exploded against the metal lockers. Apparently, the cops subdued me and called Susie. She called the projectionist at the theatre, Jim Levy, assistant manager, and the bartender, all of whom showed up to bail me out.

"We've never seen Bill like this," said the cops. Once, Dr. Kilgore asked me if I had been on acid after a car wreck turned into a brief hospital visit. "You were hard to handle," he said. "It took three or four guys to hold you down."

"Drink, Doc, just drink," I said, referring to an evening of imbibing chokecherry wine.

While the cops discussed my case with my friends, I escaped out the back door, ran across the field to my house, and hid in the empty concrete dog kennel in the backyard. Eventually, I crept inside Fitz's bedroom and listened, like La Mosca, to Jim, Susie, the bartender, and an anonymous woman (the Nichols leak) speculate on my whereabouts. Fitz grew wakeful and cried. I picked him up, cradled him in my arms, walked up the stairs and into the cruel light of the kitchen/dining room. *Et voilà!* I might have said.

Nobody was innocent of the occasional outrage. Though everybody talked, few people among the Rexall-La Cocina crowd judged you. During my decades in Taos or, ironically, while passing through Colorado, it was usually the Anglos who tried to throw me in jail, literally or figuratively, while Hispanic natives, bail bonds persons, or others got me out and let me go scot-free. What was felonious in mainstream America or even Colorado did not necessarily qualify as a misdemeanor in Taos. Later on during the *Horse Fly* years, the DA began dropping homicide cases and I thought tolerance had run amok at that point.

For lawlessness has its downside. The dreaded "86," or "banishment for bad acts" rule didn't apply to bar customers in Taos back in the '70s. Banned troublemakers would sneak into your bar and start fights or they would lobby your customers to support readmission. You couldn't guarantee the safety of women or wimps except by sheer force. Due to the increasing madness, landlords and liquor-license holders began to abandon the Plaza. The number of bars and liquor stores in the immediate area dwindled from about ten to three during the late '70s and early '80s.

For decades afterwards I experienced PTSD: Plaza Theatre Stress Disorder. To this day, my first reaction is that of the street fighter/bouncer, expressed more recently as irony, dripping from an inky pen published in the tabloid sheets of *Horse Fly*. The locals have convinced me that gallows humor—laughter— is the first and last refuge of a true Taoseño.

Prompted by my destruction of the cop shop during the Ides of March in 1975, I sought advice about my dipsomania from a shrink in Santa Fé. Due as much to a recessive Irish gene as my own lack of self-discipline, I sometimes felt as if there were no flies on me—no pain suffered, no reasonable request granted. An abstract idea like justice or injustice takes on "thingness" for me, so I tended to act as if the concept was reified—turned into a concrete object. Alcohol released the anger that was stimulated by imagined and/or real observations of injustice. Or maybe it was self-indulgence and confusion. *Quien sabe?* To the shrink I confessed my abject guilt for a marriage going bad, but the shrink convinced me that I was only fifty percent guilty for the co-dependent nature of domestic relations. My wife, she said, should take some responsibility. Mostly, she shook her head and sighed as she considered my confession of confusion.

When I exited her couch, I left forty-nine percent of my guilt behind and felt rather lightheaded—almost ecstatic—for a short time. Upon review I discovered that both my childhood and adult peccadilloes needed more analysis, but at least I got a start on the sanity project. I read Carl Jung, who commented on the ghostly figures from the dark side that haunted one's psyche, and I began paying attention to the shadow. Malcolm Lowry's proconsul in *Under the Volcano* exemplified how romantic notions of drink could lead to death at the bottom of a *barranca*. I turned, temporarily, away from self-destruction.

After Susie moved to Denver in the spring of 1976, my staff said I was a much nicer guy. Though I longed to depart Taos and do something with my life, local possibilities continued to tempt me. Unlike Odysseus, who stuffed his ears with wax and ordered his mates to strap him to the mast, I willingly listened to the sirens of commerce and ideas.

That summer Harvey offered to sell me the Plaza Theatre building and finance the purchase. And in August 1976, Dave Primas, an independent insurance guy, and Clark Funk, a plaza merchant, appeared at my office on the landing of the Plaza Theatre, representing the Taos Art Association board. They asked if I'd be interested in doing something with the four-year-old TAA theatre. Money might be in short supply, I told them—but ideas? Never.

4

The TAA theatre, only a few years old in 1976, served as a venue for Sue McCleary's *Project Discovery*, a summer art and theatre program for children, and she and her cohorts scheduled five or six concerts the rest of the year. A film series under the aegis of Larry Kaplan died when the Plaza Theatre re-opened and began showing art films. The Dave-Clark duo indicated to me that the TAA theatre was underused.

The artists who had started the TAA suspected the reserves from the adjacent Stables Art Gallery were evaporating behind the curtains and wanted to sell off the theatre, a functioning but incomplete edifice (like the Plaza Theatre Building). Meanwhile, McCleary had successfully lobbied the National Endowment for the Arts for a grant to hire the TAA's first executive director, Jane Burke, an ex-Peace Corps worker from Oklahoma.

The TAA's historic Stables Gallery was managed by Thom Andriola, who, they said, could sell a Louis Ribak painting to Bea Mandelman, Ribak's social-realist abstract-expressionist wife. The gallery grossed about $200,000 a year and members of the pantheon at Stables were considered modernists—no realists (painters of hollyhocks) need apply.

From the relative safety of the upstairs bar on the Plaza, where I battled mere drunks, I descended into colorful shouting matches among members of the art community. The distinction between life and art at the TAA was as muddied as the conflict between the realists and the modernists was perpetual. Much later, during the *Horse Fly* years, I used to stumble out of a rambunctious meeting of Taos County Commissioners and think to myself that at least the elected officials attempted to follow rules and regs, while the artists, in comparison, conducted their affairs, like an artistic process, according to the idiosyncratic manifestos of a particular vision.

A lively blond with light-blue eyes and a charming accent, Jane Burke began writing grants to the New Mexico Arts Division, and I began talking to the local thespians. In a brilliant public relations coup, board president Clark, Jane, and I came up with a new name: the Taos Community Auditorium, or TCA. The word "artist," then, had as many negative connotations as do the words "Anglo," or "newcomer" today.

After selling tickets at the Plaza Theatre for the 7 p.m. show in the middle of barrio tumult, I'd walk over to the silk-stocking district and open up the TCA at 7:30 for the 8 p.m. concert or show.

"Good evening, Mrs. Anderson, enjoy the Beethoven."

Then I'd go back and sell tickets at the Plaza for the 9 p.m. movie. While there, I'd grab the one pissing on the stairwell by the shoulders—"Sonofabitch, *cabron*!"—haul him up the stairs, and leave him wrapped around the posta.

Back at the TCA for the curtain call: "I hope you enjoyed the concert, Mrs. Anderson."

"The first violin missed several notes."

"I'm so sorry, Mrs. Anderson."

Then Leo would call. "He's back. Shall I call the cops?"

In my quest for enlightenment, I found myself drawn more and more to the artistic culture of Taos from which addiction I escaped, but not before I wreaked havoc on myself and others in the community.

Between live events at the TCA I filled in the gaps with classic films, everything from Eisenstein's *Ivan the Terrible* to John Ford's *Stagecoach*. We might show *The Littlest Angel* or *The Little Drummer Boy* during the Christmas holidays. Between the thirty or so movies exhibited each month at the Plaza, and another ten or so at the TCA during 1977 and 1978, film fans could choose from a richer variety of cinema than today's customers who patronize the ten-screen multiplex.

Rumors began to circulate in the summer of 1976 about a second indoor theatre planned by the plumber and developer Wally Chatwin for South Santa Fé Road in Taos. Wally, a quick-change Mormon bishop, had erected what was considered one of the first stick-built subdivisions, south of Cruz Alta Street, for the mysterious members of the tiny Taos middle class—accidental refugees like school teachers and government employees who had been assigned by fate to Taos. Wally had approached me about leasing the proposed theatre, but I said, "It's too soon. Wait a couple of years."

The threat posed by the intrepid plumber/developer, compounded by my wife's flight to Denver, shook the apples in Harvey Mudd's orchard. Afraid he might be left with an empty shell, he offered to sell the 18,000-square-foot Plaza Theatre building (PTB). The PTB included the theatre; the upstairs bar; the former Brandenburg-Polson Insurance Agency, which Helen Nanos had leased and turned into a gallery; an enclosed storage space, where my assistant Leo lived; and 5,000 to 7,000 square feet of unroofed space. I figured I could find the dough to put a roof on the building and make a profit on the deal. But to this day, much of the building is still unroofed and unprotected by the leaky subfloor. The millionaire wanted about $325,000, or forty cents on the dollar, for the building.

The lease on the Plaza Theatre was due to expire in 1978, which meant I was on a collision course with the future. What future, I asked myself? Who would give me a job?

Harvey and I agreed to close the bar and sell the liquor license for $50,000, which proceeds would serve as part of the down payment. He gave me a year to sell my house, raise the balance of $25,000, and agreed to carry the paper—$225,000 at eight percent—which meant I would make payments of $1,881 a month for twenty years. The theatre alone was already paying the equivalent amount of the proposed monthly mortgage in rent.

The new owners of the old Taos Country Club, Steven Plowden-Wardlaw and Jack Whitney, purchased the liquor license for their new development (Quail Ridge Inn today). The sign for the private golf course, saying "Members Only, Visitors Welcome," had long since disappeared, thanks to a group of sign-cutters, a legacy of Dr. Rosen, who was memorialized as the character Doc in Ed Abbey's novel *The Monkey Wrench Gang*. Abbey himself had lived and worked in Taos, but left after getting shot at when he walked home from work or threatened by the locals while he was editor of *El Crepusculo* (later known as *The Taos News*). He told friends he found Taos racist and hostile. The last time I heard about him as a public person, he dropped by Moby Dickens Bookstore to cash a check because the Taos Inn was dubious of his paper. No biggie. The Taos Inn once refused to cash David Rockefeller's check, too, though they cashed plenty of local checks, which were more representative of IOUs than cash.

Time grew short and my house didn't sell. I needed to make a deal. My wife and I, who maintained the charade about our relationship, agreed that I would move to Denver, the Queen City, and resume the straight life, after we bought and sold the Plaza Theatre Building. My son, Fitz, commuted between Denver and Taos via car, bus, and plane.

In March of 1977, the happy family traveled to Gardnerville, Nevada, to attend a reception for my youngest sister, who had eloped with a promising backhoe operator. I planned to lay the problem of finding $25,000 at the feet of my stepfather—the tall, quiet rancher, whose family owned property where cows once roamed in the heart of South Lake Tahoe, California. I was sweating bullets when we got off the plane in Reno on a Friday afternoon.

Just before dinner back in G'ville, a town later dubbed "slow death" by Fitz during his college years in Reno, Knox asked me how things were going in Taos. We discussed the matter for fifteen minutes. On Sunday afternoon we headed back to the Reno airport, an hour or so away. As he and I were getting the suitcases out of the trunk of the car, he said, "Well, I guess we can't let Harvey take the building back."

After we settled into our seats on the airplane, Susie asked me what we were going to do. In Nevada, words, as Emerson might say, are a kind of action, and actions are a kind of words, unlike Taos where, when I reproached Thom Andriola about his lack of follow-through on a TAA benefit auction, he claimed, "I'm a man of ideas—not action."

"We've got the money," I told Susie.

Knox forwarded the dough and we made the deal with Harvey. After taking possession of the PTB, I leased the upstairs bar to Grady and Edith Stewart of Louisiana, who converted the cantina into a ladies' dress shop called the Plaza Boutique. I dreamed of generating enough income to liberate the theatre from the vicissitudes of a monthly mortgage and to insure it against the mercurial demands of the movie distributors. That was the dream.

5

In the early '70s, Mayor Phil Cantu and the city council engaged the town's first team of professional planners, who designed, contrary to custom, a bricked-over Plaza closed to automobile traffic. Susie served as one of Phil's first assistant town planners. The outcry from the merchants and the local *gente* stopped the insurrectionists at town hall, leaving the town with an abundance of bricks. In order to dispose of the bricks, the public-works department built brick barriers around the perimeter of the sidewalks. Merchants could no longer sweep the dirt or push the snow into the gutter. Furthermore, the bricklayers also transformed the flagstone-covered, dirt-and-grass park into a series of impromptu and arbitrary elevations. The split-log handmade benches were replaced by wrought iron/wood benches decorated with generic Swiss folk figures, more commemorative of restaurateur Godie Schuetz of Casa Cordova than of the outlaw priest Padre Martinez, who presides in bronze today over the Plaza, thanks to sculptor Huberto Maestas.

Late on a busy Friday night or Saturday, a ceaseless flow of cars circled the Plaza. When the theatre was sold out and two hundred people waited in line, when five or six bars were full of music for dancing and fighting, when folks shopped inside home-owned stores—and though the tourists were in town—nobody seemed to mind searching for an empty parking spot.

"Someday," Saki said ominously, "the town's going to need parking, buddy. Look at the hotel." His car occupied one of three parking spots or sometimes the designated loading zone in front of the hotel.

"But Saki you could open the lot behind the theatre for hotel parking."

"Then they'll park there for free. Nope. The town's going to need parking."

The Greek generously let the public use the restrooms in the hotel but the pigeons disappeared after he fed them with treated grain—much to the chagrin of bird fancier and artist E.J. Bisttram. The Taos Police Department had long since moved out of their offices in the cavern under the cement bandstand to Armory Street (now Civic Plaza Drive). The empty cop shop was converted into a public restroom—mostly for the winos, who traipsed back and forth through the alley between the hotel and theatre, and between the Plaza and Saki's vacant lot. When a tourist tentatively entered the below-grade restroom on the Plaza you would see him or her re-emerge purple-faced, head popping up and out above the stairs, screaming foul but relieved to escape the pit.

Saki's back lot featured fertile weeds that served as sheltered sleeping quarters and was close to Mundo's La Lomita Bar and liquor store on the La Tuatah property, or Vigil's liquor store behind the bank next to the old *Taos News* building and Tally Richards' Gallery of Contemporary Art. After the restroom was closed, Plaza denizens found relief in the weeds or migrated toward the custom-designed alcoves at the side or rear exits of the Plaza Theatre. My trusted assistant, Leo Santistevan, regularly soaked the alley with gallons of Clorox and liquid cleaners; the antiseptic aromas smothered the unpleasant odor and helped dissolve the graffiti. Once, I billed the town several thousand dollars to recover the costs of removing the residue of piss and shit left behind by the community's outdoor residents. Then Mayor Phil Lovato, town attorney Jim Brandenburg, and editor Billy Blair had fun discussing my request in a story on the front page of *The Taos News*.

The town didn't reimburse us for the expenses or find the political will to open a public restroom for another thirty years. As the years passed, the winos disappeared from the Plaza down into the Couse pasture behind McDonald's or were transformed into the homeless, whose extant members now sit at comfortable tables under the Smith's grocery-store portal when they aren't sleeping at the shelter behind the new county complex.

If Taos was ever the Soul of the Southwest, and the Plaza was the Soul of Taos, then Saki was the Soul of the Plaza itself. The name "Saki," pronounced "psyche," is a transliteration of the Greek word for spirit. The kitschy Lawrence paintings and shiny shoes that punctuated Saki's office, conversation pieces, augmented the Greek's spiritual exercises aimed at living in a stylish manner. Despite his hubris and near demise, the miraculous recovery from the Gately debacle exemplifies how the rewards of karma speak to practical wisdom and good luck.

The multilevel dining room in the rear of Hotel La Fonda today was the result of a self-induced sucker punch Saki got from the Cowboy Bob Gately lessees, et al., who renovated the onetime La Cucaracha, where the waitresses doubled as pleasure principals. When Bob appeared in Taos—dressed up in a bent straw hat and lizard-skin boots—the bystanders and bench-sitters referred to him as a rainmaker. The bank reportedly loaned him money; local contractors and suppliers gave him credit. He reminded me of the protagonist in Robert Downey's interpretation of the Jesus story in *Greaser's Palace*.

Everybody marveled at Gately's persistence in dealing with the Greek. Saki loved to dicker but hated to close. "If you have to ask how much, you can't afford it, buddy." Sure, Gately and the Arizona wild bunch signed a lease, but there was "a ghost in the music." I remember eating lunch there at a preview, but Gately, et al., ran out of money and opened the doors only briefly to the public.

Prior to Gately's arrival, Saki had leased the bar known as La Cantina, and then Woody's, to Woody Harney, who was the "agent" on Saki's Hotel La Fonda liquor license. During the late '60s and early '70s, a liquor license owned by a single entity could legally be leased to several different agents, as long as the lessees were under a single roof or "canopy." While Saki watched the smoke rings curl above his head or reread messages on postcards from female admirers, the New Mexico legislators changed the law and restricted each license to a single "agent-lessee." The "canopy" was nevermore.

When Saki's attorney, Howard Brandenburg, drew up the contract for Gately, he put the word, "agent" instead of "agent-lessee" on the lease—though "agent" had become a meaningless term. Since Woody had already taken possession of the license as agent, he was grandfathered in as "agent-lessee," and since Saki was unconcerned, he suggested that Gately negotiate with Woody, even as he signed the lease and promised to provide a liquor license. Woody reportedly wanted $25,000 for his lease, equity, inventory, broken pool rack, crooked pool cues, and chipped pool balls. He kept telling everybody he had a lock, but nobody listened to the barkeep.

By the time Gately himself began negotiating with Woody, the Arizonans had run out of money. They left town owing money to contractors and suppliers who filed mechanics' liens against the hotel. Then the Arizonans filed a lawsuit against Saki and his attorney, Howard, who allegedly paid $10,000 to settle his case. Saki was left hanging. As the Greek always said, "Buddy, you never know who you work for."

During these tense days, I frequently visited the Greek, accompanied by Doug Terry, a young ski-shop owner from Texas. While I stared at the pinholes punched in the Lawrence paintings by an unhappy shoeshine boy, or checked out the shine on ten pairs of black dress shoes, Saki and Doug played checkers. Each time Doug lost a game, his face reddened and he pounded in frustration on Saki's glass-top desk. The Greek giggled.

One night, Doug, an athlete, probably thinking about Saki's potbelly and his appetite for ice cream, suggested that boxing was more his game. Saki asked Doug, a former Golden Gloves boxer, if he could hit the speed bag. Doug said, "I'll bet you three crab leg dinners I can beat you anytime." Crab leg dinners at

The Stakeout restaurant were our currency of exchange. Saki stood up and said, "Let's go, buddy." We got up and followed him downstairs into the hotel's huge basement.

Neither Doug nor I had ever seen Saki do more than walk vigorously around the Plaza during midnight jaunts. When Doug saw the bright red speed bag hanging from a well-oiled chain, the former SMU noseguard paled. Saki emerged from another room in boxing shorts and black-leather athletic shoes. "Shit," said the squatty ex-football player.

Doug lasted about a minute-and-a-half before he missed the bag. Saki rocked back and forth on the balls of his feet, punching the bag rhythmically. After ten minutes Doug and I quit looking at our watches. "He got us again, Whaley," said the jock. Not me, I thought to myself, for I was not one to underestimate the Greek.

We urged Saki to respond to the lawsuit filed by the Arizona gang from the Grand Canyon State, far from the safe confines of politically well-connected Greeks in the Land of Enchantment. We also suggested Saki sue Howard for malpractice, but he pleaded friendship. Then we urged him to hire his friend, attorney Billy Marchiondo, the legendary Albuquerque-Raton-Las

Vegas (New Mexico and Nevada) courtroom litigator. Marchiondo had always said, according to Saki, that the Greek should call if he was in serious trouble. "You're in trouble," we said. "Call Marchiondo."

Marchiondo had represented big-time Vegas gamblers in Nevada before retiring to the Land of Enchantment and passing the A-list on to Oscar Goodman, who served as attorney to the leading casino bosses and then as mayor of sin city. An old friend once told me he had a problem with a partner in a business deal. He called Marchiondo. Marchionodo told my friend to give him one-hundred dollars. Two days later, the partner's wife was deported. Nobody even knew she was from Canada.

When interest rates reached the usurious rate of eighteen percent at the end of the '70s, Saki and I frequently discussed our financial conundrums during our midnight rambles. "Let's go once more round the park, buddy," he used to say. After Uncle Jack Brandenburg sold the First State Bank to out-of-towners, the new owners installed an ex-Navy man as grinch. When a merchant approached, hat in hand, to ask for short-term operating capital, the grinch grimaced. Soon enough, instead of smoking Cuban cigars imported from Switzerland, the Greek and I were reduced to lighting up Te-Amos from Mexico, purchased from the cigar shop at the entrance to Taos Plaza (now World Cup).

Saki and Doug drove down to the trial in Arizona and told me Marchiondo looked like a *consigliere* and Saki, in his dark glasses, dark suit, and dark eyebrows, looked like a "made guy" in the mafia.

When the Arizona attorney cross-examined Saki on the stand, he said things like, 'Some have the cookies; some have the jar,' or 'If you can't stand the heat, get out of the kitchen,' and 'Every spider has its web.'

The court stuck Saki with a judgment of $250,000, payable to the Arizona wranglers, who, some say, made a substantial profit over their original investment of $80,000. Saki borrowed the money from the First State Bank to pay off the judgment, the local contractors and suppliers. From time to time, he renewed his notes and borrowed the interest to pay the interest from the bank's revolving Karavas fund, which soon grew in excess of $400,000.

Now Saki could no longer walk the Leon Gaspard portrait of his mother down the sidewalk and across the street to serve as collateral for his loans. The grinch demanded the Greek put up the hotel to guarantee the note. When the note came due, the banker told Saki to pay up in ninety days or said he would sell the hotel on the courthouse steps.

Despite his cologne and legendary cool, Saki grew increasingly nervous. His favorite aphorism, "You've got to make a deal if you want to live in Taos," was stuck on replay. He asked wealthy friends for help, but they all turned him down. Fellow merchant and frequent lunch companion Tom McCarthy offered to put up his El Mercado building as collateral. But the bank declined Tom's offer.

With days to go before the deadline, the bank moved in to foreclose, karma kicked in and the curator at the Cowboy Hall of Fame called. Years before, when this gentleman had been down and out, Saki let him stay in the hotel free of charge for months. "I've heard about your troubles," said the curator. "We'll buy the two Bisttrams hanging in the lobby."

The two large paintings, known as *The Cowboy* and *The Indian* hung on either side of the fireplace in the hotel lobby. Saki put the two lifesavers in his lumbering silver and gray Batmobile, and his night man, Johnny—who dragged his oxygen tank around the lobby in between drags on a constant cigarette while sweeping up the glowing embers that jumped out of the fire-place—drove the Greek to Oklahoma.

Saki returned to Taos with a check for $450,000 and thus pre-vailed over the suitors from the First State Bank. The chief suit-or died not long thereafter of a heart attack. Art dealers said the two Bisttrams were worth between $10,000 and $20,000. The curator at the museum in Oklahoma was fired and the two paint-ings were seen for sale in Santa Fé at $30,000 each.

It was the Greek's finest hour.

The king of kitsch and karma hit a hot streak and rented out the shops in front of the hotel for unheard-of monthly sums dur-ing the late '80s and '90s, all while he continued dancing the tango with a bevy of beauties in his office late at night. He lived happily and well, until he ingested so much ice cream that his system rebelled and the tango music stopped. Today the Greek lives on as an atavistic spirit of the Sahd family, who inherit-ed the hotel, and have preserved the Lawrence paintings. Saki is also memorialized by Tom and Barbara McCarthy, who in-herited some of Saki's property and display some paintings at their bed-and-breakfast, Casa Benavidez. Apparently Saki has re-versed the normal course of life and death, because the heirs are working for the Greek.

Not long before he departed, Saki said, "When I was young I had plenty of bullets but no targets and now I have plenty of tar-gets but no bullets." At Saki's funeral service, his friends and em-ployees, including lady friends, sat together as family. After the service, we adjourned to the Taos Inn, where the ladies, who ap-parently knew much about each other, told Saki stories.

If you think I am making too much out of Saki's karma, let me remind you of the way he passed from this earth to the upper re-gions. A Greek Orthodox funeral for Saki was held at Our Lady of Guadalupe Catholic Church, just off the northwest corner of the Plaza. The Greek priest said Saki died on April 16, 1996, during Bright Week, the week after Easter on the Orthodox calendar. During Bright Week, the priest said, "the soul of the deceased rises directly to heaven to join God." So Saki skipped the preliminaries. I can hear him laughing and saying, "Can you believe that, buddy?"

In the '70s, the Plaza was both a place of commerce and culture, a source of adventure and fulfillment of community. Everybody visited. You could spend three hours talking to friends or meet somebody with a come-hither look and lose yourself in a three-day joyride. Conversation was as bountiful as time and beauty were plentiful. For those who can see, the indelible impressions of the ghosts are as plain as today's traffic signals that replaced the four stop signs at the entrance to the *Mercado de Buena Vida*.

Show Biz

"Don't believe your press."

1

Though I was a country boy from rural Nevada who had dropped out of college at nineteen, I reassured the cast and crew of John Millington Synge's *Deirdre of the Sorrows* that everything I knew about the producer's portfolio could be seen in my emblematic Stetson and cigar. During the double-aught-whatnot years of the *Horse Fly*, I wore a Fedora to remind folks of my role as journalist and investigator of wayward doings. When I rather forcefully suggested that *Deirdre's* director, Larry Frank, make a casting change, he said, "I guess you're the boss." The theatrical metaphor as way of life apparently applies to Taos.

In late 1977, the cast of *Deirdre* included Barbara Paul, Josephine Roybal, Steve Policoff, Ron Kalom, Cathy Stephenson, Tom Collins, Paul Siskox, Jose Castellon, and Kevin Cannon. Pam Parker was Larry's assistant, Carol Kalom did the costumes, and American composer Noel Ferrand wrote incidental music for the production. A few hundred people attended the nine shows. Franks persuaded Albuquerque public television to tape *Deirdre* for broadcast, and a small group of us watched a muddy version of the show on television in El Patio Restaurant.

Local theatre groups lit up the community in the '70s. Steve Parks and Bill Bolender produced, directed, and acted at Taos Theatre Company; Eloise McCallister backed The Magic Mirror Players, a women's collective; the Taos Little Theatre put on *Clarence Darrow*; Ken and Nancy Jenkins produced and directed Taos High School's *Oliver* and *Man of La Mancha*.

The TAA director, Jane Burke, and I, the director of the TCA, recognized that community theatre fulfilled the mission of the organization by involving the most people per performing arts dollar. We spent $600 to produce the nine-night run of *Deirdre,* while a typical music or dance troupe on tour incurred losses of up to a $1,000 for a single evening. Second-tier performers from the region required more ass-kissing than big names and frequently played to only twenty or thirty paying customers. The joy of presenting a performance to a full house was as rare as a Maria Benitez flamenco dance concert, whose fans filled the house, stomped, cheered, and created enough energy to raise the TCA off its foundations. And Maria was easy to work with, just like Dizzy Gillespie, Earl "Fatha" Hines, and Woody Herman, who also filled the auditorium.

The stage manager for *Deirdre,* a young woman named Marty, also a member of the Magic Mirror Players, mentioned that we ought to produce *West Side Story*. Two local dance instructors, Rory Duval and Tory Olds, signed on as the choreographers, and proved to be geniuses at adapting dance moves to the limited skills of amateurs. The former *Village Voice* critic credited with creating Off-Off Broadway, one Michael Smith, who built custom harps for a living, had written a book on Polish theatre guru Jerzy Grotowski, and doubled as the editor of the arts page at *The Taos News*. Michael laughed out loud when we asked him to direct a musical, but he agreed to attend auditions. Second City vet Carol Kalom, your hostess at The House of Taos, volunteered to do the costumes. Kit Schuetz, another trained professional, agreed to design the set. Don Thompson was the musical director, and Richard Crawley, a retired banker, conducted the rag-tag orchestra.

"About fifteen and a half minutes after Joe Mondragon first diverted water from Indian Creek into his parents' old beanfield, most of Milagro knew what he had done," says the narrator in John Nichols *Milagro Beanfield War*. Between the Spanish telegraph/telephone, bar talk at La Cocina, and gossip at Dori's Café, the buzz prompted folks to call and ask about roles in *Westside Story* before an announcement was released in *The Taos News* or on KKIT-AM and KXRT-FM.

I felt as presumptuous as the empty proscenium stage seemed grandiose when the aspiring actors and actresses bravely auditioned in mid-December at the TCA. Who was I to evaluate their chops? Don Thompson played the piano for the singers. Michael Smith organized the talent. Other than one or two pieces of sheet music from Don's dusty files, Marty's beaten-up copy of the book by Arthur Laurents was the only guide we had for the casting call. Choreographer Rory and I alternately looked down when somebody sang off key or gave each other the high sign when a performer showed promise.

The staff adjourned to La Cocina after the auditions and sat on the hard-plastered bancos, softened by black Naugahyde cushions. A tall, lithe figure, the wife of a local attorney, who tried out for the role of Maria and was possessed of an operatic voice, sat down on the *banco* and began scooting over closer and closer to me. Suddenly she grabbed my hand under the table and smiled deeply into my eyes with her own brown brilliants. I was slightly embarrassed. We cast Marty's friend Cathy Stephenson, who had played *Deirdre*, as Maria. Cathy, tried and true, fit in with our grab bag talent.

After much negotiation, the agency that licensed *West Side Story* reduced royalties from $150 a night to $50. We didn't pay the cast, but promised to pay the staff a combined total of $2,500. Carol Kalom, the ingenious researcher of closets and flea markets spent $200 on costumes. Local shops, hardware stores, lumber yards, and Rexall Drug Store extended credit for supplies. As the balance in our charge accounts grew, I grew increasingly nervous.

The hippies, conventional dues-paying members of the community today, then still lived as communards. Though the transition to mainstream society had begun, the work ethic did not occupy a place of honor among any of the three cultures. Organization and efficiency were little recognized as factors in either private or public life. The bar crowd at La Cocina said *West Side Story* "couldn't be done."

They also said we couldn't get Chicanos to dance and sing on stage. So I went to see a local singing star, Vito Trujillo, who happened to be taking the winter off from touring because his wife was pregnant. We cast them both in the show. Where Vito went, other singers and dancers, both men and women, followed.

While sitting at the locals' table in La Cocina, making a list of gaps in the cast, Rory looked up at the bartender, Pat Enright, and said, "He'd make a perfect Officer Krupke." I got up, went up to the bar, and asked Pat if he would play Krupke. "Sure, Whaley." Later, Enright (RIP) told me that except for his marriage and the birth of his children, *"West Side Story* was the highlight of my adult life."

We began rehearsals without casting Tony, Maria's costar, because we needed a tenor, and nobody had auditioned for the role. The only person who could sing the part, according to street talk, was the plumber Bob Draper. But as Rory and Tory said, he was prematurely bald. We had heard that Bob was in San Francisco, experimenting with alternative energy. Though I didn't know him well, I had once kicked the plumber out of the movie theatre for commenting loudly throughout a rather sensitive Bergman drama. The patriarch of The House of Taos, Ron Kalom, intervened on Draper's behalf, and he was allowed to return to his seat. "Let's go ahead," I said to the staff. "I'm sure Draper will do it."

As the story goes, Draper ran into somebody from Taos at the San Francisco Airport, who said, "Hey, Bob. I hear you're in *West Side Story.*"

When he got back to town, Bob called me. "Whaley, what the hell's going on?"

"Bob," I said, " you've got to play Tony. Your community needs you." The tall, gangly, bald Bob Draper showed up one night and filled the auditorium with the sounds of his tenor, the female members of the cast turned into jelly, and we were set.

As both producer and TCA house manager, I could schedule as much rehearsal time on stage as the staff thought necessary for the cast. Opening night was slated for Thursday, April 6, the week following Easter Sunday. While rehearsals for *West Side Story* continued, Taos Theatre Company's Bill Bolender and Steve Parks liberated the stage at the Plaza Theatre, beneath the silver screen on top, in a production of *The Zoo Story* by Edward Albee and *Krapp's Last Tape* by Samuel Beckett, both directed by Michael Smith. At the TCA, Nancy Jenkins directed a Taos High School production of *The Man Who Came to Dinner.* Peggy Claus directed *Fractured Fairy Tales,* the product of a teen theatre workshop.

Over at the old county courthouse on the Plaza, choreographers Rory and Tory rehearsed the Jets and Sharks under the historic WPA frescoes in the courtroom. In an adjacent upstairs office, Don Thompson coached the singers. For the next two years Don managed a performing arts studio where aspiring actors and actresses honed their skills in preparation for community theatre productions.

Meanwhile the movies continued to screen and keep yours truly solvent. The comic western *Kid Blue,* Dennis's first major acting role after his self-directed debacle, *The Last Movie,* did good business in Taos. Dennis's salary, reportedly $400,000, was based on the success of *Easy Rider.*

Taos groupies frequently returned from the Hopperville train with tales of the enfant terrible. In the summer of 1977 at La Cocina, I got a professional's opinion about Hopper antics. Shel Hershorn was dining with a large, disheveled-looking man wearing baggy clothes and a straw cowboy hat and motioned me over to his table, saying "I want you to meet Bud Shrake." Shel had dropped out of a successful freelance photo career *(Time, Life)* to become Bob Draper's plumbing assistant and his partner Sonja's goatherd. I had grown up reading Shrake's colorful prose in *Sports Illustrated*, along with his colleagues Frank Deford and Roy Blount. Shrake, who wrote the script for *Kid Blue,* said that due to behavioral problems, Dennis cost the production company hundreds of thousands of dollars in delays.

Across the hallway from the downstairs Plaza theatre I had installed a game room: pinball, pool tables, and a dual-seat video racecar. You couldn't see around the corners from the box office to watch the action of my little Plaza devils—Albert, Jimmy, Steve, and Derek (among others). Occasionally, I walked in and arbitrarily threw out one of the kids.

"Hey, I didn't do anything!"

"Well, you were thinking about it or you did yesterday." If I banned one of the kids completely, I lost control over his behavior on the streets. So I used the carrot-and-stick to maintain order. "You're on probation. You can come back in two days." The video-racecar machine, which I purchased for about $2,000, grossed $600 one day during fiesta. One of the Jets in *West Side Story*, starving artist, actor, and Vietnam vet Peter Parks, needed dough, so I hired him to maintain order in the game room. Because the ruffians harassed the moviegoers on their way up and down the common stairway, and despite the steady stream of revenue, I ultimately closed the game room. Later, I met some of these homies again when they fell under the aegis of the community corrections board to which I had been appointed.

The cast had all the usual human problems. A trumpet player in the *West Side Story* orchestra, Lawrence Froelich, came up to me one night and said softly, "I've been living in my car and haven't eaten for three days. Can you loan me five dollars?" Cathy Stephenson, who played Maria, got sick early on, was hospitalized and died. Her understudy, recent arriviste Randy Raiser, assumed the role opposite Bob Draper's Tony. While Randy's voice wasn't as strong as Cathy's, the chemistry between the winsome diva and the smitten tenor energized the show.

As you might guess, life began to imitate art. The staff met at La Cocina each evening after rehearsal while the cast met at the Sagebrush over drinks and other stimulants, which activities led to steamy side-notes, including a tale known as The Mysterious Case of the Pregnant Lesbian. Several marriages and divorces (including my own) followed in the wake of *West Side Story*.

Between the sets and lights, salaries for the crew, and royalties for the rights, the cost of the show began to climb above $3,000, past $4,000, hitting more than $5,000 by opening night. TAA Director Burke wrote an application to the New Mexico Arts Division (NMAD) for an emergency mini-grant of $1,000. To show our good faith, Jane and I lobbied the legislature on behalf of NMAD, where we watched Senate Majority Leader C.B. Trujillo of Taos work the committees and senate floor. C.B. was a helluva politico. He played poker in the basement of Foster's Café and knew when "to hold 'em and when to fold 'em." Jane and I cleverly omitted reporting the rising cost of the show to the TAA board.

Board President Clark Funk once said to me, "When I see you, you frown so much I never know if you're mad at me." Damn right I frowned. I was tense. When somebody would ask me how the show was going, I'd shrug my shoulders and say, "Fine."

When I screened a controversial or bad movie at the Plaza Theatre, somebody would call me out on the sidewalk or yell at me from a passing car: "Whaley, what's wrong with you?" Why did you bring that disgusting movie to town? Or I might hear: "The projectionist [Warren] missed a changeover last night. Can't you get it together?" Or, famously: "Leo [the assistant manager] was rude to me last night." Everybody in Taos told you how to run your business.

During dress rehearsal on April 5, 1978, I sat between the director and the choreographer. As we watched the cast stumble through a dance step or miss a note and drop a line, we'd nod, smile, grimace. Rory and I agreed that we'd have a nice little show. "We'll probably sell out on opening night to friends and family," I said. "Big cast."

That night I crawled into my cave (no windows), a single room where Taos Mountain Outfitters has since resided for so many years in the Plaza Theatre Building. My accommodations were modest, but as I used to tell my son Fitz, "We've got a movie theatre and a game room in the basement." Fitz was in town for opening night and he dined well during the day due to his dad's charge account at Rexall. One afternoon, John Holland, the drugstore's mayordomo, called me up and said, "Fitz just had his fourth hamburger. Shall we cut him off?" The Plaza, our front yard, was home to man and beast, families, friendlies, and freaks.

And a couple of blocks away, I was part of a biomorphic machine with moving parts—more than sixty dancers, singers, actors, and actresses, stage managers and prop persons, lighting technicians and people with titles I didn't understand, and orchestra musicians whose names I didn't know. I did know that I didn't know what to expect.

2

On the morning of opening night, I dined on a Hash Brown Heaven at Dori's Bakery. The concoction of hash browns with an egg, topped by green chile and melted cheese, cost a dollar-and-a-half. Dori Vinella also manufactured the first fresh bagels in Taos (bagels possessed of an unusually long shelf life). On Sundays John Nichols played his own brand of boogie-woogie at her piano. The tall, robust, all-knowing La Vinella kept track of everybody and everything. If you were looking for work, a friend, a house to rent, or a lover, she could point you in the right direction.

After breakfast, I dropped by the TAA office to talk with my co-conspirator Jane—who, in addition to her role as the TAA director was also a dancer in the show. She hung up the phone and said, "The reservations are coming in. I think we're going to sell out." In those days people didn't know where they were going until they got there. Phone reservations and advance ticket sales suggested an earthquake. At the TCA, I checked in with the technical director, who checked the lights and the capricious electrical system. After making the bank deposit, I checked in with Leo, my assistant at the Plaza Theatre. "Yes, Whaley, everything's OK here." He shrugged, as if saying to his *pendejo patron*, "What do you think?" Leo's body language, punctuated by a guttural remark or grunt, expressed a complex response to any question for those who could see and hear. During lunch at La Cocina, I checked up on preparations for the opening night cast party with owner-manager Cal Loving. He agreed to furnish the hors d'oeuvres for a cast party if I provided him with a bar full of folks on a slow Thursday night in post-ski-season April.

My friends from La Cocina, who rarely left a barstool, said they were coming to the show. Folks whose names I didn't know stopped me on the street and asked me what I knew. The ladies at the bank asked me if they could get tickets. A story about the show appeared in *The Taos News* and Ron Kalom flogged it on his early-morning stint at KXRT-FM. Jane and I had already visited with Steve and Barbara at KKIT-AM on their 11 a.m. show, *What's New.* And I had arranged with Billie Blair, the editor of *The Taos News,* for John Nichols to write the opening night review. At 5 p.m. Jane said we were sold out.

"I hope they show up to pay for their tickets," I said. Then I advised her to over-book reservations—a trick I'd learned from Jean Mayer at the Hotel St. Bernard. I could feel the vibes in the soles of my feet. When Francois Truffaut and Jean-Luc Godard made their first movies, *400 Blows* and *Breathless,* one of them said they went all out because they never knew whether they'd get a second chance. I got in my '67 Ford pickup with its carved wooden racks and drove up the street to Paul's Men's Shop.

"Do you have a tux in my size?"

The cast was onstage warming up when I got to the box office about 6:30 p.m. to check the bathrooms and concession stand, sweep the sidewalk, and see to backstage problems. The crowds generally began to trickle in about fifteen minutes before shows started at 8 p.m. By combining the roles of house manager, ticket-seller, and producer, I cut out staff mistakes and lowered the overhead. Someone had artfully arranged bouquets of flowers backstage. When the cast spotted me in my tux, they froze for a moment and then the nervous energy intensified.

Back then the hippie girls in Taos still wore granny dresses sans bras, and longhaired males dressed like a favorite TV Indian or some version of a character from a *Mad Max* movie. Hispanic natives appeared in public neatly dressed and well-groomed, as did the natives of Taos Pueblo, whose modest selection of jewelry and leather, footwear and braids, gave them a touch of style. The rest of us wore a mix of Levis, working man's wear with a taste of the west, except for the bankers, who wore suits.

As soon as I opened the TCA box office at 7:30, a steady stream of people showed up to claim their tickets. The hippies were dressed up in coats and ties or dresses and bras, wearing make-up and lipstick, albeit slightly askew. The clean clothes and smell of soap shocked me. When I asked playgoers if they had reservations, some said, "Reservations? Who ever heard of a reservation in Taos?" Others peeked over shoulders and proudly said, "We have reservations." We even had printed tickets with seat numbers. By 8 p.m. the theatre was full and the audience seated.

Just before the lights went down, one of the stage managers came up and whispered, "Noel is sick; she won't go on." Noel was a talented pre-teen dancer (and the daughter of costume mistress and stage manager Carol Kalom and her husband, Ron, who played Doc). I followed the messenger down the aisle to the backstage prop room (janitor's closet). She was curled up on the floor in the fetal position. "What's wrong?" I asked. Noel mumbled something about her stomach. "You'll be okay. Better get up and move around," I said gruffly. An effective producer instinctively pleads, grovels, cajoles, or threatens the actor, actress, dancer or musician until he or she rises to the occasion. Noel groaned and moved a little. Then, "Let's go," I said, in my best imitation of a football coach. I left her sitting, now in an upright position. Back in the box office, I gave the high sign for the show to start.

The lights dimmed, the voices of the audience dropped, and the curtains drew apart to reveal Kit Schuetz's set—painted bricks and asphalt, cracked walls and windows—a sight so real you could smell and taste the New York City neighborhood. The crowd gasped. Conductor Richard Crawley raised his baton and the orchestra came alive. The Jets and Sharks emerged from either side of the stage in chorus lines. Marco Perella, the first Jet, was momentarily awestruck when he spied the crowd, who greeted him and the rest of the dancers, including Noel, with applause.

That night and for eight more nights, the cast of *West Side Story* performed at a level that was greater than the sum of its parts or the product of its rehearsals. At the end of each evening, the audience stood and clapped, long and loud. Though common today, a standing ovation then celebrated the praiseworthy. We saw the magic of community theatre as individuals were transformed from gardener or carpenter, layabout or plumber, into singer, dancer, and character right before our eyes. The chemistry between players and playgoers turned into magnetic energy that flowed back and forth under the proscenium, lifting everyone a little bit higher for each successive song-and-dance number.

No single member of the cast or crew was more surprised than me by our collective success. The accolades poured forth from our friends and families at La Cocina that night. Somebody, I've forgotten who, gave me good advice; maybe it was Ron Kalom or Peter Parks, who said, "Savor it. It may never happen again."

The next morning on KXRT, Ron read Nichols' rave review and the good John mentioned every single person listed in the program. By the time I got to the TAA office around 10 a.m., the phone was ringing off the hook. The following Thursday, Nichols' review was printed in *The Taos News* on its single art page. There was a small photo of the producer in the lower left-hand corner of the front page, with a caption that asked, "Why is this man smiling?"

I was smiling, ladies and gentlemen, because the show was very cool, but better yet, I knew that we could pay for it.

Closing night for *West Side Story,* Saturday, April 22, 1978, sold out, like all the other nights, and the New Mexico Arts Division had awarded a mini-grant for the show to the TAA of $1,000 (thanks to Jane). That, plus box receipts in excess of $5,000, meant we would do better than break even. We had money left over for utilities, the phone bill, and the purchase of a few klieg lights. Just after 8 p.m., I was at my post in the box office, waiting for everyone to find their seats before lowering the lights. We had filled the back row of the auditorium with folding chairs. The only space left was SRO near the northwest exit.

At the box office, out of the twilight, a familiar figure approached, whispering, "Bill, do you have any tickets?" Dennis, his entourage hovering in the background, said, "I've got Neil Young and Russ Tamblyn with me." Russ Tamblyn played Tony in the movie version of *West Side Story.*

"We're sold out but you can come in, Dennis. But you have to pay and stand in the back." The eight or ten folks with Dennis took up a collection, paid five dollars each, and entered the theatre. I went backstage and said, "Don't get nervous," then told them who was out front, figuring the caveat would raise the level of performance a notch. Dennis and his friends laughed, clapped, and thoroughly enjoyed the production. Afterward, they went backstage, congratulated the cast, and stayed for the closing-night party.

For the party, I used a technique I'd learned when serving as social chairman of the Kappa Sigma fraternity house at Colorado College—a fraternity whose characters resembled John Belushi and company in *Animal House*. I filled a large green plastic garbage can with ice, while mixing a concoction of cheap vodka, gin, rum, wine, ginger ale, Coke, and 7-Up to taste. As the party on stage continued and the level of liquid declined, I poured in the rest of the booze and soda pop until the empty bottles filled up the cardboard boxes. When I left at midnight, the cast and their admirers were still dancing, singing, and doing who knows what in the dressing rooms. The punch cost about $150 and served up hangovers to an estimated five hundred folks. The party lasted, they say, until almost 6 a.m. When I showed up to check the house at eight o'clock the next morning, a few supine bodies marked the spot.

The glow from *West Side Story* lasted for months and the effects for years. Notably, Maria (Randy Raiser), who won her divorce as a result of the show, became a waitress at El Portal (The Gorge), where she was besieged by autograph seekers all summer. Later, after she married the Singing Plumber, Bob himself founded the Taos Community Chorus with the help of a grant from the TAA/TCA. Though this tale of Romeo and Juliet featured several couples reborn into life with happy endings, other spouses and disappointed lovers rolled around in their sheets at home alone. The members of the cast and crew, however, still remember the sweetness of the show and savor the elegiac memories of *West Side Story*.

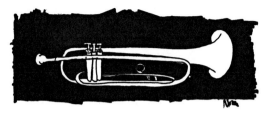

3

Following *West Side Story*, Judith Crooker directed and produced *Fiddler on the Roof* at the TCA in December of 1978. In *Fiddler*, Ron Kalom (Tevye) worked the audience each night until they cried. In the spring of 1979, Marco Perella starred as a reluctant Jesus in *Godspell*, while Kardo Romero and his driving rockers backed up the show with electronic sound. During a matinee for the elementary-school kids, one little girl said to me, "This is better than a real live movie." In December of 1979, we finished off the run of four musicals in two years with *Guys and Dolls*. The grosses were respectable but the house didn't sell out. Several talented married couples, wary of the dangers to hearth and home, avoided auditions.

During my tenure, we booked three jazz legends at the TCA. The agents asked for fees as high as $10,000, but we managed to get Dizzy Gillespie for $2,500, Earl "Fatha" Hines for $2,750, and Woody Herman and the Thundering Herd for $3,200.

The king of Be-Bop, Dizzy Gillespie (1917–1993), played Taos in February of 1979. We charged the unheard of sum of $10 a ticket and two hours after we put up the banner across North Pueblo Road, the show sold out. A young woman came up to Dizzy and said, "Mr. Gillespie, I never heard of you before but I sure like your music."

Earl "Fatha" Hines (1903–1983), called the first modern jazz pianist, was due in town around the Easter break for a concert. Due to a cancellation, Fatha and his vocalist ended up spending ten days at the Holiday Inn (Quality Inn today). I visited him daily to check on his grocery list and run errands. He wore a hairnet and watched television soaps. The night of the concert, New Mexico got hit with a severe spring storm. About 7 p.m., Fatha called and said his drummer was snowbound in Albuquerque. The box office would open in half an hour and the show began at eight. We were sold out. Once again, I called on Dennis Long— former hippie and sometime schoolteacher—who had pinch hit for me eight years earlier when I booked Bo Diddley into Old Martinez Hall. Dennis fought through the snowstorm from Arroyo Hondo that night and the crowd went wild when Fatha gave him a solo.

Artist Ken Price and his wife, Happy, hosted a reception for Fatha at their house. Ken played selections from Fatha's hits and, fueled by a couple of drinks, Fatha set the stage and recalled the various musicians with whom he'd played, the conditions under which the records were made, the showgirls and how they danced up and down the stairs at various clubs, and the names of who played what instruments. At four in the morning, Fatha played the piano for those who were still awake, including local art critic Tom Collins.

Woody Herman (1913–1987) and The Thundering Herd, twelve or fifteen young jazz guys, blew the roof off the TCA in another sold-out concert. At a La Cocina reception, the parent of a friend thanked Woody for playing at the man's Indiana high-school prom during the early '40s. The next day I drove Woody ninety miles north to the airport in Alamosa. We had a simple lunch in a local café before the flight. Woody didn't say much. He was saving his breath for the clarinet.

4

The father of the *West Side Story* choreographer, Luther Davis, wrote the successful Broadway show, *Kismet,* in the 1950s. He also produced *Timbuktu,* an updated African-American version of the show on Broadway, while I was producing *West Side Story.* When Luther visited Taos, we shared anecdotes about how lovers' spats and performers' foibles disturbed rehearsals and required the intervention of the producer. Leo Garen, a veteran of the Off-Broadway stage and Hollywood movie business, said the real difference between Taos and the professionals in New York or Hollywood was that "money holds the shows and the movies together."

Just as *West Side Story* was in final rehearsals, Wendy, aka the Black Widow, showed up in town, wearing a straw boater on a head full of long, dark, wavy hair. She limped alongside her acrylic cane alternately wearing stylish jeans or a flowing white dress. When she felt the pain spark in her back, she dialed up the buzz on an electronic gadget attached to her belt, complete with battery and wires. The shiny lip gloss and deep, sensual voice hinted at playfulness and danger. She had recently emerged from Payne-Whitney Clinic in New York, where the medical staff attempted to cure her of Percodan, cocaine, and other temptations. The cure never took and she died in her sleep, lo' these many years later, a body worn out by the trauma of a car accident and, prior to that, hard living.

The coincidence of *West Side Story* and the effect of having a beautiful woman on my arm got all tangled up with my existential search for a public-private passion—I needed to do something meaningful with my life. Though the Sacred Mountain served as the muse of my experience, it also protected me from the ultimate catastrophe. For a time, I saw the microcosmic world of "show biz," embarrassing to admit, as the organizing principle of my melodramatic life. Like a character in Plato's Cave, I had mistaken illusion for reality.

"You're naïve about love," the Black Widow used to tell me. "If I hadn't met you," she said, "I would have committed suicide." And, "you don't know how special you are." Or, "how special our love is." I believed the part about being naïve but I also knew that I was just another notch on her garter belt.

Between the euphoria of success with *West Side Story*, the electro-chemical reaction of community theatre on stage, and the spring weather, punctuated by the birds chirping, fluffy clouds, blue sky, and sunshine, I thoroughly enjoyed the first six weeks of the affair. After the first phase ended, artist Larry Bell, a friend far more experienced than I, said, "You're well rid of her."

The denouement lasted for two years. The Widow's hyperbolic acting—eyes half-closed, deep voice whispering, moaning, and a welter of physical and verbal tics, all contributed to her technique. She played pop tunes over and over as seductive mood music: Dolly Parton's "Here you come again / looking better than a body has a right to ... messin' up my mind, shakin' up my senses"; or when she felt depressed, *Piano Man* and its world-weary attitude: "They're sharing a drink called loneliness, but it's better than drinking alone." She and I were alone even when we were together.

Then I had neither read *The Unbearable Lightness of Being,* where author Milan Kundera writes that "a single metaphor can give birth to love," nor Alberto Moravia's *Boredom*, wherein a painter, despite his decided detachment, gets caught between the legs of a sexy model. The witty Black Widow, who was as sharp-tongued as Dorothy Parker, began the evening with conversation and a tincture of cocaine, which combination enhanced her charms. We spent the first summer together in a sumptuous adobe in Llano Quemado and the fall at her apartment on Lexington Avenue in New York City. Before I left on sabbatical for Manhattan, the *West Side Story* chorus performed the gym dance at the TCA and Jane Burke awarded me a lifetime pass. Though *Taos News* columnist Merilee Danneman wrote that I exited Taos in a "gossamer haze," I fled Manhattan after only six weeks and I wrecked a car on my way home from the airport to Taos. (When I woke up in Holy Cross Hospital, I naturally called Dori's for somebody to come and get me.)

Late in '78 I visited the Widow's apartment to console her at her stepfather's wake. There I met a cross-section of show-biz types: the widow of Frank Loesser (*Guys and Dolls*), for instance; stage and screenwriters Adolph Green and Betty Comden; Al Hirschfeld, Broadway's premier caricaturist; violin virtuoso Isaac Stern and his wife, Vera; and Janet Maslin, *The New York Times* film critic, who accompanied Wendy's first husband, the publisher *of Grand Street,* a literary magazine. Wendy's second husband, an executive in charge of paintings at Sotheby's, also attended.

The folks at the wake had known each other for years. Vera

Stern, a formidable woman with numbers tattooed on her wrist, reminded Wendy's mother, Gussie, of her duty to Israel. Gussie's husband, Arnold, the deceased, had donated art and mammon to museums and charitable causes in Jerusalem. Teddy Kollek (1965–1993), the mayor of Jerusalem, called with his condolences. When you looked at Vera's strong face, her determined deep-set eyes, the dyed brown-blond curls on her forehead, and listened to her harsh accent, you heard a voice that suffered no fools. Even Isaac seemed intimidated.

My fondest memory of that brief visit concerned genuine movie star Lillian Gish, whom I had just seen on screen in Robert Altman's *A Wedding*. She was an elegant, blond-haired wisp of a woman with mesmerizing blue eyes, who coincidentally had her arm in a cast like mine. I had the broken arm from a car wreck. For half an hour or so I listened in rapt attention to her discuss our mutual medical conditions. She was kindly and slightly flirtatious.

Due to reputation and the zeitgeist, a certain savoir faire accompanied travelers who hailed from Taos. Several friends confirmed this odd experience in the outside world, wherein you uttered the name Taos in response to a question and the word acted as a talisman. No further comment was required. The Black Widow moved to Taos at the beginning of the '80s and phoned at the odd hour. Like some Pavlovian dog, I got up, got dressed, drove to her house for an hour, a day, or a week, punctuated by passionate lovemaking. Rather desperately I surrendered to my survival instincts—*que sera sera*. And things ended very badly.

She had invited me over to her house in Talpa early one morning, whereupon I discovered her favorite lover's car parked alongside the front door. Later that morning she appeared at my Ledoux Street apartment, eyes blazing and looking at me with contempt. My temper boiled over and I slapped her around, horrid to relate. Later that morning I took some pleasure in rep-rimanding her lover during the Bent Street Takedown. I knocked his head upon his desk and then pounded his wriggling body with a telephone and typewriter. He squealed and tried to hide beneath the desk. As I exited, I heard the receptionist on the phone saying "some cowboy...," but this time I felt more like Lee Marvin in *Cat Ballou* after he shoots Kid Shaleen and says, "It was just fine."

The incident, tinged with ugly drama and post-violent sex, hit me in the solar plexus of guilt and shame. Her older daugh-ter called and said she understood. Later, the same daughter referred to the incident in a truly gutsy memoir about Mama, called *Her Last Death*. The first ex-husband also felt compelled to refer to yours truly in his own memoir, called *Lost Property*. In the late '90s, years after the incident, the Widow called me up out of the blue at the house of a friend in Nevada and apologized for her part in the drama—long after I had apologized and sought to make peace. The Taos D.A. made an oblique reference to the incident at a public forum during the *Horse Fly* years. The young-er daughter never forgave me or spoke to me again—except for the occasional poison pen letter or email bomb. Crimes of pas-sion do not pay.

After the final act, artist Ken Price took me for a ride in his van and told me a story about a frustrating love affair that he'd experienced and how he woke up while "breaking up" his art. The idea of Kenny shattering his ceramic sculptures—way back then—was as horrifying as the depiction of Lowry's proconsul, who saw himself tossed like a canine carcass into the bottom of a barranca at the end of *Under the Volcano*. Unlike Sam Spade in *The Maltese Falcon*, I played the sap; but apparently, like Flintcraft in the same novel, I got used to falling beams.

During the last musical, *Guys and Dolls*, in December of 1980,

I was taken with a visiting acquaintance I met at the TCA box office. I fired up the Mustang and drove at high speed, averaging 75 mph, to LA, incurring a couple of speeding tickets along the way. My friend was from New York but had spent time in Taos, having run away with her outlaw motorcycle lover and eventual husband, the renowned Michael Reynolds, rock 'n' roller and architect of alternative building fame—solar houses, beer can abodes, and best known as the progenitor of Earthships. My friend's father, a famous old-fashioned public relations man, got his start on Broadway in the '40s and seemed to know everybody connected to showbiz. When Fitz and I were visiting her and he heard that we actually bought tickets to visit Magic Mountain, he insisted we accept complimentary tickets for the next stop on our itinerary—Disneyland. She worked closely with her dad's most famous client, Frank Sinatra.

That December we joined her brother, who was a publicist for the Eagles, at the LA Forum for a concert with Fleetwood Mac and the USC marching band. On the way back to Taos, I stopped off in Las Vegas to attend Frank Sinatra's 64th birthday party and the celebration of his fortieth anniversary in show biz, which event was filmed for television at Caesar's Palace. The final cut eliminated Don Rickles' sex and toilet humor and didn't show Dean Martin drinking J&B Scotch directly from the bottle.

While Frank and his Rat Pack friends partied along with the Pearlmans, owners of Caesars, and oilman Marvin Davis, owner of 20th Century Fox, ASCAP's Jule Styne, Jimmy Carter's mother, Lillian; and ambassadors from Egypt and Israel, as well as Orson Welles, all testified on stage about how "Frank did it his way." Former heavyweight champ Joe Lewis played the greeter for tourists and groupies at the front door.

To complete this brief account of my tutelage by urban beauties, I briefly ran with a jeweler's daughter from Chicago, who wore diamond barrettes in her hair and introduced me via telephone to Geoffrey Mosher of the Goodman Theatre when I was directing David Mamet's *Sexual Perversity in Chicago* in Taos. Mosher on telephone confirmed my intuitions about staging the show he had premiered. Thanks to complimentary tickets from Chicago's dance and theatre critic, the jeweler's daughter and I once sat in the seventh row and watched Mikhail Baryshnikov in performance with the New York City Ballet.

In the early '80s, two dreamers began hanging around the Plaza Theatre, tickling my imagination with notions of FM bliss and the fortune that would follow in the wake of a home-owned publicity machine called radio. Mick Rothman, a refugee from Skokie, a Chicago suburb, worked in the box office. Young Brad Hockmeyer, heir to a flox fortune (the fuzzy stuff on greeting cards) hailed from somewhere near Boston. Brad worked in the projection room or did the odd job around theatrical productions. He and Mick dreamed of reviving the moribund FM radio station KXRT, which had been hatched but died during the previous few years at the Kachina Lodge studios. Due to my obsession with show biz, I believed that if I could control the means of publicity, I could successfully promote shows and movies via radio.

In the early spring of 1981, I produced and directed *Sexual Perversity in Chicago* on the stage at the Plaza Theatre. During its run, from March 5 through March 14, movies were shown at 7 p.m., and we put *Perversity* on stage at 9:30. Tickets were $4 in advance and $5 at the door. Opening night, we had about 140 paying customers. Actor Jonathan Gordon played his fans like a piano. Ruthie Moya and the gals from La Cocina roared with laughter at the Mamet misogynist.

Speaking for Taoseños in general, Bernie (Gordon) says to Danny, "Don't ever lose your sense of humor."

"I won't," Danny replies.

"Good," says Bernie.

Perversity, unfortunately, was well received. (I only lost $500 on the production, not counting house expenses.) Barbara Paul, an actress who overcame a drastic health challenge after the opening night show and returned for the rest of the run, said to me, "It's another feather in your cap." In *Artlines,* Tracy McCallum wrote that "*Sexual Perversity in Chicago* [is] a production in which great strides have been taken towards professional theatre in Taos." He even said the director deserved "a conjuror's accolade." Energized by hubris, I struck back and asked for more from the cast and crew when I scheduled a season of theatre for the summer of 1981.

I learned one thing: "Don't believe your press."

The cast for the summer included the original actors and actresses, Pamela Parker, Barbara Paul, and Jonathan Gordon, though the polymorphically talented (music, writing, radio, acting) Tom Collins stepped in for the suddenly vanished Michael Skinner. The latter, shaken by his harrowing experience in Taos, returned to New Jersey to train for the priesthood.

The spectacular Ingrid Boulting, a shirttail relative of the famed brothers who produced English comedies, signed up for Mamet's *Reunion.* Ingrid herself, a cover-girl model, had played the ingénue opposite Robert De Niro in F. Scott Fitzgerald's *The Last Tycoon.* In Taos she played opposite our local Brando emanation, Jonathan Gordon.

Barbara and Pamela did a turn in *Hello from Bertha.* Collins and the lovely Karen Magee lamented over the weather in *Talk to Me Like the Rain.* Noel Kalom starred in *This Property Is Condemned.* My *consigliere's* wife, Karen Messenger, handled the design and costumes. My assistant drive-by partner, Mustang Sally, kept the notes. Young Hockmeyer did the props and Albert Gallegos did whatever was necessary, whether driving to Albuquerque to grab movies off airplanes or acting as liaison for discreet errands during a summer and fall of discontent.

While we were putting the show together, Mustang Sally, the nymphet who graced my company on road trips, inspired less by Kerouac than by fueled readings of Hunter S. Thompson's *Fear and Loathing in Las Vegas*, wrote to the Woody Creek, Colorado, resident and asked Mr. Gonzo if we could turn the novel into a play. He wrote back and said wild, great idea, do it. I have consigned his handwritten letter to Fitz's care.

Though I chose plays that summer meant to conserve costs and keep the actors and actresses from too much hands-on work, the best laid plans go awry. For "getting laid" was the one thing accomplished. The male lead in *Talk to Me Like the Rain* got stabbed by his wife as he stood behind the cash register at Brodsky Books. He, in turn, socked the angry husband of his paramour in the jaw during an evening's respite at the Dramme Shoppe on Kit Carson Road. At least one teenage crewmember got lucky with a thirty-something actress. The reviews were justifiably bad. Attendance was disappointing and ticket sales for the movies were also down. I had over-stepped my limits and Nemesis began to haunt me.

We canceled the Hunter Thompson project. When I sent the fabulous Mustang into Cottam Ford for repairs, the repo man grabbed my dream machine. For the Thompson project we had acquired a stylized fiberglass fifties car from the grounds of the Mabel Dodge Luhan House, a Bruce Nauman piece, which Dennis had left behind buried in leaves and debris. Years later, when Hopper attempted to reclaim the art, we learned that a condo owner had dumped the fiber glass ignominiously into the local landfill.

5

Rejected by the public and disgusted by my own bad judgment, I began emulating Thompson's self-loathing. By the end of the summer, Mustang Sally and I had locked ourselves into the second-floor tower, receiving visits occasionally from an attractive pharmacist, who hailed us with goodies between her shifts at La Cocina. We came downstairs only to buy books from Brodsky, mostly Evelyn Waugh novels, and occasionally showed up at the box office, whenever Leo and Albert were short-handed. Due to an overdose of fuel one night, Albert discovered me passed out. He ran over to La Cocina and called on the nearest EMT/drug dealer, who knew the drill and applied ice cubes to my testicles. I must remember to thank Franny.

But the nymphets in the sheets couldn't cure the bats in my belfry. Mustang Sally and I fled to Denver and lived in an apartment near Raoul's Barber Shop of Love on Capitol Hill. During a Nyquil binge, I abandoned her and returned to Taos. That winter of 1981–82, a local smuggler, who had more customers at $120 per gram than I had paying $3.50 each for tickets to the movies, gave me shelter from the freezing temperatures.

To paraphrase the Repo Man, I hate a man who doesn't pay

his bills, so, in an anti-climatic gesture, I sold the movie-theatre business for a pittance—some promises and a little bit of cash. Thus I became a twisted financial middleman with a paper portfolio—a handful of promissory notes owed to me and bills owed by me to others. Although Joe Montana and the 49ers won the first of five Super Bowls in early '81, my own winning streak had ended. In an effort to stop the ship of self from slipping away, the entrepreneur doubled down on Taos.

Doubling Down

"I'll lose these warrants."

— ROBERT TAFOYA

1

Between my first and second year of college, high school friend Bill Shaw and I devised a scheme to beat the roulette wheel at a Tahoe casino. After red came up three times in a row, we bet on black and doubled down repeatedly—but red came up again, and again, and again. Our dough disappeared and we dared not go home to confront our parents, so we lit out for Southern California in his red MG (sans a bonnet), where we worked in Newport

Beach tourist joints as busboys and watched the smoke curl up above South Central L.A.'s smoggy sky as Watts burned. When the end of summer arrived, we returned home and went back to college.

My friend dropped out of college that fall, joined the Marines, and survived two tours in Vietnam. I dropped out and survived twenty tours in Taos. When he got back from his military adventure, he reentered life as a student at University of Nevada-Reno. "I hit the ground running," the successful attorney later said. I got stuck in Taos running in place. As Captain Willard says in *Apocalypse Now*, "I wanted a mission, and for my sins, they gave me one." By the beginning of the '80s, I knew I wanted to leave town. But, as syndicated film critic Chaucer Henderson said, "You've got to get back in before you can get out."

About the time I purchased the entire Plaza Theatre Building (PTB) in the late '70s, a local plumber and developer opened a second single indoor screen south of town, which caused attendance to decline by thirty percent at the Plaza Theatre. My tenant, Helen Nanos, had turned the old insurance office into a gallery, which she rented from me. Que Pasa Records rented the back portion of the building, across the street from the entrance to the First State Bank. The upstairs bar was now a dress shop, the Plaza Boutique. An unfinished area of several thousand square feet, concealed behind massive walls and open to the sky, contributed zero revenue. But if I could get the open space roofed, I figured I could turn a profit on the space. After agreeing to the deal and taking responsibility for the PTB, I remember less about pride of ownership and more about unfinished subfloors posing as leaky roofs. When it rained or snowed I avoided the southwest corner of the Plaza.

In a desperate effort to accelerate the mortgage payoff and preserve the Plaza Theatre, I doubled down and transformed the rental spaces into commercial condominiums. I sold off the corner to Helen Nanos; the slightly elevated area fronting the sidewalk to Dick Schroeder and Lyn Taylor for Taos Mountain Outfitters; and the former upstairs bar cum boutique and dress shop to artist Ken Price and his patient wife, Happy, for living quarters and a studio.

The millionaire Harvey, who held the paper on the building, had agreed to roll out and separate individual mortgages from the original contract on the building for each commercial condo I sold. Though Helen opted out of the condominium project, she purchased the corner and furnished us with the down payment to get the deal off the ground. (Later, Helen was able to retire when she sold off her property.) Dick and Lynn remodeled the empty space and installed windows in what had been a street-level café prior to the 1969 fire. Happy and Ken remodeled the old upstairs bar for a studio-living space and sold it at the turn of the century to the poor devil who also bought the defunct movie theatre, betting his poke on a dream that had failed twenty-five years prior to his arrival. The PTB still sits empty and forlorn on the southwest corner of the Plaza at press time.

The PTB project concentrated my mind wonderfully on what I missed by not going to law school. According to the myth, Mudd attorney Jack McCarthy of Taos and Santa Fé had helped write condo law at the New Mexico legislature. Steve Natelson, a one-time ski bum, former film actor, and owner-chef of the petite bistro, L'ensoliee (situated in Tally Richards' courtyard on Ledoux Street), had finished last in his NYU law-school class, so he represented me. A former Herman Rednick follower, attorney Big Steve Rose, represented Dick and Lynn. Rose so thoroughly nitpicked the condo articles, bylaws, and proposed purchase agreements that I resolved not to do business in the future with any potential buyer who hired him as counsel of record. My *consigliere*, attorney Hank Messenger, checked Natelson's docs, and I signed when Hank gave me the say so.

For years, Hank gave me good advice, which I rarely followed. He even accused Saki to his face of being a bad influence on me. "Imagine that, buddy," laughed the Greek. But risking my patrimony and credit on a game of pitch and toss—"You've got to make a deal to live in Taos"—became the indelible pattern I followed from my innocent beginnings until the bitter end.

Meanwhile, the millionaire-turned-poet, Mudd, had made a deal with Ken Price to draw a series of images for Mudd's book of poetry called *The Plain of Smokes*. The poet arrived one day during the World Series and asked the artist, a long-time baseball fan, to sign the contract for a book deal. They went outside on the porch, where the millionaire, allegedly, had thrown some changeups into the poetry-picture. He had the advantage of the baseball fan, whose attention was diverted by a 3-2 count, two-out, bases-loaded, bottom-of-the-ninth situation. When Ken related the story, he also said, incidentally, that Harvey mentioned he had no intention of rolling out the mortgages.

Toward the end of 1980, the millionaire confirmed his change of heart and though Hank said we had a case for breach of contract, due to letters and preliminary agreements, and should file a lawsuit, I had deals with buyers, including an agreement to purchase Edith Stewart's lease for the upstairs dress shop, so I could sell the space to the Prices. Plus, I needed cash to fix the leaky roofs and to pay for street prescriptions. In a fit of pique, I said to myself, "I'll double down and borrow the money; pay off the bastard."

At the First State Bank, the new president looked down his nose at me. As I searched for existential confirmation of my net worth, the clouds passed before the sun. So I listed the building for sale with Joe Wilson at LOTA Realty. An eccentric investor in property and art, one Richard Siegel, known as much for his deep pockets as for his dry throat, made an offer that I turned down but the offer lit up the sky and I used it as a carrot to convince the banker of the building's worth.

The banker approved the loan of $225,000 at eighteen percent interest for ten years. For the pleasure of the promissory note, I paid $4,050 each month, or $1,200 more monthly than the original agreement with Mudd. Though I owned in excess of 18,000 square feet, including 5,000 square feet of unfinished commercial condo space, and a business at the Plaza Theatre with a solid financial history, I was mortgaged to the hilt and could no longer borrow a dime during the off season to make repairs or bridge cash gaps.

Back then, I read novels like J.P. Donleavy's *The Ginger Man,* about the decadent Sebastian Dangerfield, who hustled friends for drink, and in *Schultz* about a theatrical producer, who mentions "That religion does not teach the only important truth there is, that man saves his soul by money alone and to be rich is right and true and from that derives all beauty and justice." Schultz's advice sounded ironic then but prescient in 2014.

Competition from the plumber's competing Taos Cinema forced me to sell the theatre at a discount, which deal included a list of unpaid vendors. When Joe Montana led the 49ers to a Super Bowl title in February of 1982, my reputation and my psyche were in tatters.

When Young Hockmeyer of Boston and Mick Rothman of Skokie, Illinois, came knocking, knocking at my door in the spring of 1982, I woke up from my winter snooze at the home of a local smuggler. Hock and Mick urged me to join them in purchasing the FCC license issued to Taos Communications Corporation (TCC) d/b/a KXRT-FM. They said we needed twenty-five grand in cash to capture the airwaves. Brad, the proposed program director, put up $15,000 from his trust fund. Mick, the proposed general manager, owned a tiny bit of stock and knew the phone numbers of the principals.

Though my own paper assets added up to more than $300,000, I didn't have a job, an income, or an automobile. I owned part of an unfinished downtown building and possessed promissory notes due me. Yet Rothman worked it out with the hotshots from Chicago so that I could sign a couple more promissory notes totaling $40,000, guaranteed by third and fourth mortgages. The majority stockholder, Danny FastTalk, and minor stockholder, engineer John McDermott, agreed to sell me the controlling interest based on these handsome bits of paper.

Street talk said Mr. FastTalk inherited Chicago's WXRT, which originally played ethnic music—polkas and the like—but progressive musicologists convinced him to turn Windy City listeners on with a format dedicated to an eclectic mix of pop, rock, blues, and jazz. The Chicago station found success and Danny, guided by thoughts of synchronicity and serendipity, sent McDermott and Rothman out to Taos, along with their good ideas, their savings, and their hopes. But, as Governor Lew Wallace used to say, "Every calculation based on experience elsewhere fails in New Mexico."

The proposed deal for Taos Communications Corporation would mean that I got ninety percent of the liabilities but only forty-nine percent of the stock, due to the "Burns Agreement." Mr. Burns owned, allegedly, a Christian radio station in Los Alamos and had, when KXRT foundered, offered to pay pennies on the dollar for the FCC license, but Danny wanted to salvage his pride. Burns got his claws—a right of first refusal—into Danny's agreement with the FCC, which stated that if a single person acquired fifty percent or more of the stock in the company within three years, the dreaded Burns Agreement kicked in and Taoseños would be harassed by Christian music or worse. So we flogged the fear of the cross, suggesting potential stockholders could save their community from the proselytizers.

The first version of FM radio in Taos failed due to lack of capitalization and community support, in-fighting, and bad timing. Back in the '70s the debut of FM was twenty years too early. By 1982, we were sixteen years closer to the mark. Hockmeyer, who survived the FM experience and bought the sound of static on the dial, began breaking even toward the end of the '90s— long after I'd left town (but before I returned).

By selling airtime and promoting movies, live theatre, and concerts, I figured "show biz, baby," was the road to glory and sure-enuf survival. Roll the dice and keep the cash flow coming. My vision included broadcast booths perched high above Taos Plaza in the PTB. Build it and they will come; give them good stuff to see or watch or listen to and they will buy advertising. The vision had worked variously for the movies at the Plaza Theatre and on the lively stage at the TCA. Folks thought I was high on unmentionables, but it was my imagination that sent me into the zoo-o-sphere. Like some junk-bond buyer or Ponzi schemer, I was betting on the cash flow—potential ad revenue—and the increasing value of the FCC license in the event of a sale. For months we tried to raise $10,000, the balance of the down payment. Friends and acquaintances began to avoid me. Really good friends suggested I leave town. Though broke, I had seen a former smuggler flash the color of hundred-dollar bills in the night at the home of my smuggler friend. His name was Michael Sheary and he appeared to be laundering his ill-gotten gains through the construction of his house when he wasn't buying up stuff for his nose.

2

The night before Mick and I were scheduled to leave for Chicago to finalize the FM deal, we were still ten grand short. I made an all nighter out of it with Michael Sheary. Given his tongue-tied monologues and psychological state, Michael was as unpredictable as the number of hundred-dollar bills he could pull out of his pocket. Finally, at 8 a.m., Mick and I got in the car for the drive to the airport in Albuquerque. My coat was hung on the back of the driver's seat. We planned to spend the night at Mick's parents' house in Skokie. (Everything I knew about Skokie I had learned from the famed *Blues Brother* scene where John Belushi leads the charge against American Nazis!) Mick had a certified check from young Hockmeyer for $15,000. He asked me, not really wanting to hear the answer, "Do we have the rest of the money?"

My eyeballs grated against my eyelids, my nose was filled with phlegm, and my throat was raw from cigar smoke. I sighed, reached behind me into the pocket of my jacket, and drew out a dirty green bundle tied up with a rubber band. "Count 'em," I said. In Chicago, Danny FastTalk maintained a neutral expression and stuck the bundle of banknotes in his pocket and the check in his wallet. He signed. I signed. We all signed.

Maybe Danny's bank didn't notice the unregulated dollars

but the Sacred Mountain concerns itself with the people of the valley. Stress and chemicals interfered with my intuition and nullified my intuitive safeguard—a voice, which (like the Socratic daimon) always says "no" when spiritual or physical survival is threatened. I hadn't listened to the voice prior to the moment I stepped behind the bar at El Cortez/Old Martinez Hall. But at least my struggle was rewarded with a treasure trove of cultural experience. Now God had another wager in mind for his Job-like servant. After I made a deal with the dark side, karma beat me with a broom. Survival was only one of my many punishments.

Due to deregulation, the assigned frequency of 101.7 for Taos was worth less the day we acquired it than it had been the day we made the offer. I'm not sure what happened but the FCC had changed the rules. At 22, when I bought the movie theatre on the Plaza, I made the best deal of my life in 1969. At the age of 35 when I bought the radio station in 1982, I made the worst.

Back in Taos, our motley investors, Young Hockmeyer and Michael Sheary front and center, congratulated the Mick and me. Sheary, the retired marijuana mogul, was good for a total of $15,000; Mark, the blond-haired male model, jumped in for five grand; and Doug, the squatty motorcycle mechanic from Aspen, contributed another $5,000. The motley ones elected me president of Taos Communications Corp. (TCC) d/b/a the FCC-permitted KVNM-FM (Voice of New Mexico). A local entrepreneur, Mark Yaravitz, loaned us $25,000, based on a promissory note and received a fifth mortgage on my building as guarantor. The two promissory notes, owed to prior stockholders, McDermott and Lee of Chicago, constituted the third and fourth. The First State Bank held the first. I don't remember who held the second, perhaps the guy who bought the movie theatre. I just remember counting five fingers on one hand every day for several years.

Though the 1981 buyer of the Plaza Theatre, an Española businessman, agreed to pay off some $10,000 in debt owed by me to theatre vendors, he had purchased the Taos Cinema, over by Friday Motors—a pig in a poke—from the Mormon Bishop for way more than it was worth and his cash flow began to dry up. When he didn't pay the vendors or the Plaza Theatre Building mortgage, I got harassed by those who held the notes.

The minute I signed the docs to purchase TCC/KXRT, I became liable for thousands of dollars in unpaid state and federal taxes owed by TCC. Former employees of the defunct station had filed claims for unpaid wages and Ed Lineberry at the Kachina Lodge, the landlord of the KXRT studios, had filed liens against the equipment for unpaid rent. Each day, someone new showed up with an old claim against the new owners of TCC. Due diligence, you ask? I'd never heard of it, anymore than I'd heard the term "location, location, location" before I moved into El Cortez Theatre in Ranchos.

If I had been a local hero during the TCA/*West Side Story* years, now my picture had been slapped up on the walls at the post office and I was Public Enemy No. 1. In reality, I was a gringo/pendejo twice over. Then things got worse.

Mick and Brad reclaimed from a storage unit the old KXRT equipment—turntables, tape players, microphones. The miscellanea looked like dead car parts strewn around Levi Cohn's junkyard in midtown Taos behind the Red Arrow Café. A rented 28-foot trailer without running water housed the studios on Blueberry Hill. The antenna for the topographically challenged transmitter on Blueberry Hill was set down in an arroyo just below the mesa's rim. The 3,000-watt "line of sight" signal couldn't get into El Prado, which adjoined uptown Taos, and residents of nearby Ranchos received the signal only intermittently. Our business offices (and eventual living quarters) remained upstairs in the Plaza Theatre Building, from which windows I could stare down anxiously at the First State Bank, wondering which checks might bounce each day.

Since I believed in the potential of my comrades, I kept some distance from the radio project and personnel. At the TCA, I had stumbled into a group of talented theatricals who transformed themselves from moths into butterflies, culminating in *West Side Story*. As sales staff, Mick hired Pat DeLozier, now a deacon, and Angela Romero, now a retired restaurateur. Hockmeyer, the program director, loaned his massive record collection to the station. But disc jockeys, aka radio announcers and so-called on-air personalities, turned out to be less like hardworking actors and more like dime-store divas.

If I suggested that a blues guitar riff followed by a series of four-letter expletives didn't go well at midday when local businesses were tuned to the station, they'd whine, "What's the matter man? You don't like my music?" If the announcers didn't slaughter the names of local Hispanic politicos, they mixed up roads and neighborhoods when giving on-air directions to the location of our advertisers. I frequently turned off the car radio to avoid apoplectic reactions.

While the one bright spot, engineer Sara Thomas, tinkered with the transmitter and its driver and exciter tubes, Michael Sheary, an amateur backhoe operator turned construction superintendent, did a tongue-tied radio show at night under the sobriquet "Wolfboy." During the day Sheary and his chief assistant, Dick Gordon, the dropout and former stockbroker from New York City, resolved to raise the antenna some fifteen or twenty feet in erector-set fashion.

Gordon, the renowned drinker of margaritas and reader of *The Wall Street Journal,* had made a name for himself on the slopes of our 49th state. He and Steve Hancock of Wilderness Books, and Rich Jamison, who developed the downtown Dunn House shopping complex, traveled to Alaska during the pipeline boom. Gordon read a book about engineering and explosives, then passed a qualifying exam with the highest marks of anyone who sat for the test. When he was assigned to blow a trench next to a school building, he discovered nobody on the crew had more experience than he, so based on a diagram in a book and a few calculations, he laid the charges and removed the dirt and rock without destroying the building.

A Moly mine engineer, Bill Renison, had designed the antenna extension for me on a cocktail napkin at La Cocina. After several weeks of Krazy Kids construction, the antenna project was over budget and behind schedule. "Christ, Whaley," Renison said, "if I'd known this was going to happen, I would've brought a crane down here and done the job myself in a day." The do-it-yourself studio installation and antenna upgrade of twenty feet cost us $12,000 in stock, assigned to Sheary, and another $12,000 in reserve funds from the Yaravitz loan. The new and improved antenna made a marginal difference, at best, to our listeners in El Prado.

3

From 1982 to 1986, KVNM hung by a frayed thread, dangling from engineer Sara Thomas's fingers. She was our wild card—call her sane. None of us had a grasp of the practical engineering arts so she explained the technical problems in laymen's language, even as she dramatized the options, alternately treating us to visions of hope and hell. Sara's tenure spanned the decades, including the solar era under Brad Hockmeyer when KVNM became KTAO in the late '80s.

Regardless of employees or stockholders who contributed a

last bit of savings, alimony, or pocket change; and regardless of local merchants who gave us credit; and regardless of the politicos who helped us during dark and desperate days of 1982 and '83; and regardless of those who worked for nothing, it was Sara who got the last bit of life out of $15,000 driver tubes as we searched nationwide for a supplier who would send us same on credit. When all we had for power was a 50-watt exciter, Sara tinkered patiently with the 1948 transmitter and kept FM alive and on the air.

And from midnight to 6 a.m. that first summer, Sara worked out her DJ fantasies as rocker Roxanne Rush. Unlike the average existentialist, good Polish Catholic that she was, Sara made the transition from man to woman that summer and took responsibility for her person and her life like no other person I had ever known (or know). Between her daily tinkering at the transmitter, she shared the care of her two pubescent boys with her former spouse, Sakti, a local belly dancer. When she sunbathed out behind the studio, the boys were heard to admonish "Aunt Sara," and advised her to put on her top when menfolk approached.

Our new general manager, my then girlfriend, gave Sara tips on dressing up for a fall wedding in New Jersey. Upon her return from the family affair, Sara imitated the accent of her Polish grandmother, who said, in an accent tinged with old-country speech patterns, "So, how does it veel to be a voman?"

We had known Sara first as Tom, when he worked for Dyma Engineering and played the bass guitar in a rock 'n roll band. She once said to me, "Bill, people are spreading rumors that I'm a dyke because I play with Yogy Odus [an all female band]. Would I go to all this trouble to become a dyke?" She once sent her male lover a belly-gram from Sakti. Sara is living happily in Florida, having inherited some property from her husband's (RIP) estate, which proves a point about someone whose karma is fine-tuned like a sensitive transmitter on a clear day.

The station began broadcasting during summer solstice in June of 1982. The Moly Mine laid off most of its workforce about this time. By the end of June, I had fired everybody in the office who was getting paid. Then times got rough.

Well-fueled by trades at local liquor venues, but under-financed, the motley crew at KVNM-FM rocked on during the summer of 1982. Members of the staff without personal transportation, gas money, or fix-a-flat, pedaled back and forth on the company's single bicycle between the offices high atop Taos Plaza and the Blueberry Hill studio three miles southwest. If you had a record collection or a sponsor and a capacity for pain or struggle, you too could become a spinner of discs. In lieu of revenue, we traded advertising for food and drink in local restaurants like Naomi's, La Cocina, and The Wine Shop.

The cash that came our way was shared first with the phone and electric company. Supplies for the transmitter and studio equipment came next. Employees, including management, were paid—if at all—according to need. Among those who loaned us their golden tones and spun discs for sauerkraut during those early years were full-time and specialty jocks like Kardo Romero

("Kardoriffic"), Ted Dimond, Peter Micelli, Chuck Perez, Harvey Cedars (aka Brad Hockmeyer), Mick Rothman, Bob Aldo, Thom Andriola, Sara Thomas, Michael Sheary, and Dennis, a black Anglo who drifted into town one day and said he'd do anything for a free meal. We loaned Dennis the company bicycle and turned him into a disc jockey.

Too broke to buy chemical or liquid antidotes, we resorted to the Taoseños' favorite refuge: gallows humor. Hardly a day went by when one of the staff didn't ask, "Hey, Bill, when do I get a raise? Ha, ha." Or, "Wow, the new studio is great!" or "I'm taking my paid vacation in Hawaii."

Only newsman Dick Behnke gave us whatever shreds of credibility we had. Though he tended bar at La Cocina during the afternoons and evenings, Behnke also insisted on receiving his agreed-upon salary—the only regular paycheck. Once he called in a description of the Fiesta parade over the phone to the studio from our general offices and I marveled at his professionalism.

"Where did you learn to do that?" I asked.

"Whaley," he said, looking at me with disgust, "I'm a trained news observer."

A sign above the fireplace in the office commemorated Hunter Thompson's contribution to our cause: "When the going gets weird, the weird turn pro." In lieu of a proper education or religious training, I have always been partial to the one liner—the epigram—as guide for conduct and the moral imagination or ambiguous explanation of the unfathomable. As the Paul Newman character in *The Verdict* says, "Act as if you had faith. Faith will be given to you."

Blind faith in nothing but the human experiment helped me through the dark nights when I counted up the bounced checks. The simple reminder about the weird turning pro, call it advice from the gonzo author, buttressed my morale. KVNM investor and Aspenite Doug Pumpelly—a mechanic who drank beer and tequila with the famed journalist from Woody Creek, Colorado—told me: "I didn't sue you, Whaley, because I saw that sign above your desk." While Newman and Thompson gave lip service to my plight, it was Nietzsche's reassuring whisper to the collective endeavor, i.e., "The contemplation of suicide has helped me through many a difficult night" transformed into the Taosenos last retort, i.e., "There's always the bridge" that comforted the motley staff.

Though my stockholders, despite their small contributions, lack of experience, or laid-back work habits expected to have a say in the operations of the company, the idea of groupthink gave me shivers. In anticipation of an annual meeting of the corporation, dissident stockholders, including Young Brad Hockmeyer and Michael Sheary, organized the motley members to meet with an attorney and organize a coup, aimed at ridding the station of yours truly. In terms of financial challenges and my own lack of managerial skills, not to mention the weak cash flow, they had a point.

When a local dealer leaked the details of the clandestine conspiracy, I cancelled the meeting and expressed my displeasure with Hockmeyer by punching him in the shoulder, a kind of tic I used daily to remind him of his duties. He seemed like a kind of younger brother during the KVNM years. The dissidents, meanwhile, filed objections to my high-handed ways in district court.

Basically, your Anglo Taoseño prefers that folks behave "nicely" even if the concept entails "failure." It's better to fail than find fault and fire the failures. I had fired the paid staff because they "failed" to deliver. Worse, I was guilty of the ripe retort or wise ass remark, meaning that I was an insensitive lout.

But District Judge John Wright was less interested in manners than the law and ruled that the president of a corporation can call a meeting of the stockholders or call off a meeting of the stock-holders. Since the drama featured a cast of characters subject to mood-altering chemicals, the conspirators were seen as unreli-able witnesses by their own attorneys, who negotiated a truce with Hank. My motto was then (and still is): "Millions for de-fense; not one penny for tribute."

Shortly after we dragged the KVNM-FM studio-trailer up the steep road to its Blueberry Hill location, where we had zilch in the way of running water, Manny Ocanas, a patron from the Old Martinez Hall and jazz aficionado, showed up with his treasure truck or septic hauler. Manny talked in the bebop rhythms of a lifelong hipster and always bought tickets for concerts, wheth-er at the early '70s Old Martinez Hall or in the late '70s at the TCA.

"Hey, why don't you put in an outhouse up here?" he asked me.

"Manny, the county commission outlawed outhouses."

"Don't worry. James is my man."

The chair of the county commission, James Duran, was also chair of the Taos County Democratic party—a political ma-chine with long arms that reached into the Roundhouse in Santa Fé. Manny built us an outhouse. If the corporation commission complained because we hadn't filed timely reports, or the New Mexico Tax and Revenue department came looking for pay-ments, I called Manny, Manny called "the man," and the tax dogs from Santa Fé quit barking.

Dyma Engineering's Carroll Cunningham fronted some $7,000 in equipment to help get us on the air while reminding us that we had to pay off the note on same in thirty days, but, of course, we were broke. The general manager mentioned that her ex-husband still owed her $7,000, but said he might be broke, though her ex-mother-in-law might be good for it. I cooed and whispered sweet nothings. She brought home the $7,000 and we paid off Dyma. Later she got her revenge, warning one and all that I was a one-eyed Jack before she called in the dogs. I couldn't be trusted.

For a time, thanks to a state and federally funded CETA program (Comprehensive Employment and Training Act), we managed to pay and feed the staff. The poverty angels from the Santa Fé state government funneled $2,000 per month to us for six months: $400 each for five employees. The contract said the employer must match the grant with a similar amount—another $400 each. Our share totaled $2,000 per month. We promised the world to the poverty angels but we deposited the dough in the general checking account and distributed the money among all the employees "from each according to his or her ability, to each according to his or her need." As good Christian-Marxists, the employees, named as subjects in the subsidy, conspired with management and signed off on the fiddled reports.

Although the spinners could talk for hours about which guitarists laid down what track on this album or that single, and whether Lead Belly or Robert Johnson influenced Woody Guthrie or Bob Dylan, they knew *nada* about your local congressman or county commissioners (though they knew where to find the county jail). Hence I interviewed most of the politicos during election season while the general manager, a good Democrat, shamelessly filled up the log with complimentary, unpaid spots pushing Democratic candidates in defiance of FCC regs.

Political operative Ernie Ortega, a onetime Plaza Theatre projectionist (now a magistrate judge), squired Democratic candidate for U.S. Senate, Jeff Bingaman, around Taos. The mild-mannered, slightly undersized Bingaman, smashed moonwalker Republican Harrison Schmidt in the general election and went on to serve quietly in the Senate for forty years. James Duran won his election for county commission. With KTAO's help, Bill

Richardson eventually won his first election to the U.S. House of Representatives and later the congressman helped Hockmeyer with FCC problems at KVNMs successor, KTAO.

Due to increasingly poor relations with the general manager, I began looking for solace at cantina confessionals (even as I slept hither and yon). She, in turn, began sleeping late and refused to let the staff into the office, where we lived, before midday. "What kind of way is this to run a radio station?" Brad fumed.

We gave up the lease on the upstairs office and carried desk, chairs, file cabinets, and phones into the vacant, unroofed court-yard area above the movie theatre and enclosed two roofed alcoves with plywood on either side of the rear entrance to the movie theatre's projection room. We plugged in electric space heaters to fight the January cold. From above, the former GM cussed us out, while below we continued to sell ads, record thir-ty-second spots, and pretend that we were a respectable radio station.

Though I personally owned this spot of concrete, I hadn't bothered to notify the members of the Plaza Theatre Building Condominium Association. The remodel cost us a couple hun-dred dollars but the condo board turned us in to the town's building inspector. The inspector told me we were within the compliance guidelines. More importantly, he said, "Don't worry Bill. I know you."

When the mail arrived one morning in mid January of 1983, a rumor became a terrifying fragment of reality. The general manager, who felt righteously scorned and conned like any disap-pointed investor or stiffed employee, had turned us into the New Mexico Attorney General, claiming we had engaged in fraud and fixed the CETA books. We confessed: "guilty as charged." Representatives of Ma Bell and the Kit Carson Coop arrived the same morning, saying they intended to shut us down if we didn't pay up past due utility bills by 5 p.m.

Although the sun was shining, the temperature was twenty degrees below zero. Still, sweat ran down my forehead and my stomach felt as if someone was pulling a knotted rope through my intestines. There was no place to puke unless I stepped out into the alley and joined the crew sitting under the bushes in Saki's back lot. To settle, the AG wanted cash—$8,000.

Hockmeyer, Sheary, our investors, and staff gathered to watch the gallows being erected and asked, "What are you going to do?"

"I'll think of something."

Hank, Natelson, and I, via a series of phone calls, convinced the AG's office in Santa Fé to accept a second-party promissory note as collateral for the eight grand. The note was due me in June from the buyer of my theatre for the misspent cash. Then I turned to Hockmeyer, who had let it slip that he was supposed to sign a check and forward it to the family trust account. But I knew he cashed the check to pay his rent. So I told him the radio station was about to close due to unpaid utility bills. That meant he'd have to find an honest job. Terrified, he agreed to pay off Ma Bell and Kit Carson Electric. The staff and stockholders cheered him for his selfless act.

As the sun rose higher in this sky, we began to thaw, breathe, relax. The concrete deck warmed up to minus-ten degrees. Out of nowhere, a Taos County deputy sheriff appeared, carrying a sheaf of papers. He spoke briefly to the various staff and stockholders milling about, who now looked fear-stricken. Apparently, the copper had warrants for liens and was prepared to execute them against TCC d/b/a KXRT because the company owed back rent to its former landlord, Ed Lineberry of the Kachina Lodge. The deputy explained that he had come to pick up all the radio station's equipment. You could see the dreams disappear into the cold blue sky as he proffered the terrifying documents and, besides, the white boys were terrified of *La Raza*—especially one in uniform.

Then the deputy sheriff turned and looked at me. "Bill," he says, "are you part of this group?" The deputy's name was Robert Tafoya, the son of Pilo, who had tended bar part-time and kept the peace for me at El Cortez Tavern in Ranchos de Taos more than ten years before.

"Yes Robert, I'm the majority owner."

"Oh, I didn't know that. I'll lose these warrants."

He turned on his heel and walked out the front door. Sheary, Hockmeyer, and Rothman stared at me, tongues hanging out of their mouths, eyes wide. My job done for the day, I winked at the staffers and headed over to the Wine Shop, where, during her retirement from La Cocina, Ruthie worked the day shift. Those liens disappeared—permanently.

4

Chance and luck kept us alive to serve the ship at KVNM-FM. By late winter of 1983, my nervous system, frayed from years of financial stress, began to shutdown. Later, when I tried to reconcile my memories with eye-witness accounts, I was grateful for a low pulse rate that intensified my blackouts and created the presence of absence. But here's what I remember or was told.

As a Keynesian advocate, I expanded the money supply with the "float" by opening a second front, or checking account, at Centinel Bank. Thus, I kited checks or covered bad paper at First State with half-bad paper at Centinel and vice versa. The bankers grew irritated with the practice but they made a fortune on bad-check charges.

To make the weekly payroll, I worked the bank deadlines for daily audits, checked the bank accounts at 2 p.m. on Friday, then sold ads and collected money like crazy, doing deals and offering discounts on receivables. I made deposits before 5 p.m. and wrote payroll checks after five. During the weekend, I relaxed and prayed to chance that a check or two would arrive to cover the deficit in the account by 2 p.m. on Monday.

One week I tried selling 1,000 spots for $1,000. Brad said I was crazy, calling the sale a "giveaway." Nobody took us up on it but here's a typical comment on the economic climate:

"Bill, thanks to the KVNM promotion, I had a big crowd in here last Saturday."

"Great."

"Yeah, but I didn't sell a single thing."

We were fighting against a slim-to-none economy. The Moly mine in Questa was mostly closed. February signaled the death of retail. Skiers passed through the streets of Taos like ghosts on their way to TSV.

That winter I met, as Van Morrison always reminds me, a *Brown Eyed Girl* (and full-bodied she was), Jo Owens, in the midst of a dim-eyed binge, while dancing to *G-L-O-R-I-A*. Jo gave me shelter from the storm. She had broken her arm falling into the privy outside her one-room adobe house on the rim in Des Montes. Given the snow and the fact that our cars ran precariously on rubber bands, we found time for a brief fling in the midst of our mutual misery.

After a domestic dust-up—about every two or three days—I'd leave and walk several miles to Whitey's at the Blinking Light or to town. "Fuck the time and temperature, goddammit," I'd mutter to myself, my beaten-up Stetson pulled down against the snow and cold, corduroy coat wrapped tight, muttering, "Money and pain, money and pain," as I relived *McCabe and Mrs. Miller*.

One time, "they" saw me driving north through El Prado in an old red station wagon, wheels I had purchased from friend

Fargo Gerard for $600. "They" say I was driving that old car at 80 mph, making haste toward the Blinking Light. The car listed toward the driver's side on two bare rims, front and rear, not a cop in sight. I abandoned the red station wagon across the street from Whitey's and called Leo Santistevan, my old Plaza Theatre amigo, who arrived with his primos and hauled away the evidence. Like *Cool Hand Luke,* I couldn't get my mind right that winter.

During my days and years I have crashed and totaled several cars and once wrote a monograph on the subject for *Horse Fly,* called "Car Karma." At least six times I turned a horseless carriage into smithereens and walked away. Back then, though homeless and sans transportation, I still held the paper on a major corner of the Plaza and more or less owned the only FM station in Taos County. What was that about? The sunsets were so friggin' beautiful but I was so damn miserable. Still, I remembered what the poet Shelley said: "If Winter comes, can Spring be far behind?" Sure spring came, and things got still worse, for I was a hard-headed gringo.

In the fall of 2004 I saw Amon Carter of Fort Worth at New Directions Gallery on Taos Plaza. Mirabile dictu, unlike so many of the others, he's still alive. "Amon, I owe you one for saving my life."

"Yeah, Whaley. God you were heavy. I was trying to carry you up the stairs [that spring of '83, into La Fonda]. Finally, I gave up and began dragging you by your legs, letting your head bounce."

O, ignominious drunk.

"The maids won't clean up after you anymore," my friend Saki said, and kicked me out of the hotel. Wagner had warned me about ending up with the winos. Supine, in hat and jacket, absent cigar, there I was ladies and gents, across the street from the Plaza Theatre Building with cinema and radio hidden away in its heart—passed out in the park of the central Plaza. Or so "they" say.

O, ignominious drunk.

And Amon appeared … again. He picked me up and hauled me off to the original El Monte, where ordinary folks took refuge from hard roads and harder lovers. Whitey visited. "Willie, what's wrong?" he asked. "You need to drink in a more reasonable manner." He then offered me the familiar pick-me-up from his silver spoon.

O, ignominious drunk, now a druggie, too.

At last, during the first, but lost long weekend in May of 1983, someone put a sign over the body. Here lies so and so, who was such and such. The next day I woke up in a strange house in lower Arroyo Hondo. Very hungover. You don't know pain in stomach or head until you've been beaten by the hammer and tongs; the stomach gurgles and boils and feels like it's full of ice-bergs bumping up against the rapids in a stream full of alternately hot and cold raging dirty ditchwater. I walked and belched and ached down a dirt road from lower Hondo and up the long miles of paved road to Des Montes. Nobody picked me up—there were no cars.

At the end of Malcolm Lowry's *Under the Volcano,* the consul, drunk as a lout in a cantina, gets mugged and thrown over the edge of a ravine. He bounces down the slope into the muck at the bottom. Lowry writes: "It was as if, for a moment, he had become the *pelado,* the thief—yes, the pilferer of meaningless muddled ideas out of which his rejection of life had grown, who had worn his two or three little bowler hats, his disguises, over these abstractions: now the realest of them all was close. But someone had called him *'compañero'* too, which was better, much better."

Darling Jo, my Des Montes girlfriend, did not call me *compañero* but said to me, when I showed up, "You're worth saving." She called my ex-wife, who said, "Call his sister"—though she did send a hundred dollars to help with my extraction from Taos. Jo called my little sister in Gardnerville, Nevada. Married with children, my sister talked it over with her backhoe opera-tor husband, who said, "Better buy him a ticket and get him out of there."

In a tiny, tinny, yellow car, Jo drove me to Albuquerque to meet my fate. We stopped for lunch at a restaurant between Taos and Santa Fé. Jo paid. I don't know where the money came from. She had called Brad and said, "He's got to go."

We kissed goodbye at the Albuquerque airport and I walked across the tarmac to the gangway, feeling more dead than alive. Red was the color of my chagrin and silver the color of my cof-fin. I had doubled down repeatedly and lost.

My Chief Comforters

One is always going in the wrong direction
to do the opposite thing in Taos.

1

The bad gringo crawled up the gangway and winged his way west in the passenger jet, ticket courtesy of family and friends, leaving behind his mistress—the Sacred Mountain. "What a sorry ass he is," I thought. The plane landed in Reno, not far from the California-Nevada border, where natives and visitors alternately lay on the beach in the sun or lay bets on the green felt blackjack tables. But he loved the pristine beauty of Lake Tahoe—seventy miles in circumference, more than twenty miles across, nestling in Mother Nature's womb among snow-clad peaks. When you look down at Lake Tahoe from the tops of the mountains, the deep blue lake sparkles like a many-faceted diamond and contrasts sharply with man's contrived temples—the multi-story, glass-clad, gold 'n' silver towers built to the gods of chance and fortune.

So at the age of thirty-six years, in May of 1983, I woke up on a couch at my little sister's ranch-style home on East Valley Road in a Carson Valley neighborhood called Fish Springs. At 5:30 each evening, five days a week, I attended an hour of therapy with John Ritter of *Three's Company* and Carroll O'Connor of *All in the Family*. I slept in a camper trailer behind the house at night. During the day I trailed along behind my sister and her three small boys to the beach, where the sun baked my skin and vaporized the toxins. Above the house, I walked between the sagebrush and piñon and sweated out the memories, leaving nasty images behind, stuck on the thorns of wild rose bushes.

O savage humiliation. O fear and loathing.

Though I repeated Rudyard Kipling's poem, "If you can keep your head when all about you / Are losing theirs and blaming it on you" … and… "If you can risk it on one turn of pitch and toss…" and… "fill the unforgiving minute / With sixty seconds' worth of distance run, / Yours is the Earth and everything that's in it, / And—which is more—you'll be a Man, my son!" Well, if a man, I was a *viejo* and exhausted. Ladies and gentlemen, I was not a man but a *pendejo—pelado—stupido*.

I had come back to recover my soul in Nevada, where the beauty is skin deep, unlike northern New Mexico, where beauty touches the eyes and rises up; it throbs first in the soles of your feet then crawls up your legs and shoots directly up the spine to your brain. I skipped D.H. Lawrence and read and re-read F. Scott Fitzgerald's *The Crack-Up*, trying to understand how a man cracks in the head, the body, and in the nerves. In 1975, when my business and my marriage came apart due to drink (I thought), I visited a shrink and tried a turn with therapy. Psychological explanations took care of the short-term challenges and armed me against immediate gratification, but did little for my grasp of the longer journey. I was under the illusion that I was sober because I didn't drink for another five years; but in 1978 I succumbed to a couple of vixens who poured promises into my nostrils. I reread Thomas de Quincey's *Opium Eaters* to try and exorcise the sweet seduction of the drug. As frequently as I swore off, the deep-throated siren (aka Black Widow) rang at 3:00 in the morning with alluring promises. By nature and inclination I was a dipsomaniac, but due to twisted logic I had convinced myself that a toot was merely like taking aspirin with benefits. But then the financial stress at KVNM created a context for failure; my will crumbled and I barked for booze.

In Taos, I had found the freedom to flourish and fail—to experiment with life. It wasn't the women who caused me trouble, though they diverted me from my hypnotic bête noir, the muse, my curse and cure, call it the Sacred Mountain, the promise of beauty, and the search for experience. The Sacred Muse and Mountain gave me shelter from the war and kept me safe from avalanches while turning me into a respectable citizen. After saving me from myself, she turned against me—like the mother of all karmic monsters. But hold on, I thought, for I had opened the window and betrayed not only her but myself. Self-hatred burns hot after one destroys the promise of youth. The bile of guilt and error churned up my esophagus and emerged in one long continuous belch. In a misguided attempt to survive, I had lost my moral center and earned the mark of Cain.

As Fitzgerald writes, "I began to realize that for two years my life had been drawing on resources that I did not possess." Ladies and gentlemen of the jury, just like Captain America and Billy in *Easy Rider*, I had blown it. And then I damned near died.

2

My nine-year-old son Fitz and I drove up to the Sierras above Tahoe, where my stepfather's cattle spent the summer at his range in the Fountain Place. Above, the ridges and peaks surround natural terraced meadows and pristine creeks below. Between the pine trees and the granite, the water seeps out and dribbles down into the creeks that water the meadows next to the ponderosa pines. A primordial peace descends and you feel as if you have entered Mother Nature's own cathedral.

The first afternoon, we walked up an easy trail to one of the ridges, where the barbed-wire fence keeps the cattle from plunging over the summit and down onto another rancher's range in Hope Valley. I felt not light-footed, but okay. That night, we suffered through the mouth and nose attacks of flies and gnats (which occur at dusk and dawn) and played cards inside our tent.

The next morning, we hiked up the other side, on a steeper trail, which leads up to a summit just below Freel Peak, the highest peak in the Tahoe Sierra. We had just begun the last pitch up to the ridge, where the sandy slope swallows each step, when my heart began to pound inside my rib cage like a jackhammer. We stopped and I rested. Next to the trail, Fitz, nine years old, bounded up and down the granite walls like a mountain goat. I waited. The jackhammer pounded.

"We'd better go down," I said. Instead of feeling relief and a second wind, as is normal on the downhill grade, I had to stop every three steps and rest. Christ, I thought, I'm gonna die. What if I die here? Will Fitz find his way home? The once proud athlete, who cruised nonstop from top to bottom on Al's, Snakedance, and Longhorn at Taos Ski Valley, was reduced to a middle-aged wastrel, dying on his feet.

My lungs gasped, my heart beat faster. Scared now, I sweated. I had lived too many lives in Taos: The Ski Valley, the National Guard, the Plaza Theatre, El Cortez Theater, Old Martinez Hall, Taos Community Auditorium productions, the Black Widow, and the madness at KVNM-FM. My life was a bad movie. Youth gone. I was old, used up, and done. *Fini.* I projected my persona out among the trees and regarded the image, hat and broken body, with a mix of curiosity and skepticism. Was this really the end?

Thanks to gravity I stumbled on and finally recovered my breath at the bottom of the trail.

3

At unpredictable moments that summer, while driving down a highway, watching a movie, or sitting at the counter drinking coffee in Sharkey's Casino, the nerves would reverberate and the ghosts make a grab for me. Dark glasses hid the tears and the regret I felt: seventeen years of work wasted. To pay for coffee and buy newspapers, I needed a penny-ante job. I was over-qualified for washing dishes and under-qualified to tend bar. Personnel departments saw a middle-aged ne'er-do-well, a bedraggled rat crawling through the door. Once I even got turned down to work as an usher in a movie theater.

My brother-in-law knew a local entrepreneur who hung out at Sharkey's. Between blackjack bouts, the guy bought the town's only taxi service and needed a driver. I got an intro and the job and was on call twenty-four hours a day, seven days a week. We subtracted the cost of gas from the take and split the proceeds. I got forty percent and was grateful. Behind dark glasses and a thick gray beard, I slithered around my hometown, escaping identity checks and talk of "what are you doing now?" Few of my high-school familiars bothered to check the fellow in the baseball cap, sitting in the driver's seat.

O blessed anonymity.

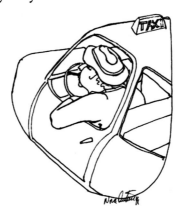

Mornings, I read the *San Francisco Chronicle* front to back at Sharkey's, relying on Herb Caen and the sports pages to chart the meaning of life. When I caught a glance of the face in the mirror behind the counter, I saw a face submerged in a foggy aura. Behind my eyeballs, images haunted me: the supine figure in Taos Plaza, the Gringo cussing out his banker at El Patio, the melodramatic day of the Bent Street Takedown, and the destructive blood sport called conversation by the Black Widow. I had left KVNM behind, teetering on the edge, and my conscience called me "quitter."

Spring storms and heavy moisture knocked out two of the main mountain passes from Sacramento and the Bay Area to Tahoe. But the pilgrims found the detours that took them round to the glistening towers, driving, flying, or hitchhiking up the alternative routes to enjoy the beauty and the beast. When folks landed at the local airport and called, I drove them twenty miles up and over a secondary road, Kingsbury Grade, to Tahoe. During the daylight hours I'd visit my favorite beach, or a trail where I'd ridden my horse as a kid, or hole up in the family log cabin and read.

One night, my boss called: "Take me to the cat house." A round trip to the Moonlight or Kit Kat ranches east of Carson City cost a hundred dollars. The girls at the brothel tipped me twelve bucks for bringing in the suckers. My boss tipped me again when I got him home. In Nevada, everybody tips. If you want to stay in the Silver State, you gotta pay. Money, not class or celebrity, is the ticket.

Back when I was a kid, Governor Grant Sawyer kicked Sinatra out of Nevada because the singer hung around with hoods and even refused entreaties from President Kennedy himself to delete Frank's name from the black book. That's the way things were when fifteen "cow counties" ran the state, prior to one man-one vote reforms. Prior to the reforms Nevada gaming laws required a single proprietor to own and operate a casino.

But by turning the clock forward and validating democratic reforms, corporate enterprise triumphed as the Washoe County/Reno and Clark County/Las Vegas population centers gained control of the state legislature. Hence Sinatra, et al., came back for an encore. And mobsters were replaced by accountants in the casino cages.

When the highway department opened up direct routes from Sacramento to Tahoe, my customer count declined and I could barely afford gasoline. The cab owner himself was addicted to the slots. Sharkey, the local casino owner, reminiscent of Sydney Greenstreet, the fat man in *Casablanca*, said to a friend, "Slot machines are worse than crack cocaine." My boss sold everything, including the taxi service, to pay off his gambling debts, and fled the Silver State.

Back on the street, I looked for work and inevitably got rejected, but I found I could get out of the car and approach a help-wanted sign without my nerves betraying me. Sure enough, I got a job selling ads for a hospitality rag called *Guest Life* magazine. After about a week, I said to myself, "What the hell—if I'm going to sell ads, I might as well do it for KVNM." The company was still, unfortunately, mostly mine—if it was still there and I could get it back, and if "they" would let me back in Taos.

After putting me on the plane for Reno in May, my guardian angel Jo wrote letters promising love and a new start. We were going to meet up. Then nothing. Nothing. When you wanted to find out what was going on in Taos, you called Dori's. The waitress-cook who answered the phone, a friend of my angel's daughter, said, "She moved to Costilla with some guy she met." Fuck You If You Can't Take A Joke. That's the surest lesson you learn in Taos—to laugh at yourself. Without an expectation of loyalty, there's no sting in betrayal.

In Virginia City, the home of the Comstock Lode, I bought postcards and sent them to Brad. One card focused on the image of a grizzled prospector, bent felt hat, moth-eaten pants and shirt, buried in the sand next to his pickaxe, a couple of vultures pecking at his corpse. A second showed a straggler in the desert saying, "I'll be home soon."

Though Fitzgerald suggested in *The Crack-up* that I needed "a clean break," and mentioned that I would never be as good a man again, I decided to return to Taos to see if I could crawl up and out of that deep arroyo. I knew I had to change my attitude and transform my psyche or live with guilt and shame the rest of my life.

O ignominious mess!

4

Thanks to the kindness of friends, I got my third start in Taos circa September 1983, and I felt like a newborn babe. On the northwest edge of Blueberry Hill, where my old friend Steve White gave me a couch to sleep on, the wind howled around the corners of the white concrete block cottage. There I read and wrote down my responses to Ralph Waldo Emerson. In his essay *Self-Reliance*, Emerson advises his acolytes to "do your work and I shall know you." So I got to work and Emerson helped me through the night.

Each evening, Steve ladled out some soup when I appeared at the back door of Whitey's International Restaurant, the former home of D.H. Lawrence groupie Lady Brett. Wurlitzer fellow and Pulitzer Prizewinner N. Scott Momaday, in a *New York Times Magazine* article, said Whitey's was his favorite restaurant, and referred to Taos as "the soul of the southwest." Steve came home during the early-morning hours. We had coffee together before he went to sleep and I began my day.

My ersatz guardian angel returned from Costilla to her Des Montes digs. We spent a night or two together before she said, "You don't even know how to wipe your own ass." We split. Tom Collins, generous soul, came to my rescue and loaned me a car so I could get around town.

Downtown on the Plaza, the radio station headquarters were still set up in the alcoves of the courtyard at the Plaza Theatre Building. Brad and Michael Sheary had picked up a couple of checks due me on promissory notes from the buyer of the Plaza

Theatre. They used the money to pay off the attorney general for CETA crimes and a note due the Centinel Bank for the five acres of land the station owned up on Blueberry Hill. I'm not sure how I lost control of my finances, but New Mexico officials see the standard rules of banking or the rule of law as if it were like a travel guide filled with illusions and false promises. In the 21st century, I would observe firsthand how judges and D.A.s cannibalize the law in the interest of perverse political persecutions.

In search of warmer offices, Brad and I toured the upstairs of the old McCarthy Building in the southeast corner of the Plaza. The noir effect of wooden floors and rippled glass doors suited my repressed alter ego, called Spade or Marlowe. (I was determined not to play the sap this time round.) Rent for a tiny upstairs office, about $75 a month, included heat and electricity. We went to see the landlord, Tom McCarthy, at El Mercado.

Tom smiled and said, "Bill, how are you?"

"Good, Tom," I said. "I know I still owe some money on my charge account at El Mercado."

"Don't worry about it."

"Thanks Tom. We want to rent two little offices from you upstairs."

"Okay."

"But we can't pay the rent right away."

"Pay when you can." He handed us the keys.

As we walked away, Brad asked, "How did you do that?" I shrugged.

People talk about the kindness of strangers but Tom, like Whitey, was a friend who looked past the sins at the sinner and in a single gesture forgave and redeemed your soul as if you were a member of the community. Tom was the only person, except for his mother, that Saki trusted.

After a trying day of selling ads for radio, I walked into the Adobe Bar at The Taos Inn. Singer T.G. Futch was playing guitar for ten or fifteen patrons. I sat down and ordered a bitters and soda. He started singing a tune made famous by Bessie Smith—"Nobody knows you when you're down and out." At the end of the song, T.G. smiled and I smiled.

5

At first, to give my nerves time to heal, I limited my office visits to an hour or so each day. While stopped at one of the few traffic lights in town, I'd see the driver in the other car catch sight of me and sneer. I felt like the Jason Robards character in *A Thousand Clowns*, as he stands on the sidewalk and says to pedestrians passing by, "I'm sorry." Whenever I picked up a phone at the office, I listened first for background noise. A faint sound indicated that a long distance caller was on the line. Long-distance meant bill collector and I'd say, "I'm sorry, he's not here. May I take a message?"

Various state and federal agencies had levied several kinds of taxes on KVNM-FM and its parent company, Taos Communications Corporation. The Plaza Theatre Building Condominium Association sent me notices of fees unpaid and penalties accrued. I hadn't filed my personal taxes in seven years. If the IRS ever found an agent courageous enough to drive north from Santa Fé to investigate the disreputable financial alleys of Taos, he'd snap my hands behind my back in handcuffs.

A story about the DEA undercover agent who sat at Ogelvie's bar for a week—while a local street dealer, aka Monkey, sat at the other end, dispensing condiments—cheered me. My sources claimed not grams but ounces flowed through those famous portals. Eventually, the undercover guy entrapped a busboy, who sold the agent half a gram.

After my duty hours I returned to the cottage, where I read, typed dark thoughts, and tried to reconcile my dreams with this nightmare. I had little to go on beyond Emerson's admonition: "It is easy in the world to live after the world's opinion; it is easy in solitude to live after our own; but the great man is he who in the midst of the crowd keeps with perfect sweetness the independence of solitude." I wasn't a great man, but I knew that solitude, properly understood, might help me.

Meanwhile, I had to stop KVNM's drift toward the shoals and keep the FM signal alive until it could be sold, which meant I must negotiate with Brad Hockmeyer, now KVNM's programmer and the virtual, if desperate, general manager and president of the two-man board, which had a crucial vacancy. (Sheary was doing four years in a federal joint, called La Tuna, in Texas for the sin of getting caught with eight and a half tons of marijuana in some Midwestern state—an event that occurred prior to his association with TCC.) Jazz and blues DJ Ted Dimond, a brick of stability, still sat in one of the chairs. I needed two votes to get back on the board so I could get the station back and get out of Taos for good. One is always going in the wrong direction to do the opposite thing in Taos.

Brad was hungry for the good life, or at least a square meal, so I invited the lover of FM radio to Whitey's International for dinner, courtesy of our host. While displaying a certain *je ne sais quoi*—born of my desperate condition—I kept my friend Tom Collins' mantra in mind: "If you look good, you are good."

We began discussing the station business over the chef's famous soup. During the main course, rack of lamb (or maybe Beef Wellington), I asked why a station manager, desperate for capital and a patron saint, had passed up hiring the daughter of Dandy Don Meredith (he of Monday Night Football fame) when she applied for a job. "That was stupid on my part," admitted Brad. Instead he had hired a college radio feminista, whose laborious monotone during morning drive time was putting drivers back to sleep.

Whitey's staff hovered over Hockmeyer, even pouring him the occasional nip from the chef's stash of Grand Marnier. The lovely Patty Stutz, an ex-nurse and kind hostess who was famous for her innocent come-hither look, smiled as she inquired after his every desire. Headwaiter Larry Crowley sashayed around like he was serving one of Whitey's celebrity diners.

Later, Hock told me, "Everybody thought I had a trust fund, but I was so broke I borrowed money to buy underwear." This was before his poor father died and left him a small fortune, which he turned into a smaller fortune by buying the radio station. Then, Hock lived in the equivalent of a cold-water shack out in Des Montes, where he depended on his girlfriend, a jewelry-maker, for food, shelter, or doses of fix-a-flat for the tires on his Volvo.

By reassuring Hock that I would come in from the cold and right the enormous financial wrong of which we were both guilty, he seemed more relieved than frightened. By the time we finished the chocolate mousse, he had agreed to vote with Ted and reappoint me to the board, while reassigning me my rightful titles as president and boss. Besides, I could also type, write copy, sell advertising, collect overdue accounts, and interview the occasional politico.

Soon I had "legal" control of the radio station and was negotiating a cease-fire between Brad and Tom Collins, the latter whom I hired as program director. Collins was one of those multitalented guys—actor, musician, radio announcer, disc jockey, and bon vivant. He could also read and write, a skill that posed a danger less to his enemies than to himself. At Christmas, we had a staff meeting at Dori's Bakery. While discussing the DJ lineup, Collins and newsman Dick Behnke cracked wise with baseball metaphors.

"You can't have your lead-off hitter batting at the end of the order," said Collins.

"Or a .200 hitter leading off," responded Behnke.

The drive-time feminist yelled, "Male chauvinist pigs!" and stomped out. I offered her the night shift but she refused to confront the isolated trailer-studio after sundown. To avoid a problem with the labor commission, I refused to fire her. When she called to protest, I quoted Kate Hepburn, who turns to the camera in *Lion in Winter* and says, "What family doesn't have its ups and down?"

Around this time, Whitey and I dropped by the Quail Ridge Inn, down the road from the restaurant, to look in on social doings at a fundraiser for the Taos Art Association. A local realtor of uncertain integrity with a supplemental and not-so-discreet cash flow sidled up and mentioned to me what nerve I had to show my face in public. I was surprised and even nonplussed, but before I could respond, a beauty with a sculpted face, light brown skin, dark hair and eyes, and feet floating lightly across the floor, caught me by the arm and gave me a kiss. We danced. The passersby stared.

From time to time over the years, she and I fell into conversation, and occasionally spent the night catching up. She came back to the house with me and nursed me back to health before leaving the next morning. Three weeks later, she was dead, a suicide—and me none the wiser. She was the best of comforters.

The Long Vamoose

*"The life of man is a self-evolving circle, which, from a ring
imperceptibly small, rushes on all sides outwards to new
and larger circles, and that without end."*

— RALPH WALDO EMERSON, *CIRCLES*

1

While I searched for my wits out west in Carson Valley, Nevada that summer of 1983, a band of outsiders hustled the Taos bourgeoisie and raised the unheard of sum of seventy grand to support an out-of-town repertory theatre company—players with mid-Atlantic accents—in residency at the TCA. The KVNM staff had offered the interlopers free airtime to flog their shows. Upon my return, Jonathan Gordon, director of his own band of players, called the Minimum Security Theatre (MST), got in touch with me. MST had a concept but not a home. After Jonathan persuaded me to produce Jean Anouilh's version of Sophocles' *Antigone*, one of the flacks from the East Coast gang appeared at KVNM's second-story offices and asked for a handout: free airtime. I handed him a rate card, saying, "You've got to pay to play, buddy."

While the new regime at the TCA shut its doors to us citizens—the former actors, stagehands, musicians, and general helpers who had donated time and energy to the community auditorium in trade for the opportunity to perform, Judge Joe Caldwell of the Eighth Judicial District opened up the people's courtroom and gave us free use of the 160-plus seats in this triumph of modern architecture, albeit an acoustically challenged echo chamber. In turn, MST promised to dedicate a portion of box office revenue to Walter Vigil's neophyte community corrections program (still extant today).

To raise dough, we turned to the art crowd, hitting up the usual suspects—standup guys like Ken Price, Larry Bell, Ron Cooper, and Gus Foster—for invaluable donations. The visual provocateurs of Taos could be counted on to support theatrical artists, folks with medical bills, or the occasional subversive cause. Our leading lady, young Hilary Fraley, who played Antigone, had fallen under Jonathan's spell and the princess with a trust fund bought the art collection.

Jonathan directed the play from the judge's bench and played the dictator Creon, glaring down into the litigator's pit—the epitome of a man, father, and fascist leader. The defiant Antigone honors the gods, buries her brother, and wreaks havoc on the house of Creon. Truly, Hilary as Antigone portrayed a frightful figure of integrity who, born by madness, challenged Creon from below. Offstage, Jonathan said to me about his paramour and co-star, "For Christ's sake Bill, Hilary is taking this part too seriously."

The loyal cast and crew included the known and unknown: Pamela Parker, David Garver, Chuck Perez, Geraldine Harvey, Karen Magee, Kika Vargas, Klein, and Elizabeth Crittenden. Each evening as death entered, the lights dimmed and haunting flute music, compliments of Tony Isaacs' Indian House recording studios, sent the audience home in shivers.

Whitey and a friend from the Hotel St. Bernard presented me with a framed collage that included the four-column review from the *Albuquerque Journal* titled "Group Heats Up Summer With Antigone." The reviewer, Marjorie Atlas, a freelance critic and playwright at NMSU, wrote: "*Antigone* is perhaps the ultimate tribute to community theatre at its best. Produced on a shoestring, financed by contributions from local artists and businesspeople, rehearsed painstakingly for five months by an unpaid (but well-rewarded) cast and crew, this group succeeds quite possibly more thoroughly, within its own definition, than its richer and more prestigious neighbor the Actors Repertory of Taos."

The first season of the mid-Atlantic dancing bears was their last.

2

Despite decaying driver tubes and marginal revenues, the radio station continued to broadcast. In the fall of '84, my Hollywood screenwriter friend Leo Garen and I began negotiations with the owner of the Plaza Theatre to lease back my bête noir, my curse and cure. As a young man, Leo, a legendary off-Broadway ace, had directed plays adapted from novels by Norman Mailer (*Deer Park*) and J.P. Donleavy (*The Ginger Man*). Then he moved to Hollywood, where he directed a couple of movies but mostly wrote screenplays for film and television. In the late '70s, he moved to Taos to write a screenplay based on the Eagles' album *Desperado*, but the project got dropped when Leo's bipolar contraries overwhelmed the writer. Now that Leo's mood soared, no project appeared too absurd.

At the time, I knew I'd strike out at the movie theatre, but like the gambler in Robert Altman's *McCabe and Mrs. Miller*, described by Leonard Cohen in *The Stranger Song*, I *"was watching for the card/ that is so high and wild [I'd] never need to deal another."* My movie should have been called *El Pendejo and the Paradox of Paradise*. I knew I had to go deeper into debt to get out of debt: to get out of town, one must do the wrong thing for the right reasons.

Called in by the condo association, the state fire marshal showed up in the person of Bill Beutler, and helped back up a rumor about "dangerous conditions" aimed at closing Gallegos's movie theatre. Beutler sold me the original 400-seat Plaza Theatre business back in 1969 and was the only man who profited from the torch and subsequent insurance pay-off. While he pushed, I pulled, and Leo Gallegos surrendered the keys to Garen and me.

We paid the condo dues, as well as the first and last month's rent to Gallegos himself as part of the ruse, and spent several thousand dollars on maintenance and repairs for the former bijou. Like the Blues Brother, I rounded up the band: Leo Santistevan, custodian, concessionaire, and assistant manager, rejoined the team, as did longtime projectionist Warren Wood. The popcorn was plentiful but attendance sparse. Between sales calls and evading the bill collectors at KVNM in the McCarthy building up the street, I booked the movies at the Plaza Theatre down the street and sold tickets at the box office.

Garen, who had met movie producer Michael Fitzgerald in a Hollywood studio anteroom where both waited to pitch their latest projects, persuaded me to schedule a colloquy on Fitzgerald's two John Huston movies, Flannery O'Connor's *Wise Blood* and Malcolm Lowry's *Under the Volcano*. My companion with the intense green eyes accompanied me to the Albuquerque airport in my rattletrap 1974 pickup, where we picked up Michael.

His father, Robert, had translated Homer's *Iliad* and *Odyssey* and Virgil's *Aeneid*. Flannery O'Connor had been a Fitzgerald house-guest. As we drove into Taos alongside the strip development on South Santa Fé Road (Paseo del Pueblo Sur today), Michael seemed dubious about the scenery.

But his eyes lit up when we reached the Plaza and dropped him at the Taos Inn. After screening the two films, the producer discussed the genesis of the movies, which included playing poker on Sunday nights in L.A. with John Huston. The event lost money but the discussion tickled my synapses and reminded me of Pauline Kael's lecture on criticism and film back in the summer of 1965 at Colorado College.

Like a moth drawn to the flame, I moved from Whitey's Blueberry Hills digs to my aerie on the second floor of the Plaza Theatre Building—though I knew by then that I didn't want to die on the Plaza (or in Taos). Two stories below my bedroom, in the subterranean basement of the Plaza Theatre, the harpies dozed where my financial sins lay locked up in filing cabinets behind steel doors, hidden away in the labyrinthian underground tunnels.

Stand-up comedian Eddie Murphy in *Beverly Hills Cop* stimulated a bonanza at the box office in February of 1985. Consequently I hired Jannika, a brown-haired Fin with a Prince Valiant haircut, an acupuncturist by trade, and friend of the green-eyed blond, to delve into the dark secrets and root out the paperwork. Praise the cop who helped me find the money to pay the Fin her wages of righteousness.

My friend Leo Garen got tired of waiting for a return on his investment and sicced a Hollywood entertainment shark on me. While we waited for lunch at The Taos Inn, the shark threatened me with unspeakable legal complications and financial penalties. As the waiter hovered, I responded, "We're doing our best," voice rising. Then: "Who the hell do you think you are? Stand in line, asshole! I'm judgment proof." The waiter retreated. The attorney gaped sheepishly at the silverware and I stomped out of the dining room not unlike Spade in his first confrontation with fatman in *The Maltese Falcon*.

When Leo Gallegos, my original buyer of the Plaza Theatre and now alleged landlord in the leaseback scheme, asked why I wasn't paying the rent, I, the original seller and, now a tenant, said, "You pay me, I'll pay you." Two guys who were starting what became the Trans-Lux theatre chain (and now Mitchell Theatres) agreed to buy out Gallegos and pay off the promissory notes he owed me the first week of August in 1985. After I paid attorneys' fees, employment and gross receipts taxes, creditors, part of the debt owed to Leo Garen, and residual film rentals, I walked away with enough dough to invest in a Kaypro computer and Okidata dot-matrix printer. I needed new tools for my venture into word processing.

I still held title to two air condos in the Plaza Theatre Building and was the middleman on a couple of pass-through mortgages but the deal with Trans-Lux signaled the end of my affair with the movie theatre. I worked off the last bit of debt owed to my friend Leo Garen by holding his hand at his house in Pilar on the Rio Grande while he completed his last screenplay in 1997. The job fulfilled his contract and qualified him for a screenwriter's pension. He moved to Columbia, indulged in the heroics of Viagra, and died of depression in the double aughts on an island off South America. Friends, including novelist John Nichols and I, celebrated his life at a memorial service south of Taos. We spread his ashes in the Rio Grande, though a portion remains with me in a plastic zip bag, locked away in my desk, next to the ashes of cranberry bogger Mark Tribe, one-time bass player and consumer of terpin hydrate. RIP *mis amigos*.

3

Call the story of KVNM-FM a tale of *Two Tubes for Sister Sara,* our transgendered engineer. Without Sara the sound would have died. According to my notes, dated January 1, 1985, business at KVNM had grown fifty percent during 1984. And in my qualitative summary I noted that "1984 was better, much better, ten times better than '83, which was seventy percent better than '82, which was fifty percent worse than '81, which was worse than '80, which was worse than '79, which was way worse than '78."

KVNM produced enough ad revenue to warrant a move from a tiny office in the rear hallway of the second floor in the McCarthy Building to a corner office on the same floor with two or three times the floor space. The rent doubled from $75 to $150, but the staff could see Taos Plaza and Taos Mountain as well as our adjacent boardroom, a back booth at the Plaza Café.

At mid-morning, and sometimes at mid-afternoon, respectable citizens like Clark Funk and Eloy Jeantete (First State Bank) still met for coffee at Mary's famed Plaza Café, as they had been doing during the previous decade. We disreputable board members, Brad Hockmeyer, or Chuck Perez, and I, met with the respectable Ted Dimond to discuss ways of keeping Rube

Goldberg radio on the air. Coffee cost fifty cents and you got as many refills as you wanted. He who had money or the company checkbook paid.

Both Chuck, the Big Chicano, and Brad, the pale-faced WASP, spent their extra cash on Fix-a-Flat, canned air from Yellow Front, the multi-merchandise store behind the Plaza, to keep the tires of their decrepit but identical Volvos inflated. And despite disheveled appearances and empty pockets, these seductive radio voices were always accompanied by good-looking women. When the conspiratorial Hockmeyer turned on me (again), I appointed the loyal Chicano, Chuck, to the board of directors. Jazz-show host and board member Ted Dimond always maintained a rational and sensible persona.

At the Plaza Café we pursued marketing strategies and worried about unpaid employment taxes, FICA, and the specter of the IRS. After deciphering seven years of my own sins, the angelic Fin reorganized the radio station records of TCC going back a decade and prepared the tax records for "the man." On a grand spring day, we confessed our collective peccadilloes and filed the whole muddled mess, thanks, also, to Jean Thompson of the aptly named bookkeeping service, Loose Ends.

Hence this weary heathen, baptized a Catholic and reared a Protestant, began to understand how the universal and apostolic church had survived, due to the psychic call and response of confession—the therapeutic cure for spiritual pain. We dined on chile and beans and toasted our victory with tepid coffee at Mary's cafe.

At Mary's I interviewed refugees from the mainstream who arrived in Taos, eyes glistening and hearts full of hope, lured here, they said, by the magic. I'd stare down at the cracked white Formica tabletop, then out the window at the dusty landscape and muddy parking lot. Finally, I'd lean back against the

red booth back and study the shiny resumes, the enviable education and experience associated with the arts of broadcasting. The
radio pros begged for a chance to work, but I knew the job seeker
might last an hour, a day, a week, a month. Most left town after
the cunning Taoseños took their money or when a spouse got lost
with a local lothario—if he or she didn't die due to the practice
of mixing Coors and cars.

"I made $50,000 during the last few years but my life wasn't
meaningful."

I nodded.

"Yeah, I'll work for $5 an hour."

I'd wait.

"Well, pay me what you can, I just want to make a contribution to the community."

"What community?" I'd mutter to myself. To cover my karmic
ass, I'd channel Hunter S. Thompson: "You look around and see
this bucolic bullshit and pastoral crap and think you're in paradise. But if you stay, you'll go broke and die of a broken heart.
This place is a fucking sagebrush jungle. IT WILL FUCK YOU
BEFORE YOU'RE DONE. IT'S A NIGHTMARE. IS THAT
WHAT YOU WANT?" If the seeker didn't run screaming out
of the café, he or she would learn that ninety-nine percent of the
time my predictions turned out to be true. Occasionally, during
a forgotten road trip to Marin or Malibu, I'd run into the typical
two-year Taos transient. "God, you were right," the whipped one
would say. "I lost my money, my wife, and my car. Taos set me
back ten years."

The vibes at the Plaza Café, like the vibes at Hotel La Fonda
and the McCarthy Building, were omens—transcendent signs—
indicative of a karmic turn toward survival. My new karma
culminated in a meeting with the redheaded buzz-cutter from
the IRS, the man dressed in white shirt, dark pants, white socks,

and black shoes. I was as calm as the coffee was tepid at the Plaza Café because I knew how an authentic Taos scene could unsettle a day-tripper.

"You've been on air since July of 1982?" said the buzz-cutter.

"More or less."

"And you haven't filed or paid taxes?"

"I'm really sorry about that."

He muttered into his coffee about the system breaking down and uttered the word "audit." My eyes closed, my life behind prison bars passed in front of me. One can't explain cash flow, check kiting, CETA violations, trade and barter to straight people. Who could even remember all the cash-and-carry deals? We were scam artists but not for profit, merely idealists with a code, like the Repo Man, except we couldn't pay our bills.

"Either you can do the audit or we can," he said.

My eyes snapped. My ears perked up and I gulped. "What do you mean?"

"Just select checks and deposit slips from each quarter representing payments for utilities, payroll, supplies."

"Sure, we can do that."

He paid for his coffee. I paid for mine. Outside he turned right. I turned left. Upstairs in the office, I said, quietly, "We're all going to jail. Get your affairs in order." Brad and Chuck sat down. The receptionist and bookkeeper (she who gave me shelter from the storm), Jo, shrugged, like she expected it. Then I said, "We get to audit ourselves" and laughed (if nervously). We high-fived or whatever the habit was back then. Chuck got the big grin on. Brad looked happy and silly. Jo smiled and said in her Missouri accent, "Allllright." The crew at Jean Thompson's Loose Ends couldn't believe our collective luck. Even as our karma kicked ass, the clock began ticking: we had thirty days to make things right for the buzz-cutter.

4

In April of 1985, a friend who imported second-hand Subarus from Pittsburgh and split time as a waiter at Whitey's International Restaurant and a cook at the Hotel St. Bernard, one David Bachrach, vacated his cabin in Valdez. The cabin—situated west of the cattle guard near the mouth of the Hondo Canyon on the north side of the Rio Hondo, just below the original Hacienda de Valdez—was a few hundred yards away from the three-room adobe where life had begun for me in Taos back in the fall of 1966. David said he'd leave the phone on if I would pay the bill. I moved to Valdez and somehow found the money each month—$500—to pay the rent for what I called my clapboard sanctum.

The landlady was a onetime companion of Fargo Gerard, who moved in to the big house on the property. Fargo of the bad back, earring, rough-looking blue jeans, and gruff voice, appeared in my life at crucial times. He lived across the street from El Cortez Theatre in Ranchos, prior to the arrival of Ken Jenkins, where he told me tales of his career as a merchant sailor based in San Francisco. Accompanied by a young beauty, he sat at the Plaza Theatre Bar in 1975. He helped raise money for the TCA in 1977 at the Renaissance Faire, located at the Mabel Dodge House. He sold my house on Valverde Street so I could satisfy a divorce agreement and buy the Plaza Theatre Building in 1979. In the winter of 1983 he sold me the red station wagon, which made a tireless run on bare iron rims through El Prado. Then Fargo appeared, circa 1987, as my neighbor and interlocutor in Valdez—just before I left Taos for good, not so long before he went off to die of a disintegrating spine in Mexico.

I had dropped out of Taos and cancelled my post-office box, left no forwarding address and set up my new mailing address ten miles away at the post office in Arroyo Seco. I mailed postcards from town to Seco to reassure myself that I was alive. Each evening, I passed through the curtain of sound—the springtime rush of roaring water in the Rio Hondo—and a protective veil dropped behind me and blocked out the ubiquitous harpies from town. I slowly relaxed and learned how to surrender to the better spirits emerging from the woods.

On the porch under the portal of the cabin in Valdez, I began my education as an autodidact, a search for an understanding of self and society, looking for an explanation and justification of a misspent life. I read a variety of literary and philosophical works or walked softly in the woods and hiked up the sagebrush hills. Surrounded by sagebrush, wild roses, pines, cottonwoods, and the thick brush that sheltered the acequia, I felt as if I had been reborn in a new dimension of time and space.

My decision to move back to Valdez turned into a lucky cure. I remember reading a bit from Gustave Flaubert, who wrote, "People like us must have the religion of despair. By dint of saying, 'That is so!' and of gazing into the black pit at one's feet, one remains calm." Thanks to the caffeine, jottings in my journal, reading selections from Montaigne, Emerson, Marcus Aurelius, and by studying Mother Nature, I began to revive.

A sign nailed high up in a tree adjacent to my driveway said in bold, blood-red letters on a white background, "Nuestro Pueblo,

No Se Vende"—Our Town, Not For Sale. The protest against condo development was aimed at an acquaintance, a car dealer who'd sold me the fabulous Mustang, long since repo'd. He who would despoil the bucolic setting of Valdez, aka the Valley of Brujas, had told me about the proposed devastation at late-night tea with the White Lady.

"You're crazy," I said .

He said, "They can't stop me, I have the approval for the project from the county commissioners."

When he started building, the folks started shooting. Provocateurs, both native newcomers and activists, had infiltrated *la gente,* who were always spoiling for a fight. They marched, erected signs, and, though an Anglo native to the manor born, the *pobrecito* fled Taos for an American province far, far away.

When my son Fitz visited Valdez that first summer, we sat on the porch and watched the flycatchers build nests under the eaves or listened to the mountain blue jays scold each other. Toward noon, we walked east up the Hondo Canyon, or north up through the arroyos and the Sangre de Cristo foothills on a trail not far from the rear of the cabin. One morning, Fitz asked me what purpose the clothesline stretched between two trees, served.

"That's a ghost catcher," I said. "It catches and keeps the bad spirits away."

Fitz's summer reading assignment focused on Mark Twain's *Huckleberry Finn* but he found the story dull. So I gave him Thompson's *Fear and Loathing in Las Vegas* and he developed a life-long appreciation of newspapers and popular culture—though his mother never forgave me for alerting him to Thompson's wayward ways.

As my health improved, I began to climb steeper slopes, bush-whacking my way up to a defunct quartz mine. From the vantage point on the side of the mountain, I could see the valley and desert stretching west toward the sun's vanishing point. Moth-er Nature's squalls, the walking rain, drifted across the desert toward me. Brilliant rainbows formed against the clearly seen edges of the landscape under the transparent blue sky.

For years I had repeatedly asked myself, "Why am I so de-pressed when Mother Nature is so beautiful?" Now the natural beauty elevated my spirits and transformed my sensibility. As I stumbled uphill through the brush, the ghosts haunted me: self-destructiveness, the betrayers, bad women, bill collectors. The flashbacks filled me with self-repugnance. But when I reached the summit, sweaty and breathing hard, the glories of the high desert, the spring green, and the sparkles from the valley el-evated my mood. On the way down, running through manzanita and sage, breathing easily, my mind and body soared.

One day, as I descended lightly across rock and sand, I recalled the words of Louis Ferdinand Celine from *Journey to the End of the Night* and I copied them down when I got back to the cabin where the Mountain Blue Jays squawked.

> In the whole of your absurd past you discover much that is absurd, so much deceit and credulity that it might be a good idea to stop being young this minute, to wait for youth to break away from you and pass by, to watch it going away, receding

in the distance, to see all its vanity, run your hand through the empty space it has left behind, take a last look at it, and then start moving, make sure your youth has really gone, and then calmly, all by yourself, cross to the other side of time to see what people and things really look like.

Home-cooked meals and fresh air vanquished the signs of hyper-manic depression. While I waited and wondered how to liquidate the PTB air condos and KVNM-FM, pay off my debts, and exit Taos, I lost twenty-five pounds that spring and summer. Still the radio station kept coming back like the serial horror movie, *Friday the 13th,* featuring Freddy Krueger. Freddy and Brad, Brad and Freddy haunted me. I needed an exorcist.

5

Though we filed Taos Communication Corporation's confession with the IRS, the taxman ignored us. I called a meeting and made a short speech: "The taxman refuses to make a deal and allow us to make payments on our liabilities. He wants the paperwork off his desk and tells me we have to file for Chapter 11. It's a paperwork nightmare and we can't afford a lawyer. We're closing the radio Sunday at midnight."

Then, like metaphysical clockwork, Mama Karma kicked in, thanks to Chuck Perez, who introduced the redoubtable South African Gerald Leibovitz and his wife, a pet-food wholesaler to us. Gerald offered to transform KVNM into a profit-making venture and claimed he could sell ice to Eskimos. Looking deep into the sad eyes of the staff—Chuck, Brad, Ted, Sara, Nancy— I said, "Okay. I'll sign the checks, but don't bother me with the details. Jannika and I will see if we can raise the money and find a Chapter 11 attorney."

While Gerald kept the station on life support, I kept to my regimen of daily walks. Thanks to the Fin, I acted like I was no longer faithless. Chapter 11 required us to confess before the IRS and ask for mercy from the federal court. The Chapter 11 bankruptcy statutes give the petitioner time to reorganize and come up with a plan to pay off creditors. If you fail at Chapter 11, you can revert to Chapter 7 liquidation, the ultimate admission of defeat.

Somehow, we begged, borrowed, or saved up $2,000 to hire attorney Bill Davis of Albuquerque, a Chapter 11 specialist. The Fin, guided by Loose Ends, reorganized our TCC records. One hot summer day, she and I walked into Davis's oak-paneled, air-conditioned chambers in downtown Albuquerque, carrying cardboard boxes. After flipping through the manila folders, Davis said, "You're the best-prepared client I've ever seen."

Davis, the Vietnam-era fighter jock, flew up to Taos in his private plane and inspected our tin-can trailer studio and failing outhouse on Blueberry Hill. Then he came to town and climbed the stairs to our upstairs offices high above Taos Plaza. We had a cheap fan, bought on credit from El Mercado. He looked through our records, receipts, and other paltry evidence of a radio station held together by scotch tape and paper clips. He kept shaking his head and muttering, "Whaley, you're a genius. I don't know how you kept this thing on the air. It's a miracle."

"The system broke down," I said, referring to the prior conversation with the IRS. Davis's backhanded compliment made me feel worse. The Black Widow's stepfather, a muffler tycoon with twenty-five percent of General Motors' business, had paid me a similar compliment at the Carlyle Hotel in Manhattan. While my "potential" might appeal to the opposite sex or an imaginative out-of-towner, that sort of praise meant little in the street when your checks bounced.

6

We, the sorry stockholders of Taos Communication Corporation d/b/a KVNM-FM, filed for Chapter 11 protection and met with creditors and stockholders, circa Thanksgiving of 1985 in Santa Fé. Hockmeyer and his attorney were the only ones who showed up to question the "plan." The event seemed somehow anti-climatic when Janikka and I took Davis over to the Bull Ring for a drink, where legislators from the Santa Fé Roundhouse celebrated their misdeeds in the company of fellow politicos. Synchronicity was the theme of the party.

A college mate, Lieutenant Governor Mike Runnels, appeared. Mike had enjoyed a brief career as rock-and-roll promoter back in 1971 and had pitched a tent on land next to my house. His father, "Mud" Runnels, was the Republican chairman of the House Armed Services Committee, whom Ailes had recommended I call when the Guard threatened me with active duty in Vietnam. (Ailes extended my visa among the living by convincing me to ignore the Marines, join the Guard, and had written a letter of introduction to Whitey, lo' these many years ago.) I had introduced Mike to Harvey Mudd, who hired him as a lobbyist for the environmental organization known as The Central Clearing House in Santa Fé, which gave birth, later, to the Western Environmental Law Center and helped start the future lieutenant governor on his desultory political career.

My friend Whitey and my onetime attorney John Ramming, a Republican who worked for Democratic Governor Toney Anaya, also showed up. Ramming was in the company of a blond pixy, one Diane Daniels, known today as the former Democratic Lieutenant Governor Diane Denish. Because he pilfered dough from trust accounts at Brandenburg, Ramming & Brandenburg in Taos, Big John ended up losing his law license and doing a couple of months as a cook at the Springer's Boys Home before getting paroled to the Roundhouse offices, first as assistant to Governor Jerry Apodaca. Later John worked for Governor Bruce King and, following the notorious riots at the New Mexico state pen in 1980, became, briefly, the voice of national prison reform.

Now Ramming was the subject of scandalous allegations concerning the diversion of emergency flood money to a friendly contractor and he was the lead story on TV news segments throughout the state. The flood contractor ultimately purchased the old Manchester House and turned it into the Ski Valley Junction bar and dance hall (KTAO today)—adjacent to what was once Whitey's International. Whitey and Ramming were old duck-hunting buddies.

When the Taos community held a roast at the Sagebrush to raise money for Ramming's defense, we used the Warren Zevon tune to emphasize the crisis: "Send lawyers, guns, and money; the shit has hit the fan." But Ramming got convicted and went to jail—again. After he got out, he finished off his career at TSV, first as hatcheck man, then as general troubleshooter.

During Ramming's second go-round with the law, I was on the community corrections board and tried to get him assigned to the probation program instead of prison, but wiser heads said he wouldn't cop, confess, or show signs of remorse. He died in a car wreck during the '90s in Arroyo Seco. Whitey said several former New Mexico governors attended the services. When a reporter asked Whitey about community support for the Ramming fundraiser, he responded to a reporter with a Taos truism, saying "John [Ramming] may be a crook but he's our crook."

Our Chapter 11 attorney, Wild Bill Davis, seemed charmed to meet these rogues at the Bull Ring and I always believed that the entertainment factor helped keep Davis interested in our case, which dragged on through the '90s. Brad Hockmeyer told me he ultimately used complimentary CDs from the music industry to pay off the attorney.

7

Between brownouts, courtesy of Kit Carson Electric Coop, I confronted on my Kaypro computer the ghosts of wasted youth; I sweated through the memories, just as I did the images that haunted my hikes through the brush-laden foothills. As my cash from the 1985 resale of the Plaza Theatre dwindled, I dreamt of finding honest work as a waiter or taxi driver. Despite layoffs at the Moly Mine and the drought that winter, ad sales at KVNM increased slightly in 1986.

By staying home and doing less, I accomplished more. I wanted to leave town but I knew better than to say it out loud. Once again, a friend, intervened with an idea, this time my green-eyed amiga, who suggested I visit a psycholinguist in Rinconada, a village south of Taos on the Rio Grande.

"What do you want to do?" asked the man from Rinconada.

"I want to get out, study, write, do something else."

"Why don't you?"

"I feel I should continue for the sake of my obligations."

"What obligations?"

I waved in the general direction of employees, community, creditors, and the vultures that ate at my liver.

"Listen to what you're saying." He noted how "should" means duty and obligation; "want" suggests desire. He said, "Maybe it's time for somebody else to pick up the responsibilities."

Driving back to Taos in my beat-up red-and-white Ford pickup with camper shell, I felt less like a turtle and more like a bird— the way I'd felt when a shrink told me I was only fifty percent responsible for a bad marriage. The KVNM journey seemed finished psychologically. All I needed was a way to surrender the reins.

Only one person had the passion and desire to free me from KVNM: Young Brad Hockmeyer. Gerald had fired Brad for trying to undermine his authority. Brad, the lover of Dylan and Springsteen, had called me up to complain. "But Brad," I said, "we all agreed Gerald is the general manager." There was nothing unusual about infighting at the station. The owners of KVNM-FM, including yours truly, all got fired from time to time. Of the original founders and loyalists, only Sara Thomas, the engineer, survived unscathed. She, like D.H. Lawrence, wisely abandoned Taos and retired, in her case, to Florida.

The crusty Gerald also got sideways with Nancy Stapp, who claimed he was a sexist. Stapp, the natural born announcer, was as good at the arts of radio on the first day—sans experience—as she was the last time I heard her on KTAO—circa the 21st century. Nancy's claim about sexism at the Equal Employment Opportunity Commission (EEOC) morphed into a complaint about an Occupational Safety and Health Administration (OSHA) safety matter when she filed another claim alleging a lack of toilet facilities. The wind had knocked over the decrepit outhouse, and she objected to squatting and peeing next to the sagebrush on Blueberry Hill. When the OSHA guy showed up, he said he had more serious problems to deal with at uranium mines in Grants and wasn't too interested in "toilet complaints and outhouses." We rented a Porta-Potty and Nancy quit and went on to fame and fortune in bigger markets before returning to Taos for several encores, finally as a shock jock talk-show host.

After the frustrated Gerald quit, I resumed my role as overseer of the faith-in-broadcasting squad, and restored Brad to his role as program director. Then I waited patiently for my trusty helper, karma, to kick me out. An offer more dreamlike than real from Eric "Bear" Albrecht—"you keep the debt, we'll take the stock"—got Brad's attention. We board members tickled Hock's lust for the radio station by promoting him to general manager. Chuck, the Chicano, who represented a diametrically opposed style, wasn't keen on Brad, the WASP, but I told Chuck it was either going to be Brad or silence.

8

While waiting for the omens to change, I mostly hibernated in Valdez and steered clear of downtown Taos—except for KVNM emergency or bridge match at the Sagebrush Inn with owner Ken Blair and friends. I made the following entry in my notebook: "Bid and made seven no-trump last night. Twenty-six point hand." With my fellow members of the St. Bernard Alumni Club, I began watching Monday Night Football games in Bob Krongaard's house. We alums formed loose bonds while working under the Renaissance master of hospitality and humanism, Jean-Marie Mayer, epitome of *joie de vivre* and the progenitor of *elan vital*. Whether the right of return by employees to the St. Bernard was real or virtual, the feeling itself guaranteed a nostalgic if momentary communal spirit. As you warmed your backside at the fireplace in the dining room of the St. Bernard, you always felt temporarily armed against the emptiness of life. Krongaard worked for Steve White behind the plank at the St. B., whom I had followed first in 1967 and who then returned and followed me. After I abandoned the spirit of the mountain for the soulful decadence of downtown Taos circa 1969, I returned for a few guest appearances during the late '70s.

At the time of my escape from Taos to Valdez in the '80s, Whitey had borrowed big to expand and establish a second restaurant, called Blanco's, just a mile or so down the road from the famed Whitey's International at the old Dorothy Brett House. The Blanco's folly was spurred on by a "potential" investment from John Ramming, the soon-to-be indicted flood-and-bag man. A fellow alum and Whitey's waiter, Larry Crowley, used to ask, as we stood outside Whitey's back door, sipping soup, eyeing the sky for an aeroplane filled with cash: "Did Ramming bring the money yet?" During the Blanco's run, the staff and Ramming himself gathered in the lobby of the Quail Ridge to watch the evening news, featuring John's stalwart denial of the thirteen-count indictment for fraud, kickbacks, and theft. Behind the scenes at the attorney general's office, a soon-to-be Taos district attorney and, later, district judge, John Paternoster, ram-rodded the investigation of Ramming.

Back in the '60s, Blanco's had been the bar and bistro for the Taos Country Club nine-hole golf course, which advertised itself with a sign saying, "Members only, tourists welcome." Multiple joints owned by a variety of proprietors have offered food and drink at Club Quail Ridge. Whitey himself once operated an early version of Blanco's at the club and condo project. But when the Washam Propane company gasman went looking for a leak, lighted match in hand, the place blew up.

By this time excess tribute to hedonism had exhausted Whitey's indefatigable constitution. Crowley, also my first neighbor in Valdez—with whom I stained the walls of Whitey's Hacienda de Valdez for a Thanksgiving 1966 opening—said to me one night in January of '86, as we watched a scene that bore a passing resemblance to Hopper's *Last Movie*, "We can't let our buddy drown." The incorrigible appetite for unmentionables and a thirst that could only be slaked by Grand Marnier prompted us alums to bust brother Whitey and we performed a classic intervention. Consequently, we had to manage his two joints as if the in absentia boss were present.

The waiter and cook, David Bachrach, said, "Whaley, if you do the firing, I'll take care of the banquets and make the deals." So in the winter of 1985-86, I found myself in the role of the "say-so" guy behind the scenes at Whitey's International Restaurant and Blanco's Bistro at the Quail Ridge Inn. Under the auspices of hostess Patty Stutz and chef Matt Franklin, Whitey's International ran like clockwork. But we had to figure out a way to satisfy Blanco's lease, signed with the Quail brothers, Pete and Steve, who wanted the bistro to remain open for their winter guests at any cost or no cost.

We raised a few grand from friends and ex-wives for our buddy Whitey to visit the Cottonwood R&R facility outside Albuquerque. The editor of *The Taos News*, Billie Blair, called one day about the Ramming rumors and Whitey's connection. She agreed, however, that Whitey's vacation was a private matter. At Blanco's, I fired a few folks and cut the payroll. Crowley, Bachrach, and Stutz all did double duty. The used-car importer from Pittsburgh, Bachrach, made the deals for parties and noted that profits were up because Whitey wasn't around to give discounts.

Our buddy succeeded in absentia by doing less. We ran out the string of winter months, broke even on the books, paid off the debts, and the Quail brothers cancelled the lease the first week in April. After Whitey returned, he sold his namesake to Tom and Elizabeth Brownell of TSV, who renamed Whitey's the Brett House in honor of the original owner, Lawrence's most famous Taos friend. Debt-free, Whitey hit the road in his wonderful Malibu convertible.

During the John Ramming trial in the spring of '86, the prosecutors had pulled Whitey out of R&R at the Cottonwood to question the chef about a loan of suspicious origins from John. Lucky Whitey, however, had borrowed the money from a representative of the Ramming family trust fund: an indisputable paper trail separated him from the kickback scheme. And more good luck or good judgment separated him from the trust when he had gone to a high-school reunion in Winnetka, where he rekindled a romance with a childhood friend. Following some pillow talk, she learned of his financial troubles and the winsome lass loaned him the money to pay back the trust prior to the Ramming indictment and Whitey's own R&R at Cottonwood. (During a memorable visit, the happy heiress gave me a first edition of Mark Twain's *Pudd'nhead Wilson*.) Whitey told the prosecutors, like Tom Sawyer might have said, "There ain't no flies on me." He paid back Pillow Talk when he sold the restaurant.

Just as I was wondering where I'd find the rent for the rest of the summer in 1986, Whitey arrived at my cabin in Valdez one morning. I cooked up a green-chile omelet, threw in some jalapeños, and made his eyes water. After breakfast, he gave me a check for eight-hundred dollars, something left over from the sale of Whitey's International. And so I got an extension that summer, the freedom to continue mending body and mind.

9

Finally, on September 17 in 1986, I sold Young Hockmeyer on his birthday my controlling interest in TCC/KVNM FM stock for $3,500 in cash and a $6,500 note, to be paid ... sometime. Between the acquisition of the radio station in the spring of 1982 and the sale of my TCC stock, I transformed a positive net worth of $300,000 in notes and property into a negative on my balance sheet. The KVNM deal ultimately cost me about $65,000 in cash and destroyed hundreds of thousands of dollars in equity, due to mismanaged mortgages and notes.

But I held on to my sanity.

When Brad's father had died on Brad's birthday the year

before, the elder Hockmeyer had been married to the prover-bial stepmother, whom he had decided to divorce. He planned to meet with an attorney on that Monday to change his will and leave his fortune in flox to the two sons. Flox is the fuzzy stuff on greeting cards upon which the Hockmeyer fortune had been crafted. But that Sunday morning the reaper called on Brad's dad while he was chopping wood. So the stepmother got the millions and Brad and his brother got the thousands. During one run of bad luck, Brad lost first a partner and second a best friend to the perils of aneurisms, at consecutive Christmas holidays. Regard-less, his own heart kept beating and there was enough dough left from flox for Brad to buy and keep the radio station on the air.

Hockmeyer never paid off the balance due me from the $6,500 note. I forwarded the note to Whitey, who traded part of it for advertising on KVNM and later KTAO, during a second incar-nation (and demise) of Whitey's Restaurant in the '90s. Brad struggled for years to pay off the Chapter 11 debt. At the be-ginning of the second decade in the 21st century, he sold the station for hundreds of thousands of dollars. According to the documents, he collected cash and promissory notes but contin-ued to work there. During lunch one day at The Apple Tree in the double aughts, Brad claimed he had never lied to me (about anything)—he said he just "forgot."

My personal IRS tax liability, based on capital gains from the 1981 sale of the Plaza Theatre and parts of the building, which dough was used to pay off the CETA fraud at KVNM, was origi-nally $7,500, but due to penalties and interest, when the Fin finally filed my taxes after seven years, the amount had tripled. My affairs were so complicated, manila folders so stuffed with complex notes and documents—noting first, second, third, fourth, and fifth mortgages—that when I visited my IRS case-worker in Santa Fé, his eyes glazed over well before the end of our conversation. He promised to visit Taos and view my assets—the unroofed condos at the Plaza Theatre Building—"sometime."

So time became my friend. In the '90s, while I was in graduate school studying the history of great ideas, I settled an IRS claim amounting to sixty grand, due to penalties and interest. The best idea came from a retired IRS agent, my accountant, who said to me, "It's not how much you owe but how much you can pay that counts." He settled the sixty-thousand dollar debt for two grand.

10

A resume I sent to the Brownells at the Brett House turned into an offer for me to manage their bar at the Thunderbird Lodge the winter of '86-'87, though Mayer told Whitey, "Bill must be desperate to take the job." (I was.) "He never liked bartending." (I didn't.) But the Brownells treated me good and by early December, thanks to tips, I had change in my pocket.

Despite my historically troubled relations with Ernie Blake, I applied for a job to teach skiing. To revive my muscle memory, I enrolled in a racing camp and followed up with a week of ski-school clinics. The concept of the technique was easy enough to grasp, even if my legs, timing, and reflexes had suffered from the long layoff. Just before the hiring clinic concluded, Jean told me, "You have to go and see Ernie," the TSV founder and the boss.

Ernie and I covered some old ground. "Mr. Valey," he said, in a sardonic Teutonic tone, "I don't know about you." He mentioned the time I had threatened to beat him up during the mid-'60s and accused me of being a bad influence on the legendary John Koch, while blaming me for his son Peter's exit from the National Guard in the early '70s (due to a bad back).

In response, I mentioned a more recent narrative. "Back in the winter of '82 and '83, I put your ski reports on KVNM-FM free of charge. You gave me free lift tickets only last year." Ernie occasionally napped during the interview but finally hired me (thanks mostly to Mayer, who had intervened on my behalf as he had done in the '60s). By December of 1986, I was in the exact place where it had all begun back in the fall of 1966, living in Valdez and working in Taos Ski Valley.

I skied on used equipment until Dick Taylor, a bartender buddy from the Hondo Lodge days in the 60s, showed up at the Thunderbird in his new role as ski and fashion rep. "Whaley, what do you need? I'm here to fix you up. " He laid skis, pants, and a jacket on me at a deep discount.

In early December, former President Jimmy Carter visited TSV and dined at the T'Bird. Jimmy drank a gin and tonic. He skied with Instructor Berkeley Stagg. At the time, the national news was deeply roiled by the Iran-Contra hostage deal. Everybody wanted to know what the former president thought about Reagan and the scandal; what did the President know and when did he know it. Berkeley, while riding up the lift, popped the question to Jimmy.

"What'd he say?" we all asked.

"'Reagan probably knew, but then forgot.'"

When the season got under way officially during the Christmas holidays, you could find me at the lineup for ski school at 9:30 a.m., where they assigned me to the Kinderkafig, the so-called "pit," and I taught kids. At noon each day I adjourned to my duties behind the T'Bird bar, where I remained until closing.

Each night, after crawling into bed, I sought solace in selections from the *Meditations of Marcus Aurelius:*

> What then can help us on our way? One thing only: philosophy. This consists in guarding our inner spirit inviolate and unharmed ... and at all times awaiting death with contented mind as being

only the release of the elements of which every
creature is composed. ... For this is in accord with
nature, and nothing evil is in accord with nature.

Although Aurelius buttressed my interior fortitude, on the outside each morning I felt like I was back in boot camp and I barely
had time to shake off the sandman, shit, shower, and shave before
heading up to the Ski Valley in my trusty Ford truck. When I
confronted the voices of the thirsty customers demanding solace
in a glass of lambent liquor, I retreated behind a persona aided
and abetted by the stoic Marcus Aurelius.

When a filling from a tooth came out in some succulent
T'Bird pastry, however, I discovered that, as Leonato says in
Shakespeare's *Much Ado About Nothing,* "There was never yet phi-
losopher / That could endure the toothache patiently." Though
I didn't know it then, I was closing in on modernity's unre-
solved Cartesian debate about dualism or the Enlightenment's
mind-and-body problem. Toothache reduces the stoic, even if
temporarily, to a materialist.

11

At the start of the six-day ski week in January, the supervisors gave me instructor Hardy Langer's weekly beginner class:
two middle-aged women. The veteran instructor had taken his
annual winter leave to go off and polish the parts on his VW en-
gine. In the Langer lesson plan, you didn't go up the beginner's
chairlift on the first day or up the mountain until the third or
over to the Kachina lift until the last day. The trains ran on time
in Hardy's world.

But as I looked at those two women, the voice of Jean Mayer
came out of the past and whispered: "Look at the way they stand
on their skis." I recognized what they felt in their lower legs and

ankles—the way they turned the edges of their skis into the hard packed surface of the slope—the flexibility of their ankles, their balance. These two ladies had game.

Before the supervisors and ski school laggards had left the lineup area at 10:15 a.m., my two students were riding up the beginner's chairlift. At 10:30 a.m., we were sitting on the main chairlift, watching Al's Run disappear below us. Supervisor Berkeley Stagg followed us and began broadcasting summaries of our progress back to senior supervisor Chilton Anderson. By the end of the morning, we were skiing the Kachina lift on the backside—Hardy's goal for day six. Between technical tips, I whispered Mayer mantra's about seduction and sensitivity in their ears, "You must make love to the mountain." They giggled. They relaxed. They skied.

As a reward for my teaching success that winter the supervisors gave me progressively more advanced classes each week. The last week of March they assigned me a class of energetic teenagers. We skied fast and furiously, bouncing on the bumps, and tucking on the catwalks. At the end of the season they assigned me to the private lesson desk.

Though my body never quite caught up with the mind's muscle memories, I grew steadily stronger as the season passed. Several feet of powder fell like manna on the mountain the last week. The day after closing, the founder's son and my onetime National Guard commander, Mickey Blake, opened the lifts for the staff. In my finale, I skied one of my favorite runs, Longhorn, flying down the pitches, running out the flats, following the looping curving slopes like the madman of 1969. I thanked Mickey personally in the office for a fine day and fine season.

At the Thunderbird, cocktail waitresses Betsy, Jenny, and Wanda kept me sane; the cooks—Chuck Lamendola and Tim Krongaard—fed us well, and we all survived. In January, we set attendance records for T'Bird host Tom Brownell's nightly concerts, featuring "The Legends of Jazz" (Ray Brown, Herb Ellis, et al.). Tish Hinojosa had appeared just as she was on the verge of becoming a star in the world of Tex-Mex music. We made sandwiches late one night for guests John Kennedy Jr., a cousin, and his roommates, with names like Shriver and Salinger, who spent a week skiing the steeps at TSV. On closing night, long after the public had left, I listened to Michael Martin Murphy and Dan Fogelberg discuss the music business.

That winter I sent out carrier pigeons with my savings of $8,000 in tips and salary and stashed it where the IRS couldn't find it. I finally felt (with apologies to Dr. King) that I was "Free at last, free at last, thank God almighty, free at last."

But free to do what?

12

In the spring of 1986, a writer, posing as a waitress at Blanco's, had invited me to join her on a tour of the spectacular Southwest: Chaco Canyon, the Gallup bars, Canyon de Chelly, Hopi Land, and the Grand Canyon. We walked down through the sandstone and granite into the trans-tropical climate of Havasupai Canyon, arriving at the bottom of the canyon exhausted. The tribe's box office charged us $25 a night to plop down on the ground next to the waterfalls amid the tropical vegetation deep in the Southwestern desert. The price to park our sleeping bags rankled and we skedaddled after one night. Sleeping in the camper on the back of the pickup, we spent a week or so getting up close and personal with the Southwest.

If you pay attention, the mysteries of Taos are vaguely accessible to Anglos and newcomers. But in the deeper Southwest, the enigmatic and enchanting nature of Hopi-Navajo country strikes one as exotic and unfathomable. Back in the 1860s, Kit Carson ordered his soldiers to cut down the peach trees in Canyon de Chelly, but he himself never entered the fabled getaway in the Diné homeland. The sublime beauty of Hopi-Navajo country takes your breath away.

Though my spirit had fled, in the spring of 1987 my body was still anchored to Taos. While I waited for a sign, I kept my head down and enjoyed the false peace produced by gridlocked creditors. Flummoxed by multiple mortgages, my IRS caseworker didn't return my calls. After a May road trip with my Havasupai hiking friend to Boston and Great Barrington, Massachusetts, I returned to confront my failure as an autodidact. Though I scratched around in books and scribbled notes, I didn't really understand much about the eternal verities or how to write a proper paragraph. My friend and I were discussing literature and writing, when she said, "If you went back to school, you wouldn't have such a chip on your shoulder." Just as I needed the occasional lesson to review my ski technique, so in my heart I knew I needed formal academic instruction. A seeming admission of the autodidact's defeat turned into the recognition of youthful prejudice against formal education.

At age forty this dropout decided to drop out from Taos. Due to personal history and bad memories, I ignored Colorado and assumed that the University of New Mexico in Albuquerque was too close to local diversions. Hence, I headed for Cal-Neva— i.e., Lake Tahoe, Carson Valley, and the University of Nevada, Reno, where a Nevada high-school grad benefited from the right of return for purposes of university tuition.

The few friends to whom I mentioned my plans in June of 1987 encouraged me. Nobody offered me any deals: chance and fate did not intervene. I was finished. Kaput. In an effort to purge my sentimental longings, I hauled out a huge cardboard box filled with priceless movie posters and stills collected during the 1969-1985 era, and threw them in the town dump. "Fuck the past," I said to myself. It was, as Karla said of Smiley in the le Carré novels, the last illusion of an illusion-less man.

At Hughes Tire, John and his band of recent émigrés stabilized the front end of my 1973 Ford pickup and sold me road-worthy tires. The camper shell offered protection for books, clothes, and skis. I checked my battery and driver's license, and stowed a couple cans of Fix-a-Flat behind the seat.

On July 10th, I said my farewells to the sign hanging in the trees near my driveway: "Nuestro Pueblo—No Se Vende," then I drove north toward Colorado, the way I had come to town on the end of my thumb back in 1966. From Denver I drove west toward the Sierra Nevadas, thinking about the Donner Party (snowbound settlers turned cannibals). All I had to show for my twenty years was an old truck, a pile of debt owed to the IRS, child support owed to my ex-wife, a salmagundi of books, and tender memories. I was more than embarrassed by my failure at forty. But I also had some faith in my bet: "Reno or Bust."

As Emerson said, "The one thing which we seek with insatiable desire is to forget ourselves, to be surprised out of our propriety, to lose our sempiternal memory and do something without knowing how or why: in short to draw a new circle. Nothing great was ever achieved without enthusiasm. The way of life is wonderful; it is by abandonment."

Epilogue

Reason is a useful instrument...(but)...I am a born pendejo.

In mid-July of 1987, after spending twenty terrifying years in Taos, I found myself at Lake Tahoe, tethered to the family log cabin, set under the hundred-foot pine trees, staring across Trout Creek meadow up at Freel Peak. When I didn't have my feet up, book in hand, I walked up the mountain trails or lay on the sunbaked beaches. That fall, I enrolled at the University of Nevada, Reno.

For the next ten years, I commuted ninety miles round trip to Reno two to five days a week, from either Lake Tahoe or Carson Valley. During the commute, a question kept coming up: What the hell had I been doing and how had I gone wrong in Taos? Thanks to a graduate teaching fellowship in the Western tradition, which focused on the Greco-Roman-Judeo-Christian history of ideas in art, philosophy, and literature, I began to make sense—retroactively—of my past.

Ironically, I was, among others at UNR, the beneficiary of a grant from the National Endowment for the Humanities. Ronald Reagan's anti-relativists, Secretary of Education William Bennett and National Endowment for the Humanities Chair Lynne Cheney, a Colorado College alum, conspired to educate me and others in the arts of the truth via the history of ideas. For sure I never knew what a true subversive was until I met up with the likes of Socrates and Jesus. Thanks to the Western canon, I began to understand some of what Emerson meant in *Self Reliance* when he said, "Do your work and I shall know you."

During my ten-year academic journey I learned that reason is a useful instrument for analyzing literature and experience. The chair of my PhD dissertation committee, Dr. Husain Haddawy, asked during a discussion of Shakespeare's *Antony and Cleopatra*, "What was Antony's mistake?" While his students mumbled awkwardly, he explained how Antony had fallen in love with the feminine principle, represented by Cleopatra—not the particular woman herself. In a moment of recognition, I understood my near fatal infatuation for the Black Widow. Like one of Plato's cave dwellers, I had spent twenty years staring at illusions and mistaking appearance for reality at the Plaza Theatre.

Professors frequently scoff at sophomoric students searching for "the meaning of life." But a colleague and I—she, a major in philosophy and I, a major in literature—both nontraditional (i.e.

older) students were unrepentant in our quest. Just as Odysseus preserved his sanity with aid from the messenger of the gods because Hermes gave him the holy herb, Moly, to protect the wanderer against Circe's songs, so I now propped myself up with the literature and philosophy in an effort to learn and protect myself against self and society. Aided and abetted by my instructors, not to mention Socrates, Montaigne, and Emerson, who advised me during my second sailing, I began the journey in Reno but carried on the quest when I returned to Taos.

The eminent translator of the *Arabian Nights*, Dr. Haddawy, suggested for my dissertation I write a series of essays about my experiences in Taos, circa 1966–'87. While doing research in Taos toward the end of the 20th century, I ran into acquaintances who mentioned a number of censored news stories affecting the community. Friends loaned me and my old friend, art critic Tom Collins, the money to start a monthly rag, *Geronimo* (Dec. 1998– Aug. 1999). As an Emersonian, or "man thinking," I studied and filed notes about the ways individuals and the polis reveal the warts and glory of the complex human condition in El Norte.

After Tom and I parted, I published a monthly called *Horse Fly* (Sept. 1999–Sept. 2009). Nicknamed the Pesky Insect by Frank Concha of Taos Pueblo, or referred to as La Mosca by *Albuquerque Journal* reporter Andy Stiny, I pursued the role of cultural critic in the tradition of Socrates, who referred to himself as a horse fly in Plato's *Apology*.

In *Horse Fly* I experimented with journalism and variations on the personal essay aimed at analyzing, mostly, the art of politics in print, and the paradoxical behavior of *la gente*. (The time limit on my dissertation expired, and I remained ABD: All But Dissertation.) While the pesky insect studied the socio-cultural character of politicians and observed the noble acts of activists and public servants, he also encountered both mendacious and magnificent representatives of the human race. As the bard said, "All the men and women [are] merely players / They have their exits and their entrances / And one man in his time plays many parts ...." (Macbeth, V. 5.).

During the *Horse Fly* years, I felt as if I were a character in a Dashiell Hammett novel, but adapted for film by the Coen brothers. The muse willing, I'll give an account of my further adventures in a second book, wherein I shall focus on the myth, madness, malice and the laughter of El Norte. As you might imagine, things got worse, much worse during the return, but then, I am a born *pendejo*.

About the Author

Bill Whaley, the author of *Gringo Lessons: Twenty Years of Terror in Taos,* has pursued adventure as an entrepreneur and journalist in *El Norte* for almost fifty years. Recently, he edited Paul O'Connor's prize-winning photography book, *Taos Portraits.* Bill teaches courses in literature, philosophy, and writing for the University of New Mexico's Upper Division Bachelor and Graduate program in Taos. He published a monthly journal about art and culture, *Horse Fly,* from 1999 to 2009. For his devotion to the local *cultura* and other stimulating challenges, the so-called Bad Gringo has endured financial failure and suffered the slings and errors of political and prosecutorial misconduct while being memorialized as a figure in a Day of the Dead tableau. If his application to a witness protection plan is accepted, he promises to write a sequel called *Taos Redux: The Horse Fly Years,* a terrifying comedy of political revenge and retaliation about a pesky insect, called *La Mosca.*

CPSIA information can be obtained
at www.ICGtesting.com
Printed in the USA
FSOW01n0234130815
9677FS